Parliament Ltd

Martin Williams is a freelance investigative journalist. His work has appeared in *Private Eye*, the *Guardian*, the *Observer*, the *Independent*, and elsewhere. He hosts a live comedy show called 'Investigations', with the comedian Josie Long, which combines investigative journalism with stand-up comedy. In 2011 Martin won the *Guardian's* Scott Trust bursary and studied for an MA in Newspaper Journalism at City University. Before that, he read History and Politics at the University of York. He is originally from South Wales.

Parliament Ltd

A journey to the dark heart of British politics

MARTIN WILLIAMS

HODDER

First published in Great Britain in 2016 by Hodder & Stoughton
An Hachette UK company

First published in paperback in 2017

1

A CIP catalogue record for this title is available from the British Library

ISBN 978 1 473 63387 2
Ebook ISBN 978 1 473 63388 9

Typeset in Bembo by Hewer Text UK Ltd, Edinburgh
Printed and bound by CPI Group (UK) Ltd, Croydon, CR0 4YY

Hodder & Stoughton policy is to use papers that are natural, renewable
and recyclable products and made from wood grown in sustainable
forests. The logging and manufacturing processes are expected to
conform to the environmental regulations of the country of origin.

Hodder & Stoughton Ltd
Carmelite House
50 Victoria Embankment
London EC4Y 0DZ

www.hodder.co.uk

The problem with Westminster has been that it's filled with people who have got self-interest. And that's apparent even now, I can see that. People, quite often, they convince themselves that what they think is best and that they're being very principled. But deep down, when you scratch beneath the surface, it's not. It's pure selfishness.[1]

Mhairi Black MP, 2015

My view on politicians is fairly well known. I stay away from them, as a rule, cos I don't really like them . . . But they're a little bit like your own farts, cos every now and then you need to smell it just to confirm.[2]

Mark Thomas, 2002

Contents

A quick note

As you would expect, the details of politicians' financial affairs are continually changing. They get new jobs, make fresh expenses claims, and so on.

This book – first published in May 2016 – aims to give a snapshot of the finances of Britain's top politicians. While every effort has been made to ensure it's as up-to-date as possible, it's inevitable that some of the details change over time. However, the most important arguments made here are about the bigger picture; about MPs' relationship with money and the effect this has on politics.

Endnotes are included to timestamp many of the specific points made, as well as providing further detail, explanation, calculations and sources. For instance, an MP might update their official declarations on the Register of Interests at any time. So if a financial interest is described as 'undeclared', this is accurate at the date mentioned in the endnotes and does not suggest it is necessarily still undeclared. The same goes for all allegations about individuals and companies – please refer to the timestamps in the endnotes.

There is also no suggestion that any individuals or companies named in these pages have broken any laws, rules or acted improperly, unless it has been specifically and clearly stated – though this does not infringe on the right to 'fair comment'.

Preface

Commissioner for Standards,
House of Commons,
London, SW1A 0AA

To whom it may concern,

Please find attached a list of politicians who appear to have potentially broken parliamentary rules over their financial interests. For each politician, I have set out clearly the allegations against them.

I am requesting that you launch an inquiry against each of these individuals. I am also sending a copy of this letter to the Standards Commissioner in the House of Lords.

For the last six months I have been investigating MPs' private finances. During this time, I have seen just how corrupt Parliament has become. Greed is endemic. If you want to understand why British politics isn't working, it seems the first place to look is in the bank accounts of our politicians.

Yet this is an issue which authorities have turned their backs on. Rules and regulations are lax, and transparency is laughable. The whole thing is shrouded in secrecy. Because of this, it is easy for politicians to milk the system and get away with it.

I regret, too, that your office – in charge of policing MPs' behaviour – has refused to be interviewed by me.

Much has been written about the public's disillusionment with politics. We constantly hear that people do not trust politicians any longer. And MPs are widely perceived as 'greedy' and 'privileged'. But it appears this problem cannot be blamed on the public for being cynical or apathetic. Nor can it be blamed on the press for treating politicians unfairly. In fact, the problem lies with politicians themselves.

This issue has been allowed to fester for too long. The MPs whose names I have attached all appear to have misled Parliament and the public by failing to declare crucial conflicts of interest. Some have promoted private companies without revealing that they are being paid by those same companies. But no one has noticed and they have been allowed to carry on as if it didn't matter.

It's not just conflicts of interest and the promotion of big business; Parliament is too often treated like a business itself, where politicians can make money and live an elite lifestyle.

I will tell the full story of my investigation in a book that I am writing, which will be published shortly. It will explain how this letter came about, and how democracy has been tainted by quiet financial dealings.

In the meantime, launching an inquiry into these allegations would be a great start towards cleaning up politics.

Yours sincerely,

Martin Williams,
May 2016

INTRODUCTION
Thursday, 7 April 2016

The news broke at the end of David Cameron's worst week as prime minister. After days of mounting pressure, he was finally forced to admit the truth: he had personally profited from an offshore fund, set up in a tax haven by his father. For years, Cameron had kept this fact hidden from the public. He only came clean after a huge leak of secret documents – known as the Panama Papers – which revealed that the offshore fund had never paid any taxes. Ever. But now, in the glare of TV cameras, his private finances were finally laid bare for all to see.

Cameron had not done anything illegal, and officials denied that he'd even broken parliamentary rules. But the news tapped into a broader perception of MPs. To many, it seemed to compound the idea that politicians are a self-interested elite who keep the public in the dark about where their money comes from. Plus, there was a question of bias. How might Cameron's offshore money have influenced his political decisions? Why hadn't he made this public before?

'The sense created by the Panama Papers, and the subsequent row about the prime minister's family and tax, is that power and wealth have, once again, quietly settled into a very snug fit,' the *Guardian* wrote. 'The suspicion here is not corruption, but the veiled pursuit of the interests.'[1]

Scandals blow over. Sometimes heads roll, but then we get back to the dirty business of politics as usual. But the scandal over David Cameron's tax affairs merely scraped the surface of a much bigger issue about MPs' private finances. It's an issue that transcends party divisions and goes right to the heart of our system of government. The problem is not just about one man's tax bill – it's about how money distorts democracy.

Right or wrong, the notion that politicians are 'greedy' has now become a run-of-the-mill part of the political narrative. We've grown used to it. Barely an edition of *Question Time* goes by without David Dimbleby fielding questions from enraged audiences about thieving fat cat politicians – raking in extortionate salaries, fiddling their expenses or cashing in on second jobs and shady business deals. It seems like it's us versus them: the rich political establishment preserving their financial interests in the face of widespread public opposition and anger.

But this has not come from nowhere.

We can trace the story of Westminster's 'financial greed' right back to the nineteenth century, when the situation was flipped on its head. Then, it was not the political establishment who wanted MPs to have more money, but ordinary working class people. Over the course of nearly two hundred years, the debate around politicians' finances has come full circle. Rich elites who once turned down salaries in order to stop commoners joining their clique now cling on defensively to every penny they can get their hands on.

Here's a potted history of MPs' money:

Beginnings

King Tom was already a hero among the working classes. Despite being an MP and a banker, the crowds still loved him. He was a bad orator, a shoddy politician and regularly insulted people with tactless comments. But when he helped push through the Great Reform Act in 1832, which improved representation in Parliament, he was joined by hordes of supporters who travelled back to his Birmingham hometown with him, in the style of a royal procession. Picking up his nickname along the way, he told them: 'The bright day of our liberty and our happiness is beginning to dawn.'[2]

Born Thomas Attwood in 1783, his distinctive look was marked with a mop of curly hair and outrageous sideburns. His personal politics, however, were a bit of a quagmire. Although he was lauded for his involvement with the Chartists – Britain's first ever mass movement driven by the working class – his real passion was currency reform, not social justice. Nevertheless, for a brief moment in history, he was a man of the people.

One Friday, in the summer of 1838, Attwood stood up in the House of Commons to make a speech. It was seven years on from his glory days of the Great Reform. By now, he was starting to slip into obscurity and was disliked by his fellow MPs. In fact, just a month earlier, one of his speeches had been so boring that his colleagues tried to shut him up, crying out 'No, no'.[3] So when he opened his mouth to talk again, they must have groaned in anticipation. But on this occasion, the blundering MP was about to make a historic announcement.

In his hand, Attwood held a list of 214 towns and villages across the UK that had taken part in a huge petition. Some 1.28 million people had signed the document, with names filling up almost three miles of paper, demanding a radical shake-up of British politics.[4] This was the first of three Chartist petitions presented to Parliament over the coming years. Their demands would ultimately go on to shape modern politics as we know it today.

The Chartist movement had drawn up a list of six demands that would take away the establishment's firm grip on power and bring democracy to the working classes. But among them was one demand that might not gain such high levels of public support today: they wanted MPs to be paid.

Back then, politics was a rich man's game. Without salaries, MPs needed huge financial support to allow them time to swan around the House of Commons. Today, we're so used to hearing about politicians being greedy, it's tempting to look back with rose-tinted glasses on a time before they pocketed wages from the taxpayer. But the reality was a crippling injustice. The lack of salary didn't stop them being stinking rich – it just stopped poor people from joining their elitist clique.

One study of the House of Commons in this era found that only 17% of MPs were 'non-elite' (i.e. not aristocracy or landed gentry).[5] And – apart from a few very rare rags-to-riches stories – even this minority were generally from extremely wealthy and privileged families. For them, power was a plaything; a part-time hobby to make themselves feel important and protect their own interests. It had been like this for centuries, but Parliament kept the doors to its powerful club firmly closed.[6]

The call for MPs to be paid was a true working class campaign. This wasn't about allowing politicians to make tons of money. It was the opposite. They wanted ordinary people to be able to survive in the job and have enough to eat and live. Chartism, they said, was 'a bread and cheese question'.[7]

Introducing the petition to Parliament, Thomas Attwood accused his colleagues of running a system that appeared 'all in favour of those who possessed money, whilst the poor were utterly disregarded'.

'Men born in the clouds, and living in the clouds, could not understand the mere interests, and wants, and necessities of people living on the earth,' he told Parliament. 'They should pay the wages of attendance, in order that the Commons of England might send into that House men accustomed to the calamities of the people, and who would better represent the wants and interests of the great mass of the people.'[8]

A month later, Attwood's campaign quickly came tumbling down. MPs voted overwhelmingly to reject the petition by 235 votes to 46. Ordinary working people *wanted* MPs to be paid, but Westminster refused. The landed class would keep their clique in the House of Commons for now. But the cries of the People's Charter would not be forgotten.

'Honourably, but not luxuriously'

Seventy-two years later, it finally happened. After decades of sporadic victories for the Chartist cause, Herbert Asquith's Liberal government voted for MPs to be paid a £400 annual salary in 1911.

'The House has become too much a preserve for rich men,' said MP William Byles, reminding colleagues of the Chartists' campaign. 'I myself know several Friends who were . . . excellent Members of Parliament, who were respected on all sides, and who had to go out, not because they did not please their constituents, but because they could not afford to stop in. I say that a small payment . . . would probably enable us to enjoy the advantage of having them still.'[9]

The reform didn't go through without a fight – insiders did all they could to preserve the status quo. Their message was clear: rich people are better at politics. They warned that helping poor people to join Parliament would harm democracy by 'lowering the intellectual standard'. In one particularly patronising and classist outburst, an MP said: 'I am afraid of this House being flooded by the failures of society . . . Those are men we do not want but those are the men who, I am afraid, will flock here under the new system, and whose entrance we shall have every cause to regret.'[10]

Does having money really make you better at politics? Of course not. Yet this line of argument will come up again later in the book because it is still being preached by politicians today. The size of your wallet indicates the size of your brain, they say.

Apart from clearly being nonsense, it represents a gross misunderstanding about democracy that elites continue to peddle as fact. Even if wealth *did* show how clever you are, that still shouldn't affect your democratic rights. Britain is not based on a disappointing version of Plato's *Republic,* where leadership is the preserve of intellectuals. The only qualification for being an MP is democratic consensus. Not money, not brains, not intellect. Just the support of a majority of voters. That's how democracy works.

Despite the protests and upper class snobbery, most MPs could see it was time for reform – spurred on particularly by the rise of the Labour Party, which helped show that a few ordinary people in Westminster might not be such a bad thing. Lloyd George, then chancellor of the exchequer, justified the £400, saying it was 'just the salary of a junior clerk in the Civil Service'. By today's standards it's about £42,500.[11]

Lloyd George explained: 'You should not apply a commercial standard to payment for public service . . . The only principle of payment in the public service is that you should make an allowance to a man to enable him to maintain himself comfortably and honourably, but not luxuriously, during the time he is rendering service to the State.'[12] It was a noble idea that was quickly forgotten in some corners of Parliament.

The vote passed and democracy was better for it. But the reform came with a warning from one political Nostradamus: 'It will be too simple, too attractive, once it is begun,' predicted MP Rupert Gwynne. 'We shall see the House constantly increasing the salaries at the expense of the taxpayer.'[13]

Alarm bells should have already been ringing over a small but critical discrepancy in the new system. The confusion would come back to bite political reformers in years to come. You see, the salary wasn't a salary. Yes, on paper, the new rules referred to the payment as a salary. But when he debated it, Lloyd George clearly told MPs it was not a substitute for a proper income. 'When we offer £400 a year as payment of Members of Parliament it is not a recognition of the magnitude of the service, it is not a remuneration, it is not a recompense, *it is not even a salary*. It is just an allowance.'[14]

So what was it, a salary or an allowance? Should MPs now quit any second jobs and treat the £400 as their main income? Or should they just carry on as normal, with politics as part-time hobby while they rake in the big bucks elsewhere?

This crucial question has never been settled. The result is that MPs can have it both ways. They can demand all the money and privileges that come with a full-time job. But they can also neglect their political work and spend their time earning money elsewhere. The confusion sparked by Lloyd George opened the door to a century of politicians cashing in from dual careers and an expectation of wealth.

David Stoddart is old enough to remember the slippery slope towards greed that Parliament fell down in the twentieth century. Now a ninety-year-old lord with wispy white hair, he's been in and out of Parliament ever since he was first elected as an MP in 1970.

'There was a lot of voluntary activity around then,' he tells me. 'A greater degree than there is now. You really did have to make sacrifices.'

We're sitting on smart red leather seats in the Royal Gallery of the House of Lords. It is unimaginably grand here. Walls are decorated with golden statues and vast ancient paintings. Through an archway is the Robing Room, where the Queen puts on her crown and ceremonial outfit before addressing Parliament. It's the sort of place where you suddenly find yourself talking really posh, in some weird subconscious attempt to try and fit in. For Lord Stoddart, it couldn't be further from his humble beginnings in the small working class town of Porth in south Wales. The son of a coal miner, he now looks completely at home in the House of Lords, where he enjoys membership of the exclusive Cigar Club. Westminster has treated him well.

'It has been an amazing journey,' he admits. 'I often ask myself "what on earth am I doing here?". If I ever have the feeling that I ought to be a bit uppity, I always think of the little boy in the Rhondda.'

It's not just his own fortunes that have improved over time, it's the whole of Parliament's. Generations of politicians have successively pushed for more and more money, upping their income as much as they dare. 'When I first came into the House [of Commons], the salary was £3,250,' Stoddart says. 'Members of Parliament – really until [Edward] Heath's time – didn't get a reasonable salary, and very few expenses. In fact, until 1970, you had to pay for headed paper.'

'It was a different House then. It's difficult to describe . . .' He pauses to think. 'It was less professional, if you know what I mean? People didn't come into Parliament as a profession. It was vocational.'

'I think it's right that they should be better paid. It's right that they should get reasonable expenses,' he says. 'But I'm not at all sure that, as a result of money, Parliament better holds the government to account.'

Over time, MPs' incomes became less about *necessity* and more about *want*. Over the decades, salaries gradually sneaked away from the founding principle that allows MPs to live 'honourably, but not luxuriously'. Politicians looked enviably at the private sector and wanted an income to match their mates in the City.

After it was introduced in 1911, the £400 wage had remained in place for twenty-six years. In fact, during the Great Depression of the 1930s, MPs actually took a temporary pay cut as part of wider government austerity measures (you'll notice that MPs did not do the same in the latest economic crash).[15] But by 1937 Stanley Baldwin introduced a 50% pay rise, and a slow trickle of cash began to make its way to MPs.

The popular history of parliamentary salaries says that MPs were never paid 'enough'. The story goes that governments have, for decades, been too scared to raise wages out of fear of a public backlash. In fact, official Westminster accounts even go so far as to partly blame the 2009 expenses scandal on the 'continuing reluctance of Governments to raise MPs' salaries'.[16] The new House of Commons watchdog says the same thing. In a recent report it claimed: 'MPs' pay had fallen behind on a number of counts, as the result of the longstanding reluctance of the government and Parliament to tackle the issue . . . In part, this contributed to the expenses scandal.'[17]

Yet this is patently untrue. It's a misleading myth, designed to justify greed and corruption. MPs have actually been awarded pay rises in thirty-five out of the last forty years.[18] And they haven't had a pay cut since the 1930s. It may be true that governments feared public anger for raising salaries, but that hasn't stopped them! (Besides which, even if the salaries *were* too low, that's hardly an excuse for expenses fraud.)

This graph maps MPs' salaries since 1911. It shows them in terms of nominal value (i.e. the actual amount they were paid), and the real-terms value, which is adjusted to 2015 levels of inflation:

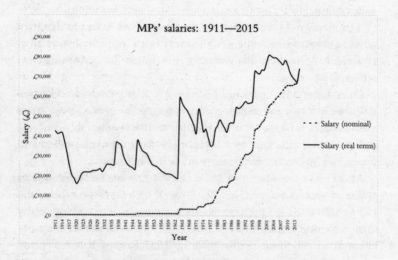

MPs' salaries: 1911—2015

- - - Salary (nominal)
—— Salary (real terms)

Over a century, MPs' salaries have increased by almost exactly 100% in real terms. To put that in context, MPs would have been on about £37,000 by the start of 2016, if their pay had matched inflation. Instead, they were on £74,000.[19]

Much of this increase has been recent, with a 60% hike in the last thirty years alone.[20] And in April 2016, MPs got yet another £1,000 raise, with salaries now standing at nearly £75,000.[21]

It's true that salaries dipped slightly in real terms after their peak in 2002. Back then, MPs were paid the equivalent of £81,000 in today's money.[22] But this is a minor anomaly against the broader picture of the last century. It also doesn't seem so significant when you remember that many MPs were fiddling their expenses during the earlier part of that period, often making thousands of pounds on the side. And towards the end there was a global economic downturn when many ordinary people were lucky to avoid a pay cut. So although there have been a few peaks and troughs over the years, the undeniable trend has been for MPs to earn more and more cash.

This, then, is not a case of governments being reluctant to hand out pay rises to MPs. Rather, politicians became so used to making money that they started demanding *even more* than the government could risk giving.

The expectation of high earnings, among many MPs, has been building for years. Lord Stoddart tells me about a time in the 1970s when he was working as a government whip. 'They recommended a salary, I think it was about £8,000 a year,' he says. 'There was hell to pay about it! What was the electorate going to say? Wilson said: "well we're not going to do it". He said "£5,200, that's all you get!" The place was seething; up in arms. So we sent a letter to Harold Wilson and told him what was happening. He came back and said: "we're not moving on it, tell them to make it up on expenses".'

From then on, expenses became another avenue for financial excess – as was eventually exposed in the 2009 scandal.

In the course of just a few decades, MPs had gone from having no wages at all to enriching themselves with ever-growing salaries and expenses. All this might have been vaguely justifiable were it not for this: it was still just a part-time hobby. As politicians cashed their pay cheques, the words of Lloyd George lived on in their minds: 'It is not even a salary.' Although some MPs gradually started to treat their work like a proper job, they could still spend time moonlighting in the private sector. It was up to them. If they wanted, they could pocket all the cash without doing anything – and then get a second job to double their income.

We never asked them to choose: which do you want? A salary, or a job elsewhere? We let them have both.

Having second jobs not only allowed them to capitalise on their greed; it also muddied the waters politically. When an MP spoke, were they speaking on behalf of their constituents, or on behalf of a private business that was paying them? And even if they weren't being *paid* to lobby, were their political opinions coloured by their outside business interests?

The fog of confusion

Nothing has ever been done to stop MPs from moonlighting and it's still prevalent today. Yet campaigners and obsessive hacks like myself have been shouting about it for ages. A book I discovered gathering dust in the Parliamentary Archives sheds some light on this age-old problem.

The Business Backgrounds of M.P.s, by Andrew Roth (who was best known for his Parliamentary Profiles volumes) reveals how politicians had come to know each other as businessmen, rather than MPs. It's a remarkable book. To produce it, Roth poured over vast catalogues of biographies to list every MP's business interests that he could find, both past and present.[23] The 1965 edition charts 770 company directorships; 57 Members from the insurance industry; 36 in PR or advertising; 129 consultants and executives; 67 from property companies . . .

Business interests were on the rise. The number of directorships was 'the highest calculated in eight years of assessing these totals', Roth said, and there was a 'doubling of banking connections'. And all the while, the MPs clung on to 550,000 acres of land that they owned between them.[24] These weren't ordinary people representing the public; they were blue-blooded barons and business moguls.

The problems around moonlighting were the same that still exist today. How could the public be sure that MPs weren't neglecting their constituents and speaking up for big business instead? And what guarantee could the public have that MPs were still putting enough time and effort into representing them? That was in 1965, and we still haven't had an answer.

Roth describes this as 'fogs of confusion' which 'play such tricks on political vision'. The worry, he said, was that MPs were becoming so 'overwhelmed by these big economic interests . . . the poor constituents hardly get a look in.'

In fact, just months before the 1965 edition of his book was published, James Callaghan – who was then chancellor of the exchequer – let slip about the real importance of business interests. At an event in Swansea, he told his audience that politicians had become more concerned with business than being an MP:

I do not think of them as 'the Honourable Member for X or Y or Z'. I look at them and say, 'investment trusts', capital speculators or 'that is the fellow who is the Stock Exchange man who makes a profit on gilt edge'. I have almost forgotten their constituencies, but I shall never forget their interests. I wonder sometimes whom they represent? The constituents or their own or friends' particular interests?[25]

What made it more galling for the public was that most of them didn't even need the extra money; they were rich enough already.

By the time of the 1979 election, there were nearly five times as many lawyers in the House of Commons as there were former miners (even though mining was still a huge industry). Only 16% of MPs had worked in manual jobs, and the ruling Conservative Party was still dominated by 73% of MPs who'd been to private school.[26]

The rise of moonlighting, higher salaries and expenses was not driven by need. It was driven by greed. The Chartist plea that working class MPs needed help to survive no longer applied: most MPs were doing just fine, but they wanted more.

The final injustice to top it all, as Andrew Roth noted in his book, was that the public had no way of finding out about MPs' financial affairs. From directorships to investments and private earnings; transparency was nonexistent. 'Editing such a book is more complicated and insight-producing than one might imagine!' Roth wrote. 'The law of libel and the absence of financing for a giant research staff prevent our telling all. But we probably have over three-quarters!'

It's now nearly two centuries on from where this story began, with King Tom's Chartist petition. In that time, the political class has done a U-turn. First they refused to take salaries, just so that undesirable poor people would be kept shut out from their clique. Now they want all the money they can get; grabbing salaries, expenses and lucrative second jobs. But often, the details are still hidden away.

PART ONE:

A bit on the side

I

Criminal journalist

An hour's train ride out of London, I arrived at the station in Lancing. It seemed pleasant enough, but I was sure I'd come off at the wrong stop. Lancing is a nothingy kind of place: a small town on the south coast that combines seaside tat with industrial blandness. If you wanted to find the secrets of British business, this would be the very last place you'd look.

The directions I'd been sent certainly sounded suspect. 'When you arrive by train, look for the Asda supermarket car park,' they began. 'Turn right down a path next to the car auction, turn right again and we are at the end of the road.'[1]

I was going to see a man called Paul Charman, a manager at Equiniti Ltd. I'd never heard of Equiniti before, but they claimed to be sitting on a gold mine of information that I wanted access to.

The story goes like this. Once every year, most British companies send a list of their shareholders to Companies House. These are then made available for free online for anyone to look at. After all, this information is meant to be in the public domain. If you want to know who has personally invested their money in a particular business, it should be free and easy to find out. As a journalist, I have to do this all the time, and it's never been a problem. That was until I searched for the shareholders in BAE Systems, the UK's largest arms dealer. I wanted to see if any Westminster politicians held shares in the company, but I simply couldn't find the right document. It wasn't that Companies House wouldn't give me the file – they just didn't have it at all.

'What do you mean?' I said. 'Surely this is a public register? Why don't you have a copy?' As I vented my anger over the phone, the woman from Companies House patiently explained that firms can skip the shareholding submission simply by ticking a box on a form, and

Companies House will ask no further questions. It's only so-called 'listed' companies that can do this, including the very biggest firms that 'float' on the stock exchange so that investors can buy and sell shares.

'So where can I get the list from, then?' I asked.

'We can't help you I'm afraid,' she said. 'The only thing I can suggest is that you approach the company yourself. Ask them if they'll let you have a copy.'

OK, so I had to email BAE Systems, but surely they would just send the file straight over? As I submitted my request I reminded myself that this was supposed to be a *public* register, so there was presumably little wriggle room for BAE.[2] They forwarded my message on to Equiniti, which acts as a third party to hold the documents. But their response was surprising:

To view the register, I either had to pay £95 for a copy to be emailed, or I had to travel down to Equiniti's office in Lancing to view the files in person. Not made of money, I got on the train.

The route to Equiniti led me across a run-down industrial estate and into a small shabby office block. Paul Charman met me at reception, checked my ID and led the way up to an ancient desktop computer on the second floor. There, I was to search through the tens of thousands of investors' names while he sat at my side throughout, keeping a watchful eye over me (presumably in case I tried to download the database to my pen drive).

'How long are you going to be?' he asked, eyeing the clock. 'How many names are you going to search for?'

'Um . . . every politician in Parliament,' I said. 'So, that's about 1,400 people. I want to see if any of them have secret investments in the arms trade. And because your system is so outdated, I've got to search for each one individually. I'm going to be here for a while.' Charman slumped into his chair and let out a deep sigh, resigned to spending the rest of his day dutifully monitoring my work.

As I began my long, laborious task, I asked him about Equiniti. The Lancing office, he said, is where the shareholder registers for some two thirds of the FTSE 100 companies are held. It's one of the very few places in the whole of Britain where the public can access this information for free. Never mind the fact they're meant to be public registers for the country's biggest, most powerful companies:

if you live too far from Lancing you can wave goodbye to corporate transparency.

If – like me – your ultimate aim is to view the register for not just one, but dozens of companies, then you'll either need to fork out thousands of pounds or book a week's break down on the south coast.

Then came the next problem: identifying shareholders was almost impossible. This dataset is so enormous that finding a specific MP is like looking for a needle in a haystack. Take the former Labour home secretary John Reid, for instance. Try typing in 'Reid' and you'll be confronted with a few dozen matches. Scroll down to 'J' and four or five 'John's pop up. Is he one of them? If so, which one? The only way to be sure is to cross-check with Reid's home address which . . . has never been published by Parliament. Home addresses can often be a nightmare to track down, especially if someone has moved house since buying the shares. What's more, some people's names don't appear on the register *at all*, if they have invested via so-called 'nominee services', which prevent their details being disclosed.

The upshot of the whole thing is this: it's really *really* easy for MPs to hide their financial investments in big business – if they want to. No one's saying they shouldn't have investments, but there's literally no way for anyone to check up on them. Instead, we have to blindly trust politicians to tell the truth about their finances.

What shares does Theresa May have in Britain's most powerful corporations? Nobody knows for certain, except her and her accountant.

Without proper transparency there's no way of knowing what kind of corruption and wrongdoing might be going on. What scandals have been kept secret over the years? It's not just the possibility of using insider information from the Treasury to influence their purchase of shares. MPs could also invest in companies straight after passing laws that benefit them financially.

In fact, the BAE Systems archive I searched through in Lancing uncovered a worrying example. This is a true story, but I'm going to give the politician a different name. Let's call her Loretta.[3]

When Parliament voted to invade Iraq in 2003, Loretta was among the MPs who strongly supported the war. As a senior Conservative, she held a powerful and influential position, able to quiz the government repeatedly on its military strategy. Yet she stayed resolutely pro-war and voted for the invasion. She gave speeches in Parliament applauding the military action and claiming that the Iraqi people were happy their country was being invaded.

But she also knew that war means business for the people selling weapons. So, after voting for the invasion, Loretta made a personal investment in the company at the very top of Britain's arms industry: BAE Systems. However, she never declared it to Parliament or the public.[4]

Loretta owned shares in the company from 2004 to 2006, while she remained in the top ranks of the Tory party. During this time, she and her fellow investors cashed in on part of a shareholder payout totalling hundreds of millions of pounds. It was a boom period for the company: the year after Iraq, BAE's order book shot up by some £4.1bn, climbing to £50.1bn. And in the period that Loretta was a shareholder, total sales went up by £286m.[5]

Around the time that she bought the shares, BAE documents noted: 'UK support activity is increasing as the partnering relationship with the [Ministry of Defence] develops ... The company's strong position in both the US and UK markets presents future opportunities for industry to support the increasingly joint nature of peacemaking and peacekeeping by our armed forces.'[6]

After voting for the invasion, Loretta had seen what an attractive investment opportunity her war was going to be. She's now a prominent figure in the Commons and nobody has ever found out about her arms investment, because the details are hidden away in a grotty little office in Lancing.

Gagging orders

STOP!

I was halfway through writing this when I realised something: I could go to prison for this. No, really, I'm not joking!

You might think it's in the public interest to reveal potential conflicts of interest in Parliament, but I could genuinely be locked up for telling you Loretta's real name. Not just *her* name; it is effectively illegal to publicly name *any* politician who has lucrative investments in Britain's biggest, most powerful companies.

Let me explain. For more than twenty years, shareholder registers were completely in the public domain. After paying a nominal fee, anyone could access them, analyse them and write about them.[7] No questions asked. It was an essential part of corporate transparency. But that changed in 2006 with an obscure clause of an otherwise tedious piece of legislation. It still allowed individuals to read the documents privately, like I'd done with BAE. But quietly and subtly, it gagged journalists.

Buried in the small print of the Companies Act 2006 (Section 116, to be precise), lies a critical sentence. Anyone requesting access to a company's list of shareholders has to first of all provide some information:

- 'Name and address' – No problem.
- 'The purpose for which the information is to be used' – Hmm, OK.
- And finally: 'Whether the information will be disclosed to any other person, and if so . . . his name and address' – Oh.

I've got to say who I'm disclosing the information to? So, let's get this straight: if I want to disclose this information in a book, I've got to use my magical psychic powers to guess the names and addresses of *anyone who might ever potentially read this book!*

I'd like to reiterate, I'm not making this up. That is the actual law.

Obviously, my first thought was to lie. I'd tell them I just wanted it for private research and say I wasn't going to publish any of the shareholders' names. That was until I read Section 119 of the Act. 'It is an offence for a person knowingly or recklessly to make in a request . . . that is misleading, false or deceptive in a material particular,' it says. So it's illegal to try and dodge the gagging clause.

Not only that, even if I *did* get the information, it's still illegal to disclose it without first providing the names and addresses of you, the readers. 'It is an offence for a person in possession of information . . . to do anything that results in the information being disclosed to another person,' it says.

And the penalty for breaking this law? 'A person guilty of an offence under this section is liable . . . to imprisonment for a term not exceeding two years or a fine (or both).' You'd be really gutted if you got both.

So that's it. I'd love to research MPs' shareholdings, and tell you all the gossip about which ministers have invested in which companies. But that's considered criminal activity.

Although this law is now ten years old, nobody really seems to have noticed it. That's possibly because investigating these FTSE 100 shareholder registers is such an effort that most people have better things to do with their lives.

But it seems that even many transparency campaigners have no idea that this isn't fully public any more. I phoned the people at Transparency International, Corporate Watch, Index on Censorship and a handful of journalists. No one I spoke to knew anything about it.

But the situation seemed ridiculous. There was no way of legally investigating MPs' shareholdings. Maybe Boris Johnson has invested his entire life savings in an oil company. Maybe Jeremy Corbyn has millions of pounds stashed away in an arms firm. Not only is it impossible to do a comprehensive check, it's also illegal to report anything that you *do* manage to find out.

If the threat of prison doesn't go far enough to prevent transparency, the bullish manoeuvring of big corporations certainly does.

Before I'd noticed the legal problem, I sent requests to a handful of FTSE 100 firms, including G4S, Tesco, BP and Barclays. I was honest with them: 'I am a freelance reporter,' my email said, diligently. 'I may therefore publicly disclose the names and shareholdings of certain selected members.'

These companies want to appear transparent, right? Surely they would realise that I literally cannot provide the names and addresses of potential future readers of this book? Surely they'll just grant me access anyway, right? Wrong.

A press officer from BP, Toby Odone, responded matter-of-factly. 'The request which you have submitted is invalid,' he told me. 'You must disclose the names and addresses of any individual with whom you are going to share the information. "Publicly" disclosing the information does not therefore satisfy this requirement as the ultimate recipient of the information cannot be identified.' Not only that, he said they were also legally allowed to refuse the request simply because it is 'not in the interest of the shareholders of BP p.l.c. and is therefore an improper purpose.'

A while later, Mr Odone phoned me up to confirm there was nothing more he could do to help. My request was invalid, and that was that.

G4S were a bit more sneaky. Clearly alarmed by my request, they decided to do some digging. Who *was* this person asking for corporate transparency? Shortly after I first contacted G4S, I got a text from a friend of mine who is a newspaper reporter: 'Call me ASAP. Just had G4S on the phone asking me for your number. I didn't give it to them.'

Bear in mind, I don't work with this reporter. We're friends, but I hadn't mentioned my research to him. Our only professional connection is that we once wrote a couple of news articles together, several years ago when we were both freelancing. So why the hell did G4S just phone him?

I called the company's press office, but conveniently the woman who had phoned my mate was now away from her desk. I decided to quiz her colleague instead and ask what was going on. 'That's a very strange thing to do,' I told him.

'I think she was just trying to get hold of you,' the press officer stuttered.

'Why has she not emailed me?'

'To be honest, it's nothing sinister,' he said. 'I wouldn't read too much into it – it was an earnest attempt to get your phone number.'

It's certainly a novel way of finding out someone's number: Google my name, find one of my old co-written articles, track down the *other* journalist's phone number and phone *him* to ask for *my* number. Hmmm. I wasn't convinced.

'The normal thing to do is to email and say "can I have your number?",' I pointed out. 'Can you confirm whether anyone else has been phoned or not?'

'Yes, I'll find out,' he said. But I never heard back.

Soon it became obvious that G4S were trying to do background checks on me. They wanted to know if I was a regular journalist, or whether my work was linked to campaigners. You see, in the past, groups of activists have tried targeting the shareholders of controversial companies – the arms trade, oil firms, animal testing, and so on. But whatever you think about this kind of activism, it's not an excuse for companies to skulk around or restrict transparency.[8]

The press officer started questioning my work. 'So you're just doing a comparison across a range of different companies? Nothing more to it?'

I muttered confirmation.

'We're just wondering because obviously there's just a bit of BDS movement with us,' he said. 'That's all. That's just what we're interested in there . . .'

'What do you mean, sorry?'

'You know BDS? Boycott, Divestment and Sanctions movement,' he explained, referring to the campaigners.

'Right, I see. That's why you're concerned?'

'I wouldn't say it's concern,' he said. 'In any enquiry like this I think it would be natural for somebody to want to understand a bit more about where you're coming from.'[9]

And so I spent the rest of the conversation trying to persuade the press officer that I was a real journalist, out of fear that my request wouldn't be processed if he thought I was a campaigner. But so what if I *was* a campaigner? Would my right to transparency be any less valid?

In the end, though, G4S replied with the same blank refusal as BP. I would not be allowed access to the register without providing the names and addresses of everyone who might ever read this book in advance. G4S's company secretary, Peter David, said: 'You must provide all the information required . . . namely the names and addresses of individuals or organisations to whom information in the register will be disclosed.'[10]

And then the final blow, bluntly spelling out the implication of the gagging law: 'A company's share register is not a public document.'[11]

How to make secrets, secretly

I'm sitting in Margaret Hodge's huge, sumptuous office in Portcullis House, Westminster. With its dazzling view of Big Ben, I'm not surprised when her assistant tells me it used to be Gordon Brown's personal office. 'It's like a penthouse suite,' she says.

Hodge is one of Labour's most highly respected politicians, admired on all sides of the House. Now in her seventies, she has a royal air about her; a warm smile and a stately presence. I've come to see her because it was Margaret Hodge who brought in the Companies Act 2006, which was now fast becoming the bane of my life. Did she realise it was gagging investigative journalism? I wanted to know how the law came about.

'Oh, I won't remember anything,' she says, reassuringly. 'It was an absolute nightmare! Go on, tell me. What happened there?'

I explain my predicament.

'*Really?*' she says, looking genuinely flummoxed.

'Does that ring any bells?'

'No,' she says, struggling to think back to her conversations from ten years ago. 'What I do remember was that we had a lot of argument about transparency of shareholder interests.'

Hodge mulls it over and remembers something: 'There was an organisation that came and lobbied me,' she says. But she can't remember who. She thinks they were calling for greater transparency about who owns shares.

'I remember the issue about openness: about shareholders' names and addresses being contentious. And we won on behalf of the little shareholder. So if there was an unintentional . . .' She drifts off into thought and reaches for her iPad, trying in vain to find the names of the people who lobbied her.

When Hodge says they 'won on behalf of the little shareholder', she presumably means that they secured new privacy measures. But those same privacy measures are simultaneously preventing transparency.

Meanwhile, the government still insists there was no intention to gag journalism. A spokeswoman initially tells me that the law merely 'aims to offer some assurance that the information is not used by third parties for criminal activities such as boiler room fraud or threatening shareholders who invest in particular types of companies'. She even claims that 'third parties have free access to the information' via Companies House.[12] But Companies House says that this is simply not true. Only huge investors are listed; not ordinary shareholders like MPs.[13] And eventually – when pushed – the government spokeswoman emails me, conceding: 'Yes you are right.'

The irony is that although these bizarre rules apply to the biggest, most powerful companies on the stock exchange, they don't apply to most other firms. Your typical small business still has to name all of its shareholders very publicly, at the click of a mouse on the Companies House website.

The gagging law is not benign, either. It's been ruthlessly applied to block the release of shareholder information. In one case a guy named Richard Fox-Davies ended up in court after making an 'invalid' request to access a list of Burberry's shareholders. The man said he wanted it for an agency he ran, but failed to provide the names of 'specialist researchers' who he planned to disclose the names to. The court ruled in Burberry's favour and blocked the disclosure. The shareholders' names, it said, were to be kept secret.[14]

In another case, a Rangers supporter was ordered to court after applying to view a list of Sports Direct's shareholders. The football club had a controversial contract with the company, and the co-founder of the Rangers fanzine, Mark Dingwall, wanted to take action. He also criticised the company for using zero-hours contracts and wanted to canvass shareholders to force a vote which would put an end to them.

Dingwall boosted his chances of accessing the shareholder register by buying a single share himself. Now that he could technically call himself a shareholder, he could apply to access the list for free.[15] But Sports Direct quickly put in a legal bid to block him and a court date was set. A letter from the company requested that Dingwall would be liable to pay all legal costs and told him: 'We invite you to withdraw your request as soon as possible.'[16]

This level of secrecy isn't about protecting ordinary, small-time shareholders. There are so many thousands of them that allowing a bit of transparency into the system is unlikely to have any real effect on the vast majority of people. Instead, the gagging laws benefit big business. It's about reputation management and concealing information from commercial rivals. But it also has another implication: politicians can hide their investments from the press and public.

Even the chairman of the UK Shareholders Association, John Hunter, believes that company law should always start from a position of complete transparency. He is one of the many people I spoke to who had never heard of the gagging clause written into the Companies Act.

'My moral opinion is: absolutely, what's wrong with transparency?

In fact, transparency is the solution to so many problems, but it also upsets so many constituencies,' he says. 'As soon as you've got some form of concealment, you've got some sort of opportunity either for money-making or for skullduggery.'

'If everything was completely open and honest you'd have perfect markets, and therefore fairly thin margins. And you'd have all the right people in jail,' he jokes. 'I think one should start with the notion that everything should be transparent and let's hear the objections and see if we can overcome them.'

Even with the prospect of shareholders being named and shamed by activists, Hunter still errs on the side of transparency. 'Maybe that's the price you pay,' he wonders, adding that there are two sides to the argument.[17]

When I tell Green Party MP, Caroline Lucas, about the gagging law preventing me from researching politicians' financial interests, she's dumbfounded. 'It's preposterous!' she says. 'Knowing that someone has particular interests in one side or another – or in an arms company or whatever – undermines your confidence in what they're talking about.

'Where you've got decision makers who are making policy decisions that will affect the future of millions of people in this country, it is absolutely reasonable and appropriate and necessary to ensure that you know what forces are exerting influence on their decision-making process.

'That ought to be publicly available information.'

2

The great transparency myth

The first time I became aware of Parliament's transparency myth was back in 2012. It was all thanks to a tiny, innocuous mistake made by the then chancellor, George Osborne. But it revealed a colossal flaw in the system.

Following the House of Commons rules, Osborne had dutifully declared an investment he had in his father's company. It was written clearly in the official Register of Interests – a public document where MPs are meant to disclose their financial affairs. 'Registrable shareholdings,' it said. 'Osborne and Little Ltd, a family business manufacturing and retailing fabrics and wallpapers.'

It had been listed there for years, looking all fine and dandy. But no one had bothered to check it. And when I traced the official company accounts, I found something odd: Osborne didn't own any shares in Osborne and Little Ltd at all. After a bit of searching around, I realised what the mistake was. He was, in fact, a shareholder in the firm's much larger parent company – confusingly called Osborne & Little *Group* Limited. The names were similar, but there was a big difference between them: the parent company brought in £10m more each year and owned a branch in America.[1]

I contacted Osborne's spokesman, but got no reply. However, when I checked back on the Register of Interests a few days later, a little note had been added on the end: 'Updated 18 October 2012,' it said.[2] The company's name had been corrected and highlighted in yellow. But there was no explanation and no apology. Coming halfway through a document hundreds of pages long, which listed every single MP's financial interests, Osborne's error was deeply buried.

Making small, honest mistakes like this is hardly the worst crime in the world. But the worrying part was that the system was so shoddy.

No one had noticed the error until now. And if the chancellor of the exchequer was making mistakes in his financial declarations, what hope was there for everyone else? It seemed that transparency failures were dealt with lightly.

A quick look at the stuff that MPs *had* declared clearly suggests there were some serious financial interests in Westminster – including investments, additional salaries and other earnings. So the idea that Parliament's disclosure rules might not be up to scratch was alarming.

Take the rules on shareholdings, for instance. Politicians don't have to declare the actual value of their investments. That would be too much like real transparency. Instead, MPs are simply asked if their shares exceed £70,000, while peers in the House of Lords use a £50,000 threshold. But as my trip to Lancing had proved, there is no way of checking whether their declarations about this are honest.

We had no idea about David Cameron's shares in his father's offshore fund until it was leaked in the Panama Papers (he didn't declare them because they were worth less than £70,000). Who knows what else his honourable friends haven't told us? Can we trust them to tell the truth? One thing's for sure though: even the stuff they admit to is pretty impressive.

Let's assume that all declared shareholdings are at exactly these threshold figures and never a penny more. Totting up the numbers reveals that – as an absolute minimum – they constitute an £81m stake in business.[3] Of course, the true figure will be far more than that. On top of this, there are an additional 416 investments that are simply described as 'controlling interests'. We're not given any indication of the value – just that they own more than a certain percentage of the company.

It's not just that the rules are lax on this; Parliament actually *instructs* politicians not to be too transparent! The rules state: 'Members should not specify the value of the shares, or the percentage of shares in a company that are owned.'[4]

Here are a few of the favourite companies that politicians like to invest in:

- **BHP Billiton:** One of the world's biggest mining companies. It paid out $25m over corruption allegations related to international government officials it had invited to the 2008 Beijing Olympics. But the firm still has fans in Westminster: eleven peers and the former attorney general, Dominic Grieve, all have a financial stake in BHP Billiton, amounting to more than half a million pounds. Probably far more.[5]
- **Shell:** It was recently dubbed the 'most hated' company by charities and NGOs,[6] but twenty-six peers and an MP have declared shareholdings in the oil giant. Their investment is worth a minimum of £1.3m.[7]
- **Tobacco companies:** At least nine peers have more than £600,000 invested in the tobacco industry. They include shares in firms like Imperial Tobacco and British American Tobacco. Conservative peer Lord Glendonbrook alone has shares in four separate tobacco companies, with each investment worth at least £50,000. The industry has long had strong ties with Parliament; Tory grandee Ken Clarke was once deputy chairman of British American Tobacco.
- **Diageo:** Together, twelve peers and an MP have a combined stake of at least £600,000 in the alcohol company, which makes drinks including Smirnoff vodka and Guinness.
- **GlaxoSmithKline:** In 2012 the drugs giant admitted bribing doctors and encouraging the use of unsuitable antidepressants for children. In the largest healthcare fraud settlement in US history, GlaxoSmithKline agreed to pay out £1.9bn.[8] However, sixteen peers still have a stake in the company, worth a minimum combined total of £800,000.

Clearly, politicians have got some big financial dealings, so good transparency is essential. After all, these guys are running the country, so we need to know who's paying them, and whether they're being corrupt. But what confidence can we have that their official declarations are accurate?

It isn't just about investments, either. More critical are the private jobs that MPs are doing for big corporations. How can we be sure they are telling us the full story? And who is checking they have declared everything?

'How would you know?'

Parliament's rules on transparency are very simple: declare every-thing. Even if it isn't a conflict of interest, MPs still have to declare anything that could even *look* that way. Even if it's unpaid. Lots of politicians seem unaware of this, but it's written quite clearly in the Code of Conduct, which ends with a catch-all 'miscellaneous' category:

> Members must register . . . any other interest, if the Member considers that it might reasonably be thought by others to influence his or her actions or words as a Member in the same way as a financial interest. This might include an unpaid employment or directorship, or direc-torship of a company not currently trading, non-practising member-ship of a profession, or a fund established to defray legal costs arising out of the Member's work, but from which no benefit has yet been received.[9]

That's pretty much anything, then. Paid or unpaid; trading or non-trading. If there's any chance that it might give the *perception* of influence, it should be listed on the official Register of Interests, which is open for anyone to scrutinise. The idea is that the public – not MPs – should be allowed to judge these things for themselves. But rules only work if they are enforced.

It's worth pointing out, for a moment, just how ridiculously archaic the Register of Interests is. With over 1,400 politicians' financial affairs to track in the Commons and the Lords, clear data is vital. If you want to analyse changes and trends, a neat spreadsheet is really the only way forward, as any techy will tell you. But Parliament hasn't caught up with 1990s technology yet. The main copy of the House of Commons register is a single 500-page PDF, published once a month. It's hard to overstate just how useless this is.

Buried deep in Parliament's website, you can find some datasets for this information. But these are hardly any better because the information isn't formatted in a coherent way. Before it's possible to analyse the Register properly, you'll first need to spend days editing and cleaning the messy sprawl of declarations into a concise spreadsheet.

If this sounds boring, that's because it is. The newspapers will never write about the formatting of data. But failure to get it right means political transparency is completely screwed.

If parliamentarians take one thing from this book, make it this: sort out your data! Improving the Register of Interests would not just do a huge service to transparency and accountability, it would also be incredibly easy. I hope I'm the last person who ever has to manually sort through the mess it's in at the moment.

The document contains some of the most crucial information to our democracy. It gives us a clue as to whether politicians are speaking on our behalf, or on behalf of their business interests. Transparency alone won't stop corruption, bias, greed and hypocrisy, but it will at least make it easier to spot these things. Yet the data in this document is scrutinised by precisely no one.

It turns out the Register of Interests is not officially audited. Ever. In fact, the only way MPs can get in trouble over their business interests is if an outsider like you or me (or a rival MP) bothers to do some research. It's then up to *us* to report things to authorities in Westminster, with fingers crossed that they do something about it.

So let's get this straight: in Parliament, 'transparency' and 'accountability' mean compiling a load of indecipherable, unaudited information, dumping it on the Internet and relying on other people to check its accuracy . . . even though it is often literally impossible for us to make the necessary checks. I know it sounds ridiculous, but this is not an exaggeration.

It gets worse.

I went for a coffee with a senior political adviser to ask him if there was any way of checking MPs' financial interests. His answer was disappointing.

'Unless they've declared it themselves, how would you know?' he says. 'It's never going to happen, but if you wanted a proper system you'd probably have to have random audits. There should be someone, somewhere. Some part of government should be auditing advisers and MPs. But no one in Parliament has got the resources or money to be investigating these things.'

He also points out that there's pretty much zero transparency for

MPs' staff either – even for high-ranking advisers like himself. 'I am the most senior I can be within the party,' he says. 'I'm at the top of the Labour Party, basically. So who's checking my income?' No one looks to see if you're secretly running a lobbying company, or profiting from government grants you've just signed off. The system is quite literally open for abuse.

'Is there any vetting at all?' I ask.

'No. The only thing we have to do to be advisers is pass the baseline staff security vetting thing. Basically, you're not a terrorist.'

Well that's a start, I suppose.

If transparency isn't bad enough, Westminster authorities are laughable. Over the years, a number of roles and committees have been established to police politicians' outside interests. But they're almost completely ineffective. It seems they exist mainly to maintain the facade that MPs are held to strict rules. In reality, the official watchdogs are like teddy bears: loosely based on the image of a big, scary creature, but actually pretty cuddly.

Kathryn Hudson is the woman charged with keeping the House of Commons in check. As the Parliamentary Commissioner for Standards, she oversees the Register of Interests and investigates complaints. But Hudson is hardly a shining beacon of accountability herself. When I contact her, she tells me: 'I do not usually give interviews to journalists,' before refusing to even answer simple questions via email. (They include: 'What confidence can the public have that MPs do not have financial interests which they have failed to declare in the Register of Interests?') Meanwhile, her office is immune from Freedom of Information laws because of a legal loophole designed specifically to protect it from transparency. Messages sent between Hudson and MPs about their business interests are kept strictly secret from the public.[10] The irony of having a transparency boss who doesn't have to disclose anything seems to be lost on Parliament.

Judging by the stats, her office is pretty ineffectual. Last year Hudson received more than 148 complaints about MPs, yet almost 90% of these did not make it to an inquiry. And when inquiries do take place, they invariably rumble on for ages. Most of the time, it takes at least three months for issues to be resolved.[11]

Hudson has perfected the art of weak discipline. It would be hilarious if it wasn't so depressing. Indeed, political commentator Dan Hodges has said: 'Kathryn Hudson is to parliamentary scrutiny what the Keystone cops were to law enforcement.'[12] Take her handling of Vince Cable, for instance – the former business secretary. In June 2014, when Cable was still in government, Hudson received a complaint that he'd taken a £6,000 donation-in-kind and failed to declare it publicly.[13] Her inquiry began timidly, emailing Cable 'to invite his comments', and warning the complainant that he 'should not circulate [the complaint] more widely'.[14]

'Frankly, I don't understand what the issue is,' Cable said bluntly. 'I have a real problem here.'[15]

A long and tedious investigation rolled on for six months before Hudson eventually came up with possibly the most feeble punishment ever. After issuing a short, half-hearted apology, Cable was told that 'the relevant entry in the Register of Members' Financial Interests should be italicised for a period of 12 months by way of rectification.'[16]

I kid you not. The retribution for senior politicians who breach transparency rules is . . . a temporary typeface alteration.

The only real retribution Cable got from this was the negative media coverage, although even that died down pretty quickly and everyone forgot about it. Indeed, the press were only interested in the case at all because Cable was a senior cabinet minister. Unknown backbenchers usually avoid the glare of newspaper headlines altogether when they fail on transparency.

Other parts of Westminster's internal watchdog are run by politicians themselves. But, all too often, they are the very ones with questions to answer. In March 2016, the chair of the Standards Committee Kevin Barron resigned over allegations that he broke parliamentary rules. He had agreed a contract with a private pharmaceutical company saying he would arrange events in Parliament in return for money. Barron had apparently already organised a breakfast and two dinner events in Parliament for the firm. He claimed he was in the clear, but referred himself to be investigated by Kathryn Hudson anyway.[17]

The same month, it emerged that another member of the same watchdog – Tommy Sheppard from the Scottish National Party (SNP) – had failed to declare more than £200,000 of shareholdings.

The MP said it was an 'administrative error'. But Lord Bew, who chairs the Committee on Standards in Public Life, warned that Parliament's watchdog needs 'to get away from the idea that it is an insider's game and that they are marking their own homework'.[18] A Conservative MP has also criticised Hudson's office, saying: 'The perception is there appears to be a lack of appetite to properly investigate reports of misconduct.'[19]

In the meantime, however, the message to politicians is plain: you have a clear pass to take whatever business interests you want. If you fail to declare them, you'll probably be fine.

3

Stinking rich

Michael Green was a prolific self-help guru. He used the Internet to sell products designed to help people get rich quick, and boasted about the millions he'd made himself. The guides were called things like 'Stinking Rich' and 'How To Become Stinking Filthy Rich Online'.[1]

'In "Stinking Rich 3" I quite literally show you how to create your own profit-generating "Game Plan" right from scratch!' he said. 'But if (like me) you're the skeptical type then you'll want to see some slam-dunk proof and evidence that my approach actually works. Click over to http://www.StinkingRich3.com and check out BOTH of my aircrafts!'[2]

To promote his products, Green posed for photos in his '$2 million' London house and on a private plane. 'Everyone needs a hobby,' he wrote. 'Mine's flying. But buying and maintaining an aircraft (and this is my second machine) isn't cheap! But I just hate to rent . . . So I took out my pocket-book and bought a plane.'[3]

Another photo of Michael Green was captioned with: 'I'm sitting in my brand-spanking-new Crossfire Convertible 3.2L . . . It even has a fridge!'

So far, so nauseating. But self-help gurus come and go and the name Michael Green gradually faded away. That was, until his almighty comeback.

Cut to a small studio at LBC Radio Station in early 2015, where the chairman of the Conservative Party, Grant Shapps, was casually sitting being interviewed by presenter Shelagh Fogarty. They were discussing whether MPs should be allowed second jobs.

'You know that having two working lives . . . it can come across as very tricky,' said Fogarty. 'And it did for you.'

Shapps flashed a boyish grin. 'Not really,' he said.

Fogarty pressed ahead with her questions about Shapps's career history. But the Conservative chairman shrugged it off. 'I thought the discussion here was second jobs while people are MPs? So to be absolutely clear, I don't have a second job, and have never had a second job, whilst being an MP. End of story.'[4]

But his answer was rather misleading. Grant Shapps and Michael Green were, in fact, the same person. The business guru was just a persona – and he'd managed to get away with it without declaring the job on the Register of Interests.

A drip-drip of information about Shapps's former pseudonymous career had been gradually exposed since 2012, largely by *Guardian* journalist Randeep Ramesh. One early story revealed that – while he was standing to be a Tory MP – Shapps posed as Michael Green and spoke at a $3,000-a-head conference in Las Vegas.[5] Another alleged that his business had breached Google's code of practice in its attempt to sell software that increased advertising revenue.[6]

But like he told Shelagh Fogarty, Shapps's defence was always that his work selling Stinking Rich products was *before* he became an MP. He said he'd never had a second job since joining Parliament.

That was until March 2015, when a recording of 'Michael Green' came to light. In the audio, he promoted his Stinking Rich products and advised listeners how to 'make a ton of cash by Christmas'. He said: 'The third product is called SR3. And those who remember the Stinking Rich range from number 1 and 2, will know that SR3 is Stinking Rich 3.' The audio dated from the summer of 2006.[7]

The problem for Grant Shapps was that he'd become an MP the year before. When presented with the clip Shapps retreated, sheepishly saying that his previous denial of never having a second job may have been made 'over firmly'. [8]

A Tory spokesperson dismissed it, saying: 'This was a decade ago.' So that's alright then.

'Stinking rich' Grant Shapps is probably Parliament's most ridiculous and audacious example of moonlighting by an MP. But it's just the tip of the iceberg.

MPs can divide their time up however they like. Some work nonstop on political causes; others take things easy. In their spare time, they're free to do almost any second (or third) job they like. Their MP wages are supplemented with often extortionate earnings from the private sector, which they make on the side. It's a hotbed of Michael Greens.

£7.4 million

That's what MPs in the House of Commons said they earn from second jobs – according to the Register of Interests.

That was in 2014. Back then, almost half of Parliament's MPs declared outside earnings, according to an analysis by the *Telegraph*. Some of them were making more than £1,600 an hour. Their jobs ranged from journalism and media appearances to banking and business consultancies. And ministerial salaries weren't included in the *Telegraph*'s figures – this was just extra money, on top of their parliamentary work.[9] Second jobs were prevalent across all the main political parties.

Perhaps this isn't so surprising. After all, MPs were just following the example set by their leaders. For years after he first became an MP in 2001, David Cameron kept hold of his position at a nightclub business, Urbium plc (later known as Novus Leisure). He reportedly topped up his MP wages with £28,000 a year as a non-executive director to the firm, which owns the Tiger Tiger chain of bars. According to one report, the business 'aggressively lobbied local councils for late night 3 a.m. licenses' and rewarded staff with 50% bonuses for selling more alcohol. It sold spirits for £1.75 and cocktail jugs for just £8. An advert for responsible business if ever there was one.[10] While Cameron was working as an MP, his company raked in money from binge drinkers, making £11m profits a year.[11]

The *Telegraph*'s analysis of the Register of Interests was published before the General Election in 2015. Since then, some of the top earners like Gordon Brown and George Galloway have left and a new intake of fresh-faced politicians have been swept into the Commons, untainted by past scandals. So I decided to repeat the exercise – I wanted to know if politicians had quit their second jobs. Maybe the election had flushed out all the double earners? Once we know the scale of their outside earnings, we can start to get an idea of the impact this could have on Westminster.

Parliament doesn't make this easy. Flaws in the data make it impossible to be confident about the accuracy of figures.[12] Still, with a bit of number-crunching we can see which way the trend is going. It's still the best indicator we've got of who is earning what.

I was using the latest version of the Register at the time, from August 2015, so MPs had only had three months to declare their interests since the General Election. I knew my analysis was going to be very conservative – it's widely acknowledged that MPs are more likely to moonlight towards the *end* of their careers. One source tells me: 'Some MPs might start off quite ambitious, but then once it dawns on them that they're not going to get into government . . . they can think "oh fuck it, I've been here fifteen years, I'm just going to kick back and not do any work – I might do some consultancy".'

After days of wrestling with spreadsheets, I finally emerged with my own rough-cut analysis of the Register of Interests. In all, the data revealed nearly 12,000 declarations. There were 3,500 from the House of Commons and some 8,000 from the House of Lords.[13] Parliament had clearly not lost its appetite for moonlighting.

In fact, almost 800 politicians said they have outside earnings: 303 MPs and 494 peers. This marked an increase from the *Telegraph*'s previous analysis, which put the MP figure at 281. In total, more than 2,000 individual entries were listed under the 'employment and earnings' category. And that didn't even include all the company directorships.

In the House of Commons, MPs earned around £5.4m of extra cash, on top of their regular wages.[14] On average, that meant for every £4 these people earned as an MP, they pocketed an additional £1 from outside jobs.[15] Per hour, the highest earner was Boris Johnson, who received £2,292 *an hour* to write a newspaper column.[16]

Of course, some of these were tiny, insignificant things. For instance, shadow minister Luciana Berger declared £75 that she was paid for filling in a survey. And she didn't even take the money for herself, instead directing the payment straight to her Constituency Labour Party. On the other end of the scale, though, the data showed dozens of politicians raking in significant salaries from private companies. Eighty-two MPs declared earnings of £10,000 or more, while forty of them were paid more than £30,000.

There's a lot of competition, but eighteen MPs were in a league of their own. They managed to make more money *outside* of Parliament than they did *inside*. Out of these, sixteen were Conservatives, and the other two Labour.[17] Here's what the highest earners made *on top* of their parliamentary wages:

- **Geoffrey Cox (Conservative): £453,000**
  Top of the pile, this Tory MP gets his extra income from legal work as a QC. This amount was all declared in 2014. That means his standard MP's salary for that year was dwarfed by outside earnings, potentially accounting for 13% of his overall income.[18] And, as if to prove how unreliable the Register of Interests is, newspapers reported in 2015 that Cox (who was a member of the Standards Committee) had failed to declare an extra £325,000 that he'd earned.[19]

- **Boris Johnson (Conservative): £451,000**
  When he became an MP in 2015, Johnson was required to take a two-thirds pay cut from his salary as London Mayor. But that still came to nearly £48k. He earned extra still from writing, but once described his £275,000-a-year pay as a *Telegraph* columnist as 'chicken feed'.[20] Since this analysis, Johnson has cut the moonlighting after being appointed foreign secretary.

- **Sir Edward Garnier (Conservative): £361,000**
  A former Solicitor General, the MP for Harborough makes most of his money as a barrister specialising in libel law. Allegedly.[21]

- **Stephen Phillips (Conservative): £310,000**
  Another barrister, Phillips is paid up to £650 an hour. His wages as an MP represent less than a fifth of his total income.[22]

- **Sir Nicholas Soames (Conservative): £240,000**
  Tory grandee and grandson of Winston Churchill, he's been in Parliament since 1983 and tried to block the introduction of a £3.60 minimum wage in 1998. He's not short on cash himself, however. At the time of this analysis he held senior positions at four businesses, including a private defence company and an insurance firm, and is paid up to £11 every *minute* of work.[23]

The Register of Interests is all very well. But what if some politicians are hiding their business interests? The key to rooting out corruption in Parliament will be uncovering the private finances that MPs keep secret.

By now I'd become convinced that I couldn't trust this document any longer. There were too many loopholes and flaws in the system. The transparency was too shaky. And I could smell a rat: there had to be more to this story than meets the eye. It was time to find the truth out for myself.

The hipster data revolution

Who would have thought that the answer to political accountability might lie in Shoreditch, east London's super-trendy hipster district? Best known as the home of far too many skinny jeans, fashionable beards and pointless tech 'start-ups', it doesn't seem a likely setting for boring old politics.

I'd come here because I was determined to find out more about MPs' second jobs. Surely, there had to be a way of unearthing the things they had failed to make public. As I'd already discovered, some of this was clearly going to be impossible to research. Even outside earnings couldn't be independently checked: there is no public catalogue listing everyone's job contracts, so if an MP is sneakily working for a private company, we may never know.

But there's one glorious exception to this tale of secrecy. And, arguably, it's the most important thing of all – company directorships.

Legally, every company has to be registered with Companies House, and all of its documents are available to the public. In theory, therefore, I figured it must be possible to tally up all this data and check it with the Register of Interests. The only problem is finding the right documents: Companies House holds records for some 3.6 million organisations across the UK and individual files can be hundreds of pages long.[24] It's one thing to pick out a single MP and research their directorships. It's quite another to do a comprehensive search, looking for every directorship of *every* MP and *every* peer. In fact, it had never been done before.

But it was time to give it a go.

So, I found myself walking into the stylish offices of DueDil, a youngish company that had agreed to try and help me. A short walk from Shoreditch station, the office is exactly what you'd expect from youthful east London – a chilled-out atmosphere, free snacks and a litany of Apple products scattered around. DueDil is a business intelligence firm that normally helps private clients get information about other companies, whether it's for analysing competition, identifying potential clients or building up a picture of particular markets. But its advanced analysis capabilities also meant it could help me find out about MPs' hidden businesses.

I was here to meet two of the company's tech specialists, Naaman Taamuz and Andrew Muir Wood. These guys are the epitome of the term 'boffin' – Naaman joined the team after doing a PhD in atomic physics at Cambridge, while Andrew has a PhD in the evolution of consumer products. Together, we sit round a table and plot a way to identify Parliament's hidden directorships. It's a huge task, but they accept the challenge. Their goal: compile a mammoth dataset, listing every UK company that has an MP or peer on the board.

'How do you approach a thing like that?' I ask them.

'There isn't one answer,' Naaman explains. 'It's not like we take the data, and we do this, and out comes this. Every piece of data has its story. There's a lot of manual labour involved, and a lot of machine algorithm work.'

One of the biggest problems is simply finding the right people. 'You might be registered as Tom or Thomas,' says Andrew. 'It's a matching challenge. You have to triangulate based on the information that you have available.' It turns out that scores of politicians are each registered under multiple names on the company database. They might be listed as both 'Lord Bloggs' and 'Joe Bloggs', for instance. In fact, it can be so hard to identify people that Naaman says the system is sometimes exploited by fraudsters who deliberately try to confuse the accounts by registering under different names. 'They don't dare make up a whole identity that's different, but they'll intentionally change some characters in their name in order to make it difficult to associate two parts of their concerns,' he says.

*   *   *

Because DueDil's data is based on information from Companies House, our analysis would include any organisation that's registered there. This means that alongside private corporations, there would also be not-for-profit businesses and even the commercial arms of certain charities. For now, though, the aim was to collect as much information as we could get our hands on.

After a month of toil and sweat, I finally got the call. They'd done it. With the catalogue safely downloaded to my hard drive, I began the task of double-checking each one of DueDil's finds. Mixed into the pot, I also added an extra batch of directorships I had traced, which were registered under different names. My computer was now overflowing with data. Having started the process in early September 2015, we finally finished just before Christmas. This is the length you have to go to, just to get some transparency in politics.

Did you forget something?

The results were staggering. We identified 2,465 British companies with politicians sitting on the board of directors. From multinational corporations to small community businesses. In total, MPs and Lords hold nearly 2,800 active directorships.[25]

The scale of Parliament's outside interests is more than anyone could have guessed. Compare it with the UK average, and you'll get the idea. Nationally, there is the equivalent of one active company per 18 members of the public.[26] In Westminster, the average is almost two companies per politician.[27]

What strikes you about this data is just how massive many of these companies are, as a combined block. It's not just a few small family firms. Our politicians are directly involved with companies representing a sizeable chunk of the economy. And the beauty of DueDil's analysis is that we can start to build the most comprehensive review of politicians' companies that's ever been possible.[28]

For a start, they are responsible for hiring and firing a vast number of people. We can safely say that politicians direct a workforce of *at least* 1.2 million employees. That's equivalent to one in twenty of the UK's full-time workforce.[29] It's like everyone in Sheffield, Bristol and Aberdeen all working under the noses of our MPs, for companies like Marks & Spencer, HSBC and TalkTalk.[30]

Not surprisingly, about 90% of these firms are registered in England or Wales, with half of them in London. Only 6% are in Scotland, and fewer than 2% in Northern Ireland.[31]

Politicians might not give their financial interests much thought. To them, a few directorships here and there may not seem like a big deal. But collectively, their companies are responsible for bringing in at least £220 *billion* of revenue every year. From this, the businesses enjoy profits of more than £45bn. Every year.

Oh, and they have at least another £372bn safely stashed away in the bank.[32]

Sitting on the boards of these companies, we cannot underestimate the enormous power that politicians have – as a combined force – over British business and the economy. It seems we have allowed a small gang of people to take control over Parliament *and* business at the same time.

But the most worrying thing is this: hundreds of these directorships are hidden from the public eye. In fact, politicians have failed to declare around 40% of the companies they run.

Checking the directorships against the Register of Interests is not an exact science. I want to emphasise that this partly comes down to personal judgement – it's sort of unavoidable. For instance, what if a company has been declared but written incorrectly, so that it appears misleading? How about if a business group is named, but not the subsidiary firms, which the MP also directs? For the purposes of this analysis, I set myself a simple rule: if a politician were to name the company in Parliament, would the Register of Interests make it abundantly clear that they are one of the directors?

I sorted the directorships into three categories: 'declared', 'undeclared' and 'partially declared' (for cases where it was alluded to, or it was clear they had other financial interests in the company). Here's what I found:[33]

- Declared = 53%
- Partially declared = 7%
- Not declared = 40%

Of course, going by the official Code of Conduct, some of these may not technically *need* to be declared if there's no risk of it looking like an influence. And, with most of these companies, there's nothing sinister about them at all. But even if they're completely kosher, what's the harm in declaring them anyway? Don't MPs think that openness is always the best policy?

They always claim they are in favour of transparency. Yet give MPs a form called 'Register of Interests' and, very often, they leave it blank. To them, it's an irrelevance. But even if they're not making money from their positions, involvement with organisations could still influence the way an MP votes. This is not about banning politicians from doing anything outside Parliament. But why not just write it down on the Register of Interests? Transparency isn't that difficult.

Why did Lord Evans of Watford not think to declare his directorship in Strategic Matters LLP? Set up in 2014, it was a sponsor in that year's Kazakhstan–US convention, singing the praises of the central Asian dictatorship.[34] Is the public not allowed to know that?

Why did Conservative MP Mark Field not say that he runs a small business called M. C. Field Consulting Limited?[35] The consultancy's clients are all dutifully listed on the Register.[36] But it would have only taken a moment longer to write the firm's name down as well. Then everything would be clear.

The same even goes for Jeremy Corbyn. He's celebrated for his 'new politics', yet – despite being in Parliament for thirty years – he still hasn't got around to formally declaring his various unpaid directorships at non-profit organisations. Corbyn has made absolutely no secret of his long-term involvement in groups like the Campaign for Nuclear Disarmament (which he resigned from shortly after becoming Labour leader). But anyone who wanted to make a quick check on his outside interests would have been left short-changed by the official disclosures.

The Register of Interests does not make moral judgements about these companies and organisations. The whole point is that it shouldn't be for politicians (or even journalists) to decide which outside interests are important and which are not. We should all be given the relevant information and allowed to judge for ourselves.

We can never be sure when and what outside interests might clash with MPs' parliamentary business, so openness to the public is the only fair way to do things. But the intelligence gathered by DueDil's data scientists revealed the depressing truth: for many politicians, transparency is an optional extra.

And with so much missed off the Register, the door is wide open to corruption and the potential for conflicts of interest.

4

Honest graft?

At the turn of the twentieth century, a small-time New York City
district leader, named George W. Plunkitt, gained a reputation for his
candid political speeches. Plunkitt was convinced that local politicians got a bad press, simply because many of them were extremely
rich. Muckraking journalists might bandy around words like 'bribery'
and 'corruption', he said, but politicians weren't crooks. Rather, they
just made money through honest graft.

> There's an honest graft, and I'm an example of how it works. I might sum
> the whole thing up by sayin': 'I seen my opportunities and I took 'em . . .'
>
> My party's in power in the city, and it's goin' to undertake a lot of
> public improvements. Well, I'm tipped off, say, that they're going to lay
> out a new park at a certain place. I see my opportunity and I take it. I go
> to that place and I buy up all the land I can in the neighbourhood. Then
> the board of this or that makes its plan public, and there is a rush to get
> my land, which nobody cared particularly for before.
>
> Ain't it perfectly honest to charge a good price and make a profit on
> my investment and foresight? Of course, it is. Well, that's honest graft . . .
> Most politicians who are accused of robbin' the city get rich the same
> way. They didn't steal a dollar from the city treasury. They just seen their
> opportunities and took them.

Exploiting your political status to boost your business is perfectly
acceptable, Plunkitt said. Just so long as you don't go breaking any
laws. His name may now be forgotten, but the Plunkitt philosophy
lives on.

Parliament is plagued with conflicts of interest. With MPs and
peers able to take up almost any job they like, the opportunities for
using politics to further their business interests are endless. Even if

they're not explicitly twisting policies to suit their commercial needs, politicians can quite easily engage in 'honest graft'. They sneak under the radar to help shape an industry that they just so happen to work for.

Their true intentions can rarely be proved: all we can do is question cases where the *potential* for conflicted interests is glaringly obvious.

These come in many different forms. Some are openly declared and acknowledged, others are well and truly hidden. But using my new data from DueDil, I began to uncover scores of examples that have never been noticed before. They come in all shapes and sizes:

1. The Candid Capitalist

On the whole, the most worrying conflicts of interest are cases where politicians have failed to disclose their interests. But transparency alone does not stop MPs talking about their own companies in Parliament. Often, they admit their business affairs, but carry on regardless as if it doesn't matter.

The former home secretary, Kenneth Baker, is an example of this. Here's part of his maiden speech in the House of Lords in 2015. Reading it, you get the impression he only took part in this debate thanks to his business interests:

> I particularly wanted to welcome the Energy Africa initiative. I draw your Lordships' attention to the forthcoming register of interests which will include my interests in Equinox Energy Capital, which is actively seeking opportunities to invest in the African clean energy sector . . . It is with the benefit of this new commercial perspective that I welcome the way that UK policy is focusing on energy in Africa.[1]

Ian Blackford is another Candid Capitalist. He joined the House of Commons as one of the SNP's new intake of members in 2015, having previously worked as an investment banker.[2] But as well as being an MP, he is also paid £1,000 a month as non-executive chairman of Commsworld plc, a company that describes itself as 'Scotland's leading telecommunications network provider'.[3]

The company offers 'connectivity solutions' and has previously urged Scottish businesses to make use of government grants to buy its broadband services, saying it was 'free money'.[4]

Blackford hasn't shied away from talking business in the Commons. With Commsworld fully declared in the Register of Members' Interests (although he doesn't always draw attention to that when making speeches),[5] he is perfectly free to use his position to raise telecoms issues. And that's exactly what he's done, making comments that might potentially impact on his own business:

> A broadband universal service obligation, working alongside significant Scottish Government investment, would help to address the digital divide and ensure that everyone in Scotland could access broadband services . . . The Government have to consider how we create competitive opportunities in rural areas.[6]

Candid Capitalists don't try to hide their business affairs. But that doesn't prevent the potential for a serious conflicts of interest. Nevertheless, their speeches go unquestioned, even if it's directly related to their own company. That's because the popular view in Parliament is that it's fine to mix politics with business. One politician even interrupted a House of Lords debate to say: 'I have to leave after I have spoken because my boss has called me.'[7]

2. The Agenda Setter

Baroness Susan Greenfield was in full preaching mode. It was April 2014 and she was lecturing the House of Lords on the virtues of commercialising universities. Higher education should be more open to private sector involvement so that businesses can profit from their research, she said. 'Our ability to exploit our science falls well short of our ability to do the science.'

If you didn't think universities were commercialised enough already, Greenfield is on the case!

The baroness was particularly interested in intellectual property (IP) rights, explaining that there is an 'appeal of university-based research to investors'. And she had a bold proposal for the government:

Set up a venture capital or angel syndicate . . . Members of the syndicate would have privileged access to the research as it was developed and therefore first refusal on purchasing the IP and developing a spin-out as and when they saw the work maturing . . . The Government might be the perfect third-person broker to get such a scheme up and running.[8]

In other words, Greenfield wanted to make it easier for private companies to profit from universities' intellectual property rights.

So what made her so interested in this particular issue? What Greenfield failed to mention was that – just one month earlier – she had been appointed to the board of directors at Tekcapital plc.[9] This is the company's slogan:

Helping clients profit from university intellectual property[10]

Not only did Greenfield fail to mention this at any point during her speech, it's also not listed in her official Register of Interests.[11] So did she conceal it deliberately? Or was she just so inept that she not only forgot parliamentary rules, but also forgot about the whole principle of transparency?[12]

Tekcapital is headed up by Clifford M. Gross, a free market obsessive. He seems like the kind of guy who actually truly believes the vacuous management talk that he comes out with. You can tell that, because he says the same things on his LinkedIn profile as he does in real life. (His LinkedIn page reads: 'I'm passionate about creating marketplace value from university intellectual capital.' And in real life, he said in an interview: 'We are passionate about creating marketplace value from university intellectual property.')[13] He's the kind of person who likes to represent random thoughts and phrases in a meaningless diagram. Like the one on the opposite page.[14]

It's thanks to people like Greenfield, in positions of power, that these kind of crazed free market capitalists get such a look in. Greenfield's proposals (which included installing an 'entry-level intake of management consultancies to act as talent scouts on campus', working alongside university professors) might have been laughed off some years ago as a crude parody of Thatcherite policy. But Parliament is now so crammed full of corporate bods that this type of thing is taken seriously. Nobody stopped to question her financial interests.

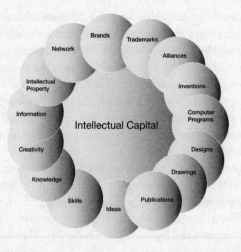

Tekcapital itself is fairly new to the game, but it stands to quickly dominate a potentially huge market. Already, it has a total equity of £1.7m. 'The market opportunity for the Group is both very large and continuing to grow,' its financial accounts say. As a new business, Greenfield's salary is still modest – just $13,162 – but she also holds £18,750 of share options.[15]

'We source technologies from more than 4,000 research institutions in 160 countries to help our clients profit from university developed intellectual property,' says Tekcapital.[16] 'We can find, screen, acquire & transfer new technologies and IP designed to create a competitive advantage.'[17]

When I asked Baroness Greenfield why the business had not been declared, she claimed to have got the rules mixed up. 'I now learn that I should indeed have included the directorship of Tekcapital plc in the Declaration of Interests and am very sorry for the misunderstanding on my part,' she said.[18]

3. The Business Plugger

What is Royston Smith doing in Westminster? A former RAF engineer, he's now a balding Tory politician with deep-set eyes and a cheeky smile. Nine months after he became MP for Southampton in 2015, he was declared the 'least active among Parliament's new members'. He had only made five speeches.[19] So what exactly is he getting out of his privileged position in the House of Commons?

His parliamentary career began with a short, pithy maiden speech about how great his constituency was. In it, he found no time to discuss any serious issues like poverty, industry or the housing crisis. Nor did he raise questions from his constituents. Instead, he used his first moment in the spotlight to reel off a list of trivia about Southampton.

'It is a port city, and it has been so since Roman times,' he told the House of Commons – presumably for the benefit of anyone without access to Wikipedia. 'The world-famous Spitfire, like me, was made in Southampton. It is true. A masterpiece of aerodynamic engineering, it was designed and built in Woolston by R. J. Mitchell and first flew from Southampton airport in 1936.'[20] Parliamentary time used wisely, I'm sure you'll agree!

But Royston managed to squeeze in one little mention: a plug for Southampton's tourism industry. 'We have new residential and commercial premises in Ocean Village, with a new luxury hotel and spa coming soon,' he said. 'We have a new restaurant and leisure quarter, plans for an exciting £400 million waterfront development and a brand-new arts complex.'[21]

In Southampton, residents weren't feeling quite so positive about the developments in Ocean Village. A week before Royston's speech, a local paper reported that the main contractor behind the project was the 'development giant Bouygues UK'. It was set to build the five-star Harbour Hotel, spa and 300 new flats, which Smith had name-dropped in his maiden speech.[22] Bouygues UK's regional managing director, Darren Gill, said: 'As a company with longstanding ties to the local community in Southampton, we're pleased that we are able to contribute further to the efforts to revitalise this important part of the city.'[23]

Comments left on the *Southampton Daily Echo* website were less than flattering, however. 'Bouygues! It will be a disaster,' one said. Another: 'Once again Bouygues will walk off back to France with a lot of profit!' A third person commented: 'Great. More trinkets and bolt-holes for the super rich while the working and lower-middle classes starve and make-do.'[24]

As chance would have it, Bouygues' 'ties to the local community' are pretty strong. The company may not be popular with the locals, but it does have a special relationship with a certain Mr Royston Smith. A month after making his speech in the Commons, directly plugging the development, Royston added a new entry on the Register of Interests. '£9,000 received from Bouygues Development . . . for consultancy services,' it read.

Quite what this consultancy work involved is not clear. Royston claims he hasn't worked for Bouygues 'since the election', even though the timing of his declaration could suggest that the payment came a while later. But a clue about what type of 'consultancy services' he provided might be found in a small company called RMJ Public Relations. It describes itself as 'a complete public relations and relationship management service including political liaison.'[25]

On his declaration of interests, the MP says he owns shares in the firm. But that's the extent of it. The company is not linked to any actual *work*. However, when I email Royston to ask for more details, he lets slip an admission. 'I keep the business operating at a low level (a few hours per week) which is all properly registered,' he says. Not only that, according to DueDil's data, he's actually the company's director as well.[26]

'In the past the business carried out tracing and serving of legal and court documents but has been exclusively Public Relations and consultancy for some years,' he says.

So when Royston Smith only found time in his maiden speech to promote one single Southampton cause, was it purely coincidental that he also had business links to it? Or was he motivated by his £9,000 cheque from Bouygues Development?

4. The Power Gangs

Built in 1722, the beautiful five-floor Georgian building was once a Huguenot silk weaver's house. Now renovated into an uber-trendy vintage-style home, it's rented out as the backdrop for glamorous fashion shoots, featuring in *Esquire* magazine and Gok Wan's womens-wear collection shoot, among others. In the heart of Spitalfields, east London, it boasts a four-poster bed, open fires and a harpsichord.

The house even has its own *Pinterest* page on the Internet – a kind of 'house porn' picture collection.[27]

Renting the building out for a fashion shoot will cost you a tidy £400 a day, plus a £95 booking fee. After all, the value of this spectacular home is estimated to be around £3m. And the owner of the plush property? Step forward SNP politician, John Nicolson.[28]

This is the same SNP that ran for election on an anti-establishment ticket, claiming to speak out against the London elite. They would stand up for the ordinary man in the street, they said. The reality is that many in the party are well-off property investors, with a stake in London's lucrative housing market. At least sixteen of the party's MPs boost their main salaries by working as landlords. They join a large crowd of MPs from across the political spectrum with a vast property portfolio. Together, they form a powerful gang who ensure their financial interests are looked after by Westminster. They are not individually corrupt; instead, they act as a combined force.

Landlords are massively over-represented in the House of Commons, compared to the wider public. Nationally, only 2% of people rent out property, compared to 30% of MPs. In 2016, research by the *Guardian* showed that 196 MPs earned extra income from rent, with the majority taking home at least £10,000 a year. The Conservative party had the highest proportion of landlords among its ranks (39%), followed by the SNP (26%) and Labour (22%).[29]

Yet politicians are specifically told not to be too transparent about their property. The rules say they 'should not register . . . any land or property which is used wholly for their own personal residential purposes, or those of their spouse, partner or dependent children.' All that's left to declare, then, is property *investments*. And even then, they don't have to declare it unless it's worth more than £100,000.[30]

Nevertheless, 224 MPs have still declared 332 properties on the Register.[31] They include:

- 239 houses and flats
- 19 farms
- 9 cottages
- 5 forestries
- 1 nature reserve
- 1 golf course

Transparency rules are similar in the House of Lords, but even less has to be declared. Peers are told not to include anything worth less than a quarter of a million.[32] Despite this, 236 peers still made 359 separate property declarations – some for multiple houses. They own places right across the UK, as well as in France, Italy, Spain, America and even Guyana. Listing them sounds like an estate agent's rendition of 'The Twelve Days of Christmas':[33]

- 261 houses, mansions, flats and cottages
- 60 farms
- 18 estates
- 18 forestries
- 3 vineyards
- 2 villas
- 1 Scottish castle
- (and a partridge in a pear tree)

So what happens when you ask a gang of landlords to vote on new laws for . . . landlords? It's no surprise that Britain's housing legislation has consistently been nice to wealthy owners.

A stark reminder of this came in January 2016. New laws were proposed that would have legally required rented homes to be 'fit for human habitation'. But a gang of 72 MPs – who each earned at least £10,000 a year from tenants – clubbed together to help block the rule.[34] The government claimed the new law would be 'unnecessary regulation' and, with the backing of the gang, Parliament voted to shut down the debate.

A few months earlier, a different law had been tabled, designed to stop rogue landlords evicting tenants who asked for basic repairs. But again, the proposals were blocked by politicians with financial interests at stake. This time, Tory MP Philip Davies – who rents out a flat himself – 'talked out' the Bill so it could not progress.

The rules on this particular renting issue had not been updated since 1957, but Davies said that modernising the law would be 'a huge burden to landlords'.[35] And, with that, he instantly became a friend to rogue property letters everywhere.

'Landlords appear to be an easy target for the Left in this country,' he said, adding that new regulations would cause 'a lot of grief' for good property owners. 'It is very difficult to keep tabs on all the things expected of a landlord,' he said.

Together with his Conservative colleagues, Davies successfully filibustered the Bill with a rambling 8,000-word speech.[36] With the full force of their combined political influence, Westminster's gang of landlords had secured yet another victory.

5. *The Muddled MP*

The Committee for Culture, Media and Sport is one of the most powerful and high-profile groups in the House of Commons. Its real moment of fame came in 2011 with an inquiry into phone hacking at the *News Of The World* newspaper.

It brought us prized events like Rupert Murdoch eating humble pie in front of the committee panel; and his son James Murdoch having an *actual* pie thrown in his face by an activist, Jonnie Marbles. It also made something of a celebrity out of Tory MP Louise Mensch, who now resides in the gutters of Twitter, shouting about politics to passers-by.

In summer 2015, the committee started fresh work on an array of important new inquiries. From doping in athletics and corruption in FIFA, through to cyber security and the BBC's finances. But one of the new inquiries must have sparked particular interest for Nigel Adams, a Tory MP from Yorkshire who had just joined the group:

> The Culture, Media and Sport Committee is launching an inquiry into the coverage, delivery and performance of superfast broadband in the UK, and into progress being made in extending and improving mobile coverage and services.[37]

The scope of this inquiry was quickly set out, with key questions like: 'Is there sufficient competition in these markets?' and 'What role should Government, Ofcom and industry play in extending superfast broadband to hard-to-reach premises?' At the time of writing, the inquiry is still ongoing.[38]

There's one snag though: Nigel Adams is the director of a tele-coms business called NGC Networks Limited. And it's not mentioned on his main Register of Interests.[39] Nor is it named in a second declaration, published by the committee itself.[40]

NGC Networks boasts that it has provided a 'wide range of Telecom and Internet connectivity services to businesses for over a decade'.

> We are a privately owned profitable debt free business and we have unrivalled experience in providing telecoms services to over 500 companies on a long term basis, with a customer service led ethos.
>
> We supply/or provide business telephone systems, connectivity and customer contact solutions from the world's leading vendors and including AVAYA, SWYX, BT, Virgin etc.[41]

But with Adams on board the eleven-person committee, the inquiry continued as normal. Formal invitations to give evidence were sent out to the world's leading telecoms vendors, including . . . BT and Virgin Media, along with others like O2, Vodafone and TalkTalk.[42]

The potential conflict of interest might not be so embarrassing were it not for Adams's continual opportunities to be transparent. In fact, the company *used* to be declared on the Register, but he removed it. In June 2015, it was fully listed. But by July, it had disappeared.[43] It must have been sheer coincidence, then, that July 2015 also happened to be when Adams joined the Committee on Culture, Media and Sport.

He seems in a bit of a muddle about the whole thing. Although there's no mention of it in his declarations, he casually brought it up during a committee meeting: 'It is probably worth, at this point, my making the Clerk aware of my shareholding in two telecoms businesses.'[44] On another occasion, he appeared to declare his wife's involvement in the business, but not his own.[45]

It's hard to see how it could have slipped his mind: Adams has been running NGC Networks for ten years. As well as sitting on the board of directors, he owns 12.5% of the shares. His wife, Claire (who is also his office manager), owns a further 37.5% of the company.[46] What's more, his work in the telecoms industry is proudly portrayed on his website as an aspirational/smug rags-to-riches tale.[47]

I emailed him, asking why he'd deleted all mention of the company. Three days later, a garbled reply dropped into my inbox.

Thank you for your email and interest in my shareholdings.

Your information is somewhat out of date and inaccurate. Any declarations that I am required to make under the house rules have been made accordingly and there is no requirement for me to declare my shareholding in any company.

Thank you

My [sic]

Nigel Adams MP

'Inaccurate'? I messaged again, explaining that my information about NGC Networks came directly from the firm's own financial accounts. And I asked him why it had been removed straight before joining the committee. Minutes later, he replied. But this time, he simply said: 'It does not need to be declared and should have been removed from the register two years ago.'

But if it doesn't need to be declared, why did he feel the need to mention it during a committee meeting? I asked him a third time:

Thanks Nigel.

Given that the Select Committee you are part of is running an inquiry into the exact same area of business that your company is involved in, do you not think this represents a conflict of interests?

Or that it could at least be perceived that way?

Many thanks,

Martin

And this time there was no response. Just a long, long silence . . . And that, ladies and gentlemen, is transparency!

6. The Silent Voter

Conflicts of interest are not confined to those who openly shout about their business; others are more subtle. Lord Wolfson of Sunningdale is a prime example, keeping a low profile in

Westminster. You won't see him delivering riveting speeches or shaking his fist at the government. In fact, he's only spoken in the main House of Lords chamber once in the last decade. That was in 2012, when he asked a short question about the Health and Social Care Bill.[48]

But his voting history tells a different story. This is not a man who has bowed out of politics – he still wields significant influence over issues that matter to him. And the Health and Social Care Bill was clearly top of his priorities. Since 2012, around two thirds of his votes in Parliament have been devoted to that same piece of legislation.[49]

It was a hugely controversial Bill that was condemned for effectively privatising the NHS. One critic wrote that it marked 'the death of the NHS as we know it'.[50] The largest health sector union, Unite, said: 'The Health and Social Care Act removes remaining barriers to privatisation by giving GPs control of £65 billion of the NHS budget and forcing them to contract out services for patients or face legal challenges from the private sector.'[51]

To get an idea of how private companies might seek to profit from the NHS, a good place to look is www.healthlogistics.co.uk, the 'link between Suppliers and NHS Trusts'.[52]

'We make it easier for healthcare suppliers to trade with the NHS,' the website says, offering a range of information and catalogue services to NHS trusts which help facilitate private sector involvement.[53] 'Healthlogistics' managed solutions enable NHS hospital trusts to dramatically reduce costs and boost revenue.'[54]

The website may seem fairly innocuous – just another private firm trying to profit from the NHS – but documents filed with Companies House reveal an interesting fact. Healthlogistics.co.uk Limited is a £1.8m company run by one Lord Wolfson of Sunningdale.[55] And despite voting twelve times on the Health and Social Care Bill, he did not make information about his company clear on the Register of Interests.[56]

Wolfson's influence in politics also extends far beyond his voting rights. As a former senior staffer in No. 10 Downing Street, he has his fingers in many pies, including a gig as Vice President of the Patients' Association.[57] His son, Simon, also sits in the House of Lords and between them they have donated well over half a million pounds to the Conservative Party, including £10,000 towards David Cameron's campaign to become the Conservative Party leader back in 2005.[58]

7. The Foreign Policy Friends

Here's a case of a politician meddling in foreign affairs, despite having business interests that might be linked.

The Earl of Oxford and Asquith (real name: Raymond Benedict Bartholomew Michael Asquith) is the non-executive director of Group DF. The company operates in Ukraine and other nearby countries. 'Group DF holds interests in regional natural gas distribution companies across Ukraine,' its website says. 'Investments in the natural gas distribution business are currently one of the most promising directions of the Group's development.'[59]

It just so happens that Ukrainian affairs are of particular interest to the earl. He's keen to settle the conflict in the country and get control over its economy.

After briefly flagging up his entry on the Register of Interests, which mentions the firm, he used a speech in the House of Lords to warn: 'Economic pressure, I believe, will characterise the next steps' to resolve Ukraine's situation. 'In the next twelve months or so, there will be a Russian push to buy out distressed Ukrainian assets,' he said. 'Russia's aim will be to become as close to a 100% shareholder of Ukraine as is possible . . . It is time that genuine mechanisms were devised and enforced so that investment funds reach the real economy.'[60]

This is not a case of directly plugging a business; there's no suggestion the earl technically broke any rules. But Parliament is perfectly happy to let those with financial interests overseas join debates about foreign policy in those very same countries.

William Hague has made a similar move. The former foreign secretary quit as an MP in the 2015 elections and joined the House of Lords a few months later. In the intervening time, however, he was also appointed as a director of ICE Futures Europe, a financial exchange for 'futures and options contracts based on global crude oil and refined oil'. Last year it made a $66m profit, on a turnover of more than $118m.[61] 'Over half of the world's oil futures are traded on our markets,' the company says.

Oil prices are clearly at the heart of ICE's business and the market is intrinsically tied up with Middle Eastern politics. Not only that, the company has itself flagged up Syria as one of a handful of key countries that can have a major effect on the markets. Under the heading 'Events that move oil prices', a company document lists: 'Middle East geopolitical tension, Iran nuclear programme; Syria, political ties and key position in Middle East.'[62] Indeed, the firm also notes that energy prices shot up after the widespread protests that hit Syria during the 2011 Arab Spring.[63] Another document says that 'Iraq, Nigeria, Syria and Libya all pose significant upside risks'.[64]

Despite all this, Hague went ahead and spoke in Parliament during the most controversial foreign policy vote of the year: the decision to bomb Syria. He did this without any mention of his position at ICE. Although his initial appointment had already been approved by a parliamentary watchdog, it did not appear on the Register of Interests until more than a week after his Syria speech.[65] Of course, Hague might reasonably claim that bombing Syria wouldn't directly boost his own earnings, but he left Parliament and the public in the dark about his company.

'We would need a very compelling reason not to act,' he told fellow peers in his first speech to the House of Lords. 'If we are to take this action, it must be effective. That means that it has to be, sadly, against economic infrastructure that Daesh controls.'[66]

8. The Ghost of Christmas Past

At 7 p.m. on Christmas Eve 2015, I received an email from Conservative MP, Jeremy Lefroy.

> As a result of you raising this issue, it has become clear to me that I must declare this directorship on the register of interests. Even if it [is] not trading, it is vital – as you point out – that there is no appearance of conflict of interests. So I am doing so.
>
> Since I have now been appointed a Trustee of the Liverpool School of Tropical Medicine, I believe that it is also right no longer to be a director. So I will step down.[67]

Jeremy Lefroy is a polite, wiry man with grey hair and spectacles. An accountant by training, he spent much of his life living in Africa before becoming Stafford's MP in 2010.[68]

His Christmas Eve email came almost three weeks after I'd first contacted Lefroy about a business he ran called Advanced Bio Extracts Limited. He'd been one of the company's directors since February 2000, but had never declared this on the Register of Interests. There was no mention of it anywhere.

There's precious little information available about this company. It isn't currently trading, but is still listed as 'active' with Companies House. And, when I contacted him, the files still named Lefroy as a director.

Eventually, I stumbled across an investment proposal that had been posted online back in 2006. It described the firm as the leading producer of pure artemisinin in East Africa – a herb used for antimalarial drugs.[69] It said: 'The company sources Artemisia annua leaves from three wholly-owned subsidiaries in Kenya, Uganda and Tanzania, is currently operating a satellite extraction plant in Kabale, Uganda and is setting up a plant in Kenya to extract and purify artemisinin from these.'

I wanted to know why Lefroy had never thought to declare it. You see, for the past five years, he's been taking every opportunity to talk about malaria and artemisia-based drugs in Parliament. Using his position, he's called for more financial backing and support for the drug business, he's sung the praises of artemisia treatments and questioned the government about political stability in parts of Africa surrounding the area where his company operated. He is even chairman of the All-Party Parliamentary Group on Malaria and Neglected Tropical Diseases, as well as sitting on the International Development Committee, which has allowed him to quiz experts on antimalarial drugs.

Malaria is an urgent problem, of course, yet at no point in these debates did he ever mention the private business he ran. True, the company wasn't trading at the time, but how could Lefroy seriously just dismiss it as some insignificant relic from years gone by?

'Do you consider there to be a conflict of interests here – or that it could be seen that way?' I asked him in my initial email.

His answer came back quickly: no. He said he did 'not consider there to be a conflict of interests.'

It's striking that, in five years of plugging the antimalarial business, nobody had ever noticed Lefroy's company directorship. Just five months after getting elected in 2010, he used his new platform to raise the issue with Nick Clegg, the then deputy prime minister:

> What outcomes does my right honourable Friend expect to result from the more than tripling of malaria funds by that date?[70]

In 2014, he told the Commons that he was 'extremely concerned about the growth of resistance to artemisinin-based drugs' and asked whether 'the international community is giving enough weight to this issue?'[71] In October 2015 Jeremy Lefroy even opened a House of Commons debate on tropical diseases. Without mentioning Advanced Bio Extracts he launched into a 3,200-word speech about malaria and the virtues of artemisinin-based drugs.

> There have been some tremendous advances in cures, notably in the artemisinin combination therapies . . . Given the effectiveness of UK support for tackling malaria over the last 15 years, will the Minister undertake to do his utmost to maintain that for the future? I am not asking the UK to increase the level of funding, but to maintain current levels.[72]

I'm not suggesting that there's been any commercial benefit from his parliamentary activity. Lefroy no doubt has good intentions to tackle malaria, which is clearly an issue close to his heart. But that doesn't necessarily excuse him from not declaring his business. If there *had* been a conflict of interest, how can we be sure that we would have known?

Haven't we learned not to let MPs police themselves? Why can't the public be free to scrutinise politicians and decide for themselves whether they're being corrupt? Lefroy's initial claim that 'there was nothing to declare' is the bureaucratic equivalent of giving two fingers up to us voters, because it's like saying: 'I'll be the judge of that, not you.'

I don't know whether Lefroy's Christmas Eve admission was fuelled by festive spirit, or the end of an agonising ordeal consulting with his advisers. Maybe he was just working late. Either way – after sitting on an undeclared directorship for five years – he finally realised it could be a flagrant breach of Parliament's rules. 'It has become clear to me that I must declare this directorship on the register of interests,' he said. He signed off: 'With best wishes for Christmas and the New Year, Jeremy Lefroy.'

A few days later, I checked back on the Companies House website to find a new document filed under Advanced Bio Extracts, which had been received on Christmas Day. 'Termination of a Director,' it said, 'JEREMY JOHN ELTON LEFROY'.[73]

5

Time to spare

With all these second jobs, how much time do politicians have left over for, you know . . . politics?

Before he became prime minister, David Cameron said that 'being a Member of Parliament must be a full-time commitment . . . The public deserves nothing less.'[1] But through his time in office, did his own politicians live up to that standard?

All MPs are meant to represent their area and listen to people's concerns. If they don't, it makes a mockery of the whole idea of democracy. Parliament's website advises the public: 'You can contact your MP when you, or people living in your area, are affected by decisions made by the UK Parliament.' It says you should get in touch with them 'to let your MP know about a problem affecting people in your local area,' adding: 'Most MPs hold regular sessions called surgeries where they meet constituents to talk about issues of concern.'[2]

But if they're off doing second jobs, how much time do they have left over to actually meet the people they represent? I decided to go undercover, posing as a constituent who I named 'Paul Michaelson'. I got on the phone.

The 'emergency-only' MP

'How can Mr Johnson help you?' said a clerk in Boris Johnson's office.

This was February 2015, when Johnson was still the Mayor of London, as well as being MP for Uxbridge and South Ruislip. I wanted to know if his constituents were getting a look-in. After all, his entry on the Register of Interests lists his *Mayoral* job like this: 'Hours: full time'. How could he be a full-time MP as well?

I give my name to Johnson's secretary and tell her I want to attend a surgery meeting to speak to him. 'It's about air pollution concerns,' I say earnestly. 'It's not necessarily really urgent or anything.'

'That's the thing,' she replies. 'Surgeries are for emergencies.'

'Really? I thought they were for anyone to just come along?'

'No. It's not I'm afraid,' the woman says firmly. 'If you could drop us an email with all your details and your concerns, and we can look into that for you. That's the quickest way . . .'

'So he only meets constituents for emergencies?'

'Yes.'

Boris Johnson spends more time than any other MP doing non-parliamentary work. Until he stood down as Mayor of London in May 2016, he had no fewer than *four* jobs listed on the Register of Interests. As well as his two full-time political positions, he writes books and spends ten hours a month writing a newspaper column.[3]

So it's hardly surprising that he doesn't have much time left over to meet his constituents. His office clerk blames 'the high demand of emails', adding: 'We obviously have to prioritise those who have a greater need.'

I ask again about surgery meetings: 'How often does he do them?'

'Um . . . It depends on diary commitments.'

'Cos I suppose he's being Mayor as well,' I say.

'He is doing them whilst being Mayor of London,' she says. 'Yep.'

The woman doesn't want to argue. She tells me to send an email and quickly brings the phone call to an end. But who was the real representative for Uxbridge and South Ruislip? Boris Johnson or the office clerk?

There is no obligation for MPs to do any political work at all. Parliament says: 'They have no contract of employment and no formal job description.'[4] This means it's not always easy to find out how many hours your MP is putting in. A good majority of them work tirelessly and put in a big commitment, so they can get pissed off when their colleagues spend half their time working in other jobs.

'The system does not recognise the role of Member of Parliament as a full-time job,' one of Parliament's new MPs tells me, astonished at the system. 'It is entirely legitimate to do this on a part-time basis! It's legitimate! It's not a breach of any rule to just not turn up. I mean, what other job in the world is there no penalty for not turning up?'

The MP Caroline Lucas says she puts in around eighty hours a week on purely political things. I believe her. And she's not impressed with those who don't make a similar effort. 'If they're managing to do thirty [hours] on top, I would be fearful of their health,' she says. 'And whether they get to eat or sleep!

'The sense that you could have a job that's taking ten, twenty, thirty hours a week on top of your MP job is just so grossly insulting to your constituents. The idea that you don't think it's a big enough job to look after the interests of 70,000 people (on average) I just think is the most arrogant, complacent message.'

Tory MP Jacob Rees-Mogg – who works in the private sector for thirty-five hours a month – admits: 'Something must give in this, nobody has endless time. Fortunately, I've never had any hobbies.' And on this point, I can easily believe *him*, too.[5]

He tells me: 'Inevitably, some things get squeezed: my wife and I don't go to the theatre very often.'

But how do we keep tabs on those who spend time working elsewhere? Yet again, the 'transparency' is shoddy. Although the Register of Interests asks MPs to declare how much time they spend on outside interests, there's no set format. The data is a mess, so it's not possible to directly compare different MPs. Ranking them in order would never be totally accurate.

However, using the information available, I've plucked out a few of the worst offenders. (These are based on interpretations of the Register of Interests in 2015. Check out the endnotes for calculations):

- **Boris Johnson (Conservative)**[6]
  Outside work: c.352 days per year
  Job: Mayor of London, author and columnist
- **Geoffrey Cox (Conservative)**[7]
  Outside work: c.85 days per year
  Job: barrister
- **Stephen Phillips (Conservative)**[8]
  Outside work: c.70 days per 14 months
  Job: barrister and recorder

- **Kit Malthouse (Conservative)**[9]
  Outside work: c.60 days per year
  Job: chairman of a financial firm, and a London Assembly Member
- **Bill Wiggin (Conservative)**[10]
  Outside work: c.59 days per year
  Job: works at three financial services firms
- **Richard Drax (Conservative)**[11]
  Outside work: c.58 days per year
  Job: director of a property company

The 'experience' argument

'The fundamental question, I think, is: "Is a Member of Parliament expected to be a full-time employee of his or her constituency?" And my own view is that it is not a full-time job.'

Michael Heseltine, the former deputy prime minister, was being interviewed on *Newsnight*, and he was tying himself in knots. 'You work all hours and all days,' he said. 'But there's plenty of time in which you can do other things.

'I think it is healthy that one is widening one's experience. Broadening one's ability to say "I know what happens" . . . Otherwise, what you're left with is Members of Parliament who don't actually have the personal experience, and rely on advice from someone else.'[12]

This is the most common argument you'll hear in favour of MPs keeping their second jobs. And there's some validity to it. They say there are too many 'career politicians'; generic suited bods with no experience of the real world. And they're right.

Far too few MPs have any idea what life is like outside their little bubble. Surrounded by fellow politicos 24/7, you get the impression they need briefing notes just to find out what being an ordinary member of the public is like. Without doubt, it would be good if more of them ventured outside to talk to the rest of us.

Actually, they're often confined to their offices partly because we are too needy, as a population. We expect our politicians to be available all the time, even if we don't much care what they *do* in that time. So if a cat gets stuck up a tree in Norwich, or a Z-list celebrity dies, the prime minister can look cold-hearted if he doesn't immediately cut short his holiday to provide a helpful soundbite.

There's a lot to be said for MPs (and even prime ministers) spending less time in the office and more time doing other things. Politicians need maturity and a sense of perspective. They need depth of character and a broader understanding of the world, and no amount of sitting in committee rooms will give you that. We need our representatives to have interests, loyalties and commitments.

Cameron's interests? He was a dubious supporter of Aston Villa and he chose Benny Hill for *Desert Island Discs*.[13] That's as deep as it gets.

The question is, does moonlighting solve this problem? And even if it does, is it the *right* solution?

To many, this will seem like a deeply cynical question. Why should MPs need additional lucrative salaries just to get them to step into the real world for a moment? Is that how low our expectations are – that we need to bribe them with extra wads of cash to make them interact with the public?

No one could argue that it's bad for MPs to spend time helping local charities. Or joining a campaign group. Or even writing occasional newspaper articles. We don't have to be too puritanical about this. But do they really need directorships and consultancies with vast salaries?

In Westminster, the debate over second jobs is often portrayed as a paradox. 'They want us to have experience in the real world, but they don't want us earning any money,' MPs say. But it is not a paradox. They forget that 'experience' does not need to involve getting rich and neglecting their constituents. There are plenty of ways to step out of the Westminster bubble without it being labelled 'greedy' by the press. After all, lots of MPs get along perfectly well without any paid outside work at all.

Liverpool MP, Steve Rotheram, has pointed out: 'Members do not need second jobs, but if they do there are food banks in every one of their constituencies. Go and volunteer in them.'[14]

Another MP I speak to puts the case bluntly:

The people who defend [second jobs] always say 'oh well, we don't just want professional politicians who don't understand what's happening in the real world'. Well I mean that's bollocks. Right? No one's saying people shouldn't have hobbies and interests. You can be on the board of a local charity, you can even be on the board of a company. You can run marathons or do whatever you want to do in your spare time, and nobody's saying the job's 160 hours a week. So the question is, you shouldn't be paid for it. You should only have one paymaster.

Besides, how useful is it anyway? How much 'real life experience' is Richard Drax getting by running a property company? Or Kit Malthouse, as the chairman of a financial services firm? Geoffrey Cox says that being a QC gives him 'practical experience of a world outside politics.'[15] But it also gives him a hell of a lot of cash. Up to £1,333 per hour, to be precise.[16] Being a QC is hardly an 'everyday' kind of job. The truth is, Cox is merely moving from one elite circle to another.

The suggestion that most MPs only take second jobs in order to stay in touch with the public is quickly dismissed by Labour MP John Mann, when I put it to him. 'That's rubbish!' he says. 'If you want to get in the real world, you could be a bus conductor as well. How strange that nobody is. No, I don't buy that in the slightest. That's a convenient excuse.' Mann has an alternative explanation: 'They're doing it for money.'

Many politicians are so out of touch, they fail to realise that these extra jobs can often distance them even *further* from ordinary people – not the other way around. But to them, their lucrative positions seem perfectly normal. A former Conservative minister tells me: 'Most of the business interests that MPs have are as non-executive directors of companies, or as a consultant: ordinary mainstream kind of things.'

Dr Dean Machin, a political academic at University College London, points out that the system favours 'people who can earn lots of money in a short space of time, and then take lots of time off going up and down the country campaigning.' This is particularly true of lawyers and company directors. If you're the boss of your own business affairs, it's easier to fit your work around political priorities. You could skive off the most boring parliamentary duties each week and sit in a board meeting instead. But if you're a postman or a dinner lady, you probably don't have that same flexibility – you'd have to ditch your second job.

The irony is that the best way to hear the voices of ordinary constituents is by actually *meeting* them. That's what 'surgeries' are for. But that's exactly what some MPs like Boris Johnson seem to be neglecting, because they are too busy doing other jobs. 'I know MPs who hold no surgeries, including Labour MPs and Tory MPs,' says John Mann. 'Those people tend to have other income streams.' For a handful of politicians, it seems working in the House of Commons is regarded as nothing more than a part-time gig.[17]

'There are some – particularly Conservative MPs – who are still of that mindset,' a former Downing Street adviser tells me. 'I was always staggered when MPs had second jobs, because [being an MP] is an absurdly hard job. The hours are insane and it's seven days a week.

'There are some MPs who are rich enough, they've got an office that deals with all the constituency work, and they don't have to worry about slogging their guts out because they've got a safe seat.

'The people at the top of parliamentary parties don't care about that . . . If you haven't got a load of backbenchers causing you trouble, you say to them "vote this way" and they do it. You're not going to be that worried.'

It's not just constituency matters that can be affected by time spent doing second jobs. My former Downing Street source reckons: 'It's probably the legislative scrutiny bit they probably spend less time on.' Indeed, one Tory MP I speak to hints that he sometimes skips work in Westminster so that he can attend business meetings. 'I always try and schedule the board meetings so they don't clash with any business I expect,' he says. 'But such is the nature of Parliament, sometimes there is a clash. And then I have to decide which is worth cancelling.'

The 'practice' argument

The next argument you'll hear in favour of MPs keeping their second jobs is this: why should they have to give up their old professions? 'How about doctors and barristers?' they say. They need to work a certain number of hours each year in order to keep hold of their professional licences. Surely we should let them do that?

The problem is, the evidence simply doesn't support this argument. These MPs are not moonlighting just so they can retain their licences. Just look at the hours they've worked – it goes way over what's required. For instance, experienced barristers only need to do one-and-a-half days' work each year to keep hold of their licence.[18] Whereas Geoffrey Cox did around eighty-five days.

So even if we *do* allow MPs to keep their professional licences, that doesn't explain why some MPs are spending weeks on end doing other jobs and potentially neglecting constituents. Yet again, the statistics point to the only conclusion: they're in it for the money.

Public enemies

This is not a black and white issue. There are lots of complications and nuances to consider and we could quibble over the details all day. But the one thing that really matters is what the general public want. After all, MPs are meant to represent the people.

Overwhelmingly, surveys show that people want to ban second jobs. One poll on the *Telegraph*'s website showed that 67% of readers wanted to put an end to them.[19] Another survey by YouGov found that only 26% of people agreed that outside work helped MPs to stay in touch with ordinary people. The pollsters announced: 'The nation is overwhelmingly against its parliamentary representatives having "second jobs".'[20]

Bear in mind also that people have been left in the dark about the true extent of MPs' financial interests. What would these stats be like if there was full transparency in Westminster?

The truth is, when MPs work for outside businesses and organisations, it regularly goes in direct contradiction to the political aims that the public may identify with. Politicians are often the enemy within.

PART TWO:

The enemy within

6

Banks

It was a hot, sunny day in July 2013 and, by 5 p.m., many of the peers in the House of Lords had probably already had enough and gone home for dinner. But those who stayed on in Parliament knew that the next few hours would be critical.

For the first time, they were about to debate new legislation that promised to overhaul the British banking system after the financial crisis. Officially named the Financial Services (Banking Reform) Bill, it was designed to clean up the City and prevent further scandals, crime and misconduct. At last, this was a chance for the massive reforms people had been crying out for. A chance to put the hated 'fat cat' bankers in their place.

Their lordships were all too aware of the significance of the legislation. 'The Bill is a central part of the Government's response to the financial crisis of 2007–09,' a minister announced, introducing the debate in the House. 'Noble Lords will recall the terrible events of those years.'

There are around 800 peers who could have joined in with this landmark debate, from all different walks of life and professional backgrounds. Yet for the entire time the Bill was being debated – eight days over the course of six months – only forty-nine peers spoke. And many of them only spoke once. In fact, only twenty-five peers bothered to join in at more than one stage of the proceedings.

So what was it that made this small handful of Lords so concerned about the Banking Reform Bill? Why did they care so much, when most of their colleagues didn't? Surely their financial connections didn't have anything to do with it?

Let me introduce them to you.

Here's a comprehensive list of all twenty-five of them, along with their banking credentials (as they were at the time).[1] I've ranked them in order of who spoke at the most stages of the debate:

1. **Lord Flight (Conservative)**

   Director at Metro Bank. He is also a director of Marechale Capital investment bank, the director of Investec Asset Management and the chairman of a 'fund manager'. Plus, he's the commissioner of the financial regulator in the tax haven of Guernsey.[2]

2. **Lord Deighton (Conservative)**

   Previously an investment banker at Goldman Sachs for 22 years, where he became the firm's Chief Operating Officer for Europe.[3] He's now the government's Commercial Secretary to the Treasury.

3. **Lord Eatwell (Non-affiliated)**

   Non-executive director of 'one of the largest issuers of credit cards in the UK'. He's also the commissioner of the financial regulation authority in Jersey (another tax haven) and economic adviser to a private equity firm.[4]

4. **Lord Lawson of Blaby (Conservative)**

   A former director of Barclays Bank. Lawson was also chancellor of the exchequer under Margaret Thatcher.[5]

5. **Lord McFall of Alcluith (Labour)**

   Senior independent non-executive director of Atom Bank, where he also owns at least £50,000 of shares.[6]

6. **Lord Brennan (Labour)**

   Non-executive director of investment firms NBNK Investments and Juridica Investments Limited, where he is also the chairman.[7]

7. **Lord Higgins (Conservative)**

   Owns at least £50,000 of shares in Lansdowne UK Equity Fund Ltd.

8. **Lord Newby (Lib Dem)**

   Treasury spokesperson

9. **Lord Phillips of Sudbury (Lib Dem)**

10. **Lord Turnbull (Cross bench)**

    Directorship at Prudential PLC, a multinational financial services company, which he also owns shares in. Turnbull also has a directorship at Frontier Economics, a private finance consultancy.[8]

11. **Lord Sharkey (Lib Dem)**

12. **Lord Watson of Invergowrie (Labour)**

    In the 1990s, he ran a management company designed to 'liaise' with a trust in the Channel Islands tax haven.[9] Exact details are not known.

13. Baroness Cohen of Pimlico (Labour)

Non-executive director of the London Stock Exchange. Formerly the director of Charter House Bank and the Yorkshire Building Society.[10]

14. Lord Barnett (Labour)

Treasury minister in the 1970s. (Died in 2014)

15. The Archbishop of Canterbury, Justin Welby (Bishops)

No banking connections but, before finding God, Welby was once an exec for a big FTSE 100 oil exploration company called Enterprise Oil plc.[11]

16. The Lord Bishop of Birmingham, David Urquhart (Bishops)

17. Baroness Noakes (Conservative)

On the board of directors at the Royal Bank of Scotland Group (which owns other banks including NatWest, Ulster Bank and the Queen's private bank, Coutts). She owns shares in a portfolio of financial firms like Barclays and JP Morgan.[12]

18. Viscount Trenchard (Conservative)

Senior adviser and consultant to Mizuho Bank, a Japanese retail bank. Also Director-General of the European Fund and Asset Management Association.[13]

19. Lord Blackwell (Conservative)

Chairman of Lloyds Banking Group and its subsidiaries, including Halifax bank. He was previously chair of Scottish Widows and Independent Director of Standard Life.[14]

20. Lord Forsyth of Drumlean (Conservative)

Former deputy chairman of merchant bank JP Morgan.[15]

21. Lord Hamilton of Epsom (Conservative)

Director of Jupiter Dividend & Growth Trust plc, an equity investment vehicle. He also appears to be on the board of three offshore firms in Bermuda.[16]

22. Lord Hollick (Labour)

Senior adviser to a leading investment banking business, GP Bullhound.[17]

23. Lord Tunnicliffe (Labour)

24. Lord Stewartby (Conservative)

Has previously worked for a range of financial firms, including a stint as an adviser to the board of Standard Chartered plc.[18]

25. Lord Desai (Labour)

> Independent director of an investment bank, Elara Capital.
> Previously, he was on the board of directors for an investment
> management firm for more than ten years.[19]

Let's discount the likes of Justin Welby, Lord Higgins and Lord
Watson of Invergowrie, for a moment. Their connections don't
really amount to working for financial institutions. But the list is still
overwhelmingly made up of bankers and City bods. Of the twenty-
five peers, twelve were working directly for financial firms *at the time
they debated the banking reform legislation*.

Two thirds of the most influential peers debating the banks were
in the pay of the very institutions they were claiming to regulate.

Repeat that again.

In the House of Lords, the Banking Reform Act was designed, scrutinised, and passed *by the bankers themselves*.[20] This supposed government shake-up of the City was, in fact, nothing more than a gang of fat
cat bankers writing themselves a new chapter for their businesses.

The result of this farcical process was a scrappy piece of legislation that failed to reform the banks in any meaningful way. Professor
Prem Sikka of Essex University, who is director of the Centre for
Global Accountability, says that politicians have completely overlooked the most important issues that needed changing after the
financial crash. 'The Banking Bill does not address the regulatory
architecture,' he says. 'The Banking Bill does not address anything.

'It's kind of re-arranged the deck-chairs on the *Titanic*, but the ship
has not really been re-steered.'

It's not just the Banking Bill that's been ineffective. By and large
the City has avoided any major reforms. It's been allowed to carry on
as if the financial crisis never happened. By the end of 2015, even the
official finance watchdog had given up, quietly ditching its review of
Britain's banking culture just months after it was launched.[21] 'The era
of "banker bashing" is over,' *Private Eye* declared.[22]

But if things carry on the way they are, the outlook is bleak.
'Britain's regulatory architecture is not appropriate,' Sikka says. 'That
has been evident for decades. Nobody's willing to do something . . .
All the important issues have been side-lined, so I would give it about
a decade before we have an even bigger crash than the one we had.'

Sikka is part of a group of accountants, economists and academics who have long been calling for a radical shake-up of the banking sector and a crackdown on tax avoidance. In 2014, he wrote a policy paper condemning the government for being too cosy with the banks. It claimed: 'The financial sector has colonised the state in such a way that political power has been subordinated to corporate interests.'[23] This idea seems to correlate with the financial interests I'd uncovered from peers during the Banking Reform Bill. The city haven't just *lobbied* Westminster; they've *colonised* it.

'The problem is, many [politicians] end up working in some capacity for some giant corporation,' Prem explains. 'It's not just about direct financial interest – important though that is – it's this idea that you've got to sympathise with these big corporations.'

He adds: 'The parliamentary committees have done important work, but there's been no government-led real investigation of the crash.'

Parliament is so interwoven with the City that it's no stretch to say the two are working as a single unit. Other people have to campaign and lobby to get their voices heard. But the banks don't need lobbyists to bang on the doors of Parliament – their lobbyists are already inside.

This is not about politicians pocketing brown envelopes stuffed with cash; no one is suggesting that these peers were being paid specifically to influence the legislation. None of the peers on this list has done anything against the rules. But it's such a whopping conflict of interest, overall, that it fundamentally undermines the integrity of any reforms.

Their argument in defence goes something like this: 'Our jobs don't make us biased, but experience in the financial sector gives us unique insights and expertise that helps make the legislation as good as possible.' They might have a point: banking reform is a complicated issue that does take time to get to grips with. How clued up are you about the pros and cons of an 'electrified' ringfence between retail and investment banks?

But just because it's complex, that doesn't mean bankers can have this issue for themselves. Lots of issues are equally complicated, but that doesn't stop ordinary people understanding them. It doesn't discredit the views of 'non-experts'. After all, you don't need to be a doctor to have a valid opinion on the NHS. You don't have to be an immigrant to take a stance on immigration. And just because you're not in the special forces, that doesn't mean your views on counter-terrorism are worthless. But in Parliament, financial affairs are frequently left to the 'expertise' of bankers.

'To my mind, if anyone's looking for evidence about "how corrupt is Britain", we just discussed part of it,' says Prem Sikka, as we wrap up our conversation.[24] 'The problem is, it's not portrayed as corruption. People are saying it's lobbying and so on. Well I'm sorry, it is not *lobbying*, as such. This is people pushing for advancement of their own interest at the expense of somebody else. That is one way of looking at corruption.

'How is democracy and transparency and accountability served? Those issues are sort of ignored.'

Sikka is not suggesting that any politicians are *individually* corrupt. Rather this is *institutionalised* corruption. It's the bigger picture that's worrying. 'It's systematic,' he says.

The dominance of bankers in the banking reform debate seemed disturbing, but did the people involved care? Did their closeness between politics and the City bother them, or was this just business as usual? It was time for some answers. I decided to email the peer at the top of my list, Lord Flight – a director at Metro Bank who had spoken in all eight stages of the proceedings for the Banking Reform Bill. I had one or two questions to ask him.

'An unpaid lobbyist'

Inviting yourself round to a stranger's house at 8:30 in the morning, eating their food, arguing for an hour and accusing them of, frankly, being a bit of a disgrace is behaviour that I'd normally consider impolite. But, strangely enough, that's exactly what I have planned for the day.

Nervous and running late, I rush through the torrential October rain before finally finding the right address. It should have been easy to spot: the house is a big, grand old thing, four floors high and casting an imposing shadow on the street below. I find out afterwards that it had once been home to both Viscount Eccles, a hereditary nobleman, and the founder of the BBC, Lord Reith. Nestled between Pimlico and Westminster, this place seems like an oasis from the surrounding hubbub of London. I ring the bell and quickly

I'm ushered in to meet the man himself: Lord Howard Emerson Flight.

Everything about Lord Flight is establishment; from his forty-five-year career in the City, right down to the gold buttons adorning his blazer.[25] Alongside his financial career, he's been a Conservative politician for decades, originally standing unsuccessfully to be an MP in 1974. Flight eventually won the safe Tory seat of Arundel and South Downs in 1997 and went on to become the party's deputy chair.

Eight years later, scandal hit. He was secretly recorded suggesting that his party would only announce 'politically acceptable' spending cuts, but secretly had plans to make 'continuing' cuts once in government.[26] Unsurprisingly, the gaffe didn't go down well with the Tory leadership and he was booted out. His elevation to the House of Lords a few years later came as a shock to many, who saw him as a bit of an embarrassment – albeit a rich and influential embarrassment.

Lo and behold, their fears were confirmed a week after he was appointed. Flight was forced to apologise for suggesting that changes to welfare benefits would encourage 'breeding' among poor people – and that this was 'not very sensible'.[27]

In his kitchen, I take a seat at the large wooden table, as family life bustles along in the background. Flight's wife, Christabel, appears in the doorway with a yapping dog called Doris and stops for a chat. The atmosphere is relaxed and jokey, with Flight (or 'Howie' as his wife calls him) chain-smoking cigarettes into an overflowing ashtray.

As the lord puts croissants in the oven, we start talking about his long career. I wonder whether his dual professions in politics and banking have complemented each other. 'They very much do,' he says. 'The areas that I will speak about [in the House of Lords] . . . are the areas that I know about from now sort of forty years career history. So it's sort of pensions, financial regulation, financial services, banking industry; all that interrelated territory. And I think – not in a sort of boastful way – I do get a hearing because people know that I know a bit about it.'

We've only been talking for a couple of minutes when he suddenly comes out with a startling admission. 'I get a lot of people come to me with things that they think need addressing or are wrong,' he says.

'You mean your business colleagues?'

'Yeah. To get me to take it up with government. And sometimes I get something changed; sometimes I don't. So I spend a certain amount of time as an unpaid lobbyist.'

Taken aback, I slurp down my tea in the kind of way that you probably shouldn't when you're having breakfast with a lord. 'I can take up issues which have come at me from my business experience and I know the individuals to talk to or write to,' he continues. 'Quite a lot of industries, their policy is to steer well clear of politics except when something comes up that is problematic for them, when they'll scramble around and get their public relations firms to go around mass lobbying . . . That's not terribly satisfactory. It's better if there is an ongoing engagement.'

I ask him for an example of his 'unpaid lobbying', and he obliges. Through his work with a trade body (the Tax Incentivised Savings Association), an issue 'came to my attention' about the inheritance of ISAs. 'I took it up with Osborne,' Flight says. 'Clearly on the second go, actually, Osborne had sight of it . . . I think it was [the] Finance Bill last summer. We got that in.'[28]

With that example, it seems unlikely there was any *commercial* benefit to his business interests. But Flight is clearly relaxed about lobbying for his banker friends (he says he'll 'only take it up if I think it's right'). The problem is, when peers like Lord Flight speak in the House of Lords, why should we believe that they have anything other than commercial interests in mind?

He dodges my questions. 'In the main in this country, it isn't particularly like that,' he says. 'I can't think almost of any occasions where I have thought "Christ, that guy is really simply speaking in his own, or his company's interest".'

But how can we, the public, be sure of that? He's already admitted he acts as an unpaid lobbyist for his City mates.

'The rules almost are over the top,' he claims. 'You have to declare an interest if you have conceivably got an interest, when you open your mouth. And so that, if you like, is putting anyone and everyone on notice: "this person's declared an interest, they may be coming at it from that angle, etc." So I think that works reasonably well.'

Flight adds: 'You simply won't get Parliament to design some legislation that you've thought of for your own benefit. I mean it just wouldn't happen, and even if you tried to you'd be blown out of the water.'

He's right that individual peers don't have anywhere near the power to simply dream up rafts of legislation crafted to serve nothing but their own interests. But let's not underplay their power *too* much. Peers are still able to vote and suggest amendments to almost all legislation, and use their position to influence and lobby other politicians. In fact, when the Banking Reform Bill was being debated, a group of Labour peers managed to attach a major amendment to it shortly before it passed into the statute books.[29] The leader of the Lords has said himself: '[The House] doesn't necessarily block or stop the machinery of government, but it influences the decisions that are made.'[30]

For Flight, his imagined lack of power means we shouldn't be worried about his business interests and lobbying. 'What drives the legislation is not politicians sitting in the chambers – it is the Treasury,' he says.

'But it is still a privilege and an opportunity that most people don't have,' I argue.

He pauses to think for a moment. 'The way I see it is the other way round,' he says, implying that it's a privilege for *Parliament* to have *him* there. 'If you didn't have anybody sitting in Parliament who knew anything about the economic activities of the land, then there would be no effective debating and discussion of what it is that the Treasury's laid down.'

'But presumably if the public had their way with banking reform, it would be a lot more radical than it has been?' I suggest.

Flight disagrees. He reckons he was pushing for the great radical shake-up that the public had been crying out for; a raft of stricter rules to regulate bankers. 'If anything that's what I was arguing,' he claims.

'Correct me if I'm wrong,' I say gingerly, 'but weren't most people arguing *against* regulation?'

'No,' he says, later telling me: 'You might read what I said, which will surprise you.' Funnily enough, I'd already done my reading. Here's what Flight said during the banking debate:

How do we get integrity back into our banking system? I do not see that rules are going to do it . . . I personally do not see the regulator as being a huge force in turning round integrity. Punishing those that basically act immorally is quite an important ingredient, but above all we need to get sound management into banks.[31]

He's entitled to his opinions, but I'm not sure that he's quite the voice of the people. And I can't help feeling his views are at least partially flavoured by his work at Metro Bank. So I ask him again: did business interests play a part in shaping the Banking Reform Bill when it went through the House of Lords?

He's starting to look at me like I'm an idiot. 'An argument that people from/related to the banking industry have been shaping the political legislation, I don't think's true at all,' he says.

We're going round in circles now and the atmosphere in the kitchen is tensing up. Christabel has nipped outside to take Doris the dog for a walk. But in the kitchen, our argument intensifies. Flight is mid-sentence when disaster strikes: a huge clob of butter falls off my knife and splodges on my trousers. Has he seen? Like a pro, I try to distract him with a question about tax while I subtly scrape it off under the table.

'Are you still the commissioner for Guernsey?' I ask.[32] 'Do you think the public might say it's wrong for a politician to be involved on that level with a tax haven? Would you buy that?'

'I wouldn't buy it,' he says. 'Guernsey is an extremely clean place basically, contrary to lots of perceptions.'

'Is it not blacklisted by the EU?'

'No, it's not.' (Actually, it had been blacklisted by the European Commission just a couple of months earlier and branded 'non co-operative'.)[33]

Whatever the merits of his arguments, it seems weird that he doesn't even recognise the controversy around these issues. To him, all this stuff is just completely normal. He feels as comfortable with banking, lobbying and tax havens as he does munching on a croissant in his own kitchen.

'Do you think the public are supportive of all this?' I ask.

'Of all what?' he asks, confused about what the problem could possibly be.

'Business interests,' I say. 'Links to tax havens. Do you think that the public know about it? . . . Do you think they mind?'

'There's quite a lot of wrong and out-of-date thinking,' he shrugs. 'The media will mislead on occasions, if it can.'

The City mindset

Back in Parliament, the House of Lords stands out as having an especially cosy relationship with the banks. A study by the Bureau of Investigative Journalism in 2012 found that some 12% of peers are in the pay of City firms. The analysis, which included politicians with clients in the financial sector, concluded that the House was 'awash with voices from the City'.[34] It said:

> The banking sector's influence doesn't stop at the red benches. Committees scrutinising issues of particular importance to the financial services industry are also packed with Lords with links to the sector.
>
> Four of the 11 members of the Lords committee set up to consider the 2011 finance bill, for example, held positions in banks, and a fifth was about to join a bank. The Finance Act gave large tax breaks to businesses with offshore interests, including multinational banks and insurers.[35]

One of the peers highlighted by the Bureau's investigation explained: 'Finding myself in this space between the industry and the political/ social environment has been the norm for me.'

But it's not just the House of Lords who are under the spell of financial firms. Many MPs, too, are in the pay of banks, investment firms and mortgage companies.

Sir Edward Leigh, the Conservative MP for Gainsborough, has a position at the Europe Arab Bank plc (EAB).[36] It's part of the Arab Bank – one of the Middle East's largest and most controversial financial institutions – but is a multimillion-pound operation in its own right. Recent accounts show it has more than €3bn of assets and made almost €9m net profit.[37] 'EAB has a European passport that enables it to open branches anywhere in the European Union,' the Arab Bank says of the EAB. '[It] provides all types of banking products and services, including retail banking and treasury services, to its customers.'[38]

While Leigh was working for the bank's UK arm in 2012, a US federal jury found the Arab Bank liable for financing terrorism. The allegations reportedly related to two dozen attacks around Israel during a Palestinian uprising beginning in 2000.[39]

The legal case had been brought to court by hundreds of victims who accused the Arab Bank of facilitating funding to fighters. One of the jurors later told reporters that the bank had provided 'oxygen for the terrorists'.[40] After the court ruling, the victims' lawyer told journalists: 'Terrorist organisations are dependent on the financial system to operate. They've been able to thrive largely because folks like Arab Bank and others have turned a blind eye.'[41] Eventually, a settlement was reached with the plaintiffs three days before the damages trial.[42]

But during this whole disturbing saga, the Tory MP kept hold of his role at the bank's Europe subsidiary. Having previously sat on Parliament's Defence Committee, he presumably thought that just because his bank's parent company had supported terrorism, that wasn't a reason to quit a good job. So he stayed on.

In fact, Leigh now tells me: 'It is an association which I am proud to maintain.' He says that his position at the EAB was 'entirely appropriate for an MP', explaining: 'The [Arab] Bank consistently stated that it did not knowingly or intentionally do business with terrorists.'[43]

Under his nose, the EAB operates within a network of financial firms owned by the Arab Bank, including a large bank in the Swiss tax haven.[44] It could prove embarrassing for Leigh, considering he's just become a member of Parliament's famed Public Accounts Committee, which has made a name for itself by shaming companies that operate through tax havens. Precisely what benefits the Swiss bank brings to the overall banking group is unclear. But Leigh says the EAB pays all UK taxes in the ordinary way. He explains the bank's seemingly low tax payments, saying that unused tax losses were 'appropriately offset against profits in accordance with the rules'.[45]

'With businesses, their views are listened to a lot more seriously and they get more access,' a source who has worked at the top of government tells me. 'A lot of Tory MPs have links to the City and are therefore all about the light touch regulation.

'A privately run organisation is always going to be better run than a public organisation, whatever the circumstance. And that became kind of received wisdom.

'Any conversations with their peers all come from a particular mindset. They're all from a private sector, business mindset. And it's quite an effort of will not to think that's how everyone thinks.'

It's a chicken and egg situation. Which came first, the banking career or the banking mindset? What's certain is that a host of MPs still stay cosy with the financial world, keeping them in tune with City thinking. They include the likes of newbie Tory Kit Malthouse, who is chairman and founder of County Finance Group Ltd, which describes itself as an 'independent finance house'.[46] Another MP, Bill Wiggin, is non-executive director at a £1.5m firm called Philip T. English International Financial Services Limited, which specialises in international finance.[47] His colleague, Jonathan Djanogly, is chairman of Pembroke VCT plc, a venture capital trust which offers clients an 'investment strategy with significant tax benefits'.[48]

Meanwhile, Jacob Rees-Mogg MP is a founding partner and director of Somerset Capital Management LLP, an investment advisory firm which brought in nearly £19m last year. The firm normally hands him a pay cheque of more than £9,000 each month.[49]

Another directorship of Rees-Mogg's goes undeclared on the Register of Interests – The American Trading Company Limited. Asked why it had been left off, his secretary said: 'It does not do anything any longer.' When I told her that its accounts say the company is still active with thousands of pounds of investments and more than £1m in assets, she said she'd ask the MP again. 'He has said that it is now an investment vehicle,' came the eventual response. She claimed that the firm did not qualify to be declared under the rules, and he was not paid.[50]

It's all very well spotting the enemy within, but are they armed? The reason that MPs get away with working for the banks is because any influence they exert is so subtle. They may not have broken any rules. As far as they're concerned, they're just doing two jobs that have overlapping interests. But nobody really knows where one job ends and the other begins. Slowly but surely, the City's influence takes a hold on the government.

Can we ever prove the influence of banker politicians as a cold, hard fact? 'You couldn't prove it, but it would be unlikely if it were not the case,' one MP tells me. 'If you've got a whole set of people who've got financial vested interests in a particular outcome, it's very hard to believe that they are not going to be influenced by those financial interests.

'What it does do is undermine whatever decisions they are making in terms of the public perception of what's going on. And for that reason alone, it's a very good reason to stop them doing it.'

7

Tax

It was as if I'd just taken a crap on the table in front of her. A mixture of horror, disgust and anger – but, above all, just complete confusion. Yet all I'd done was ask a simple question:

'What is Vestra Wealth?'

A stunned look sprang on to her face. 'Is that on the *Register*?'

'No,' I said. 'It's not.'

I was in the House of Commons canteen, having a cup of tea with Labour MP Gisela Stuart. Born in West Germany in the 1950s, Stuart has been in Parliament for around two decades and is now highly respected on all sides. She edits Westminster's own *The House* magazine, covering the latest political drama, and recently lost a bid to become chair of the prestigious Public Accounts Committee. In 2016, she was named co-head of the campaign to leave the EU, alongside Tory minister Michael Gove.

For the last twenty minutes, we've been chatting about politicians' financial interests and the importance of transparency. 'It's always openness that matters,' she says. 'We have a regularly updated Register of Interests so people know exactly where our money comes from.' And if someone failed to declare something? 'You'd be an absolute idiot!'

The problem is, Gisela Stuart has now just admitted that Vestra Wealth was not declared on her own Register of Interests.[1] Documents I had found at Companies House revealed, without doubt, that she was a member of the exclusive partnership. A short, two-page file, dated July 2012, confirms her name.[2]

The Labour Party must be pleased that Stuart has kept quiet about it for so long. After all, the business model for Vestra Wealth doesn't quite fit with the party's image:

Labour has been the most vocal of all the main parties in its criticism of tax avoidance. In the 2015 General Election, it pledged to scrap the so-called 'non-dom' status – a practice which allows the super rich to avoid paying certain taxes by claiming they are not legally domiciled in Britain. In the run-up to the election, Ed Miliband pushed the non-dom issue to the top of the party's policy agenda, claiming he was in a 'fight' against the fat cats who wanted to keep the abusive system. 'It does not matter how much I get attacked for this; I am not backing down,' he said.[3] 'It all comes back to the claim that we are powerless in the face of the richest and most powerful.'[4]

But who exactly were these rich non-doms he was fighting? And who were the 'richest and most powerful' people who supported them? It turns out that Labour's own MP Gisela Stuart has harboured an association with this very group. You see, Vestra Wealth is an investment scheme that helps non-doms and millionaires.

With the company documents safely stashed away in my folder, I ask Gisela Stuart to explain her involvement.

'It's a big partnership. And it's, err . . .' She looks panicked. She wasn't expecting to be quizzed on this, and she's clearly ill-prepared.

'Essentially, it invests serious[ly] rich people's money,' she says. 'My late husband – he was one of the people who helped set it up. So when he died, I inherited his partnership points.'

Stuart claims the scheme only 'paid out £43.50, or something like that' last year, for the first time ever. And she says she has no active involvement with it. Fair enough. But Vestra's website paints a rather more grand picture of the partnership. Photos show pinstriped execs posing in the City. The website boasts: 'It is good to know that your wealth is in trusted hands. Our investment managers have an average of more than 20 years experience working with the world's leading financial institutions.'[5]

And there's no doubt what this business does: 'We offer a fresh approach to wealth management,' it tells clients. 'Offshore and inter-national planning for non-domiciled and nonresident clients.'[6]

'Your wealth. Your future. Your way.'[7]

Company literature goes on to boast the 'ability to advise on strategies which will enhance net returns through appropriate tax planning.'[8] The firm's advisers help 'High-Net-Worth and Ultra-High-Net-Worth private clients', and say they have 'a strong interest and expertise in advising UK-Resident Non-Domiciled individuals.'[9]

After setting up in 2008, reports say that Vestra now 'manages the wealth of a large number of UK resident non-doms'.[10] And the venture has certainly paid off. By 2014, it was managing some £4.1bn of clients' money, and had raked in £8.8m of profit for the business.[11]

Of course, the firm doesn't use the phrase 'tax avoidance' itself. That's one of the tricks of the trade: don't publicise the reality of what you're facilitating. Instead, industry insiders cloak their work with an endless array of dull-sounding terms like 'beneficial tax planning', 'wealth management', 'tax mitigation' or 'efficient corporate structuring'. Meanwhile, regulators and politicians like to describe the most extreme tax abuses as 'aggressive avoidance' – as if everything else is like a vicarage tea party.

True, there are many different types and methods of avoidance and some are clearly worse than others (we don't criticise people who make use of duty-free in airports, for instance). But, the way most people see it, we should loosely describe any kind of systematic, focused and structured attempt to significantly cut tax bills as 'tax dodging'. The practice might be hard to define, but we know it when we see it. Most of the time it involves the same basic principle: extremely wealthy people trying to avoid contributing their fair share. One of Stuart's own Labour colleagues has pointed out: 'Is the term "aggressive tax avoidance" not just semantics? Tax avoidance is tax avoidance, whether aggressive or not. By doing this we are encouraging complexity, which is to the benefit of sharp-witted accountants and lawyers.'[12]

Vestra Wealth doesn't just help people with their tax issues; its top execs have publicly urged politicians not to bring in regulations banning non-doms. The chair of Vestra's investment committee, Jenny Tozer, defended the controversial tax status, saying: 'Many non-doms are entrepreneurs.' She claimed, 'Allowing them to bring in money to fund businesses and create jobs is a very pro-business policy. This has undoubtedly persuaded many of the value of the UK as a base.'[13] In other words, the government shouldn't just *allow* non-doms to dodge taxes, it should be *grateful* for them. When asked in a media interview about proposed tax hikes for the super rich, a senior partner at the firm, David Scott, said: 'We need to push back against it.' He explained. '[The super rich are] concerned that having spent their life building up businesses and having a degree of comfort in knowing what the regulation and tax is likely to be, they're just feeling things are changing very rapidly and if they take steps to try and deal with that effectively, then things will unwind.'[14]

As I tell Stuart what I know about Vestra Wealth, she shoots me a venomous look. 'Clearly, that's not something that worries you,' I say.

'. . . Well, if I say to you this is the first time anybody's ever mentioned it,' Stuart says. She claims that none of her financial interests are of any relevance to anyone. 'There's no journalist in Westminster who would regard this as a conflict of interests.'

She adds: 'If I was on the board and advised on anything, then that would be an involvement . . . It's a matter of what I actually do. But with Vestra, I don't even go to a meeting.'

'But is it a business where you support what they do?' I ask. 'Presumably it must be, otherwise you wouldn't be a member.'

'Mm, mm,' she mumbles in apparent agreement.

As far as Stuart is concerned, she has every right to be involved with Vestra. It's all perfectly legal, so what's the problem? Never mind that she's just run for chair of Parliament's coveted Public Accounts Committee, promising to focus on a tax system which 'eliminates aggressive avoidance'.[15]

She interrupts me: 'Hold on. Let's just be very clear here,' she says, sternly. 'I'm not a church and I'm not a pressure group. I'm not here because I claim to be better than you are . . . You have a right to expect me to comply with the law. You also have a right to have an expectation that, at times, I may campaign for a change of law. But within that, you have no right to expect anything else.'

That's right. MPs are allowed to get involved with legal tax avoidance businesses – and we have *no right* to expect better of them. That's what Gisela Stuart seems to think.

But is she out of sync with public attitudes towards tax avoidance? I tell her I think she might be. Stuart explodes with anger. 'I find it quite extraordinary that you sit here and tell me what the public thinks! Whereas I've had nineteen years of a public of 70,000 who have never ever raised this with me.'

It's a fair criticism of me: I don't know what the public will make of this. But then again, neither does she because – as she admits – Vestra has never been publicly declared in the Register of Interests. Yet again, the public have been left in the dark.

There were still some important unanswered questions, though. How much does she have invested in Vestra? And – although there's no evidence that she has personally dodged tax herself – what benefits does she get out of the partnership?[16]

A month after our meeting, while I was writing this chapter, I checked back on the Register of Interests to read Gisela Stuart's declarations again. A couple of sentences had been quietly added on the end: 'Vestra Wealth LLP; a private wealth management company,' it said. 'This interest achieved registrable value on 25 January 2016.'[17]

What an amazing coincidence! The 25th of January 2016? That just so happened to be the very day I had interviewed her!

In the morning, she had downplayed her stake in Vestra. Although she didn't tell me the *overall* amount of her investment, she said it had only paid out '£43.50, or something like that'. That might suggest that the investment was peanuts. Yet by the end of the afternoon, the overall value had risen to at least £70,000.[18] Now that's impressive!

The phoney war against tax dodging

Most people agree that tax dodging is bad. So why hasn't the government done more to stop it?

The scandal first kicked off properly in the summer of 2012, after *The Times* revealed that celebrities like Jimmy Carr and Gary Barlow were investing money into shady offshore tax avoidance schemes.[19] They were followed by a handful of well-known companies like Starbucks, Amazon and Google, who were named and shamed for going to extraordinary lengths to cut their tax bills.

Public outrage was so great that politicians have lined up to voice their opposition to the practice ever since. Not doing so would be political suicide. Soon after the first exposé about Jimmy Carr, David

Cameron came out to personally attack the comedian, suggesting that schemes like the one he had signed up to were 'morally wrong'.

'I think particularly of the Jimmy Carr scheme . . . I just think this is completely wrong,' he said. 'People work hard, they pay their taxes, they save up to go to one of his shows. They buy the tickets. He is taking the money from those tickets and he, as far as I can see, is putting all of that into some very dodgy tax avoiding schemes.' Cameron went a step further too, by promising to crack down on tax dodgers like Carr. 'The government is acting by looking at a general anti-avoidance law but we do need to make progress on this. It is not fair on hardworking people who do the right thing and pay their taxes to see these sorts of scams taking place.'[20]

For a while it looked like something might actually be done about it. In fact, as anti-avoidance rhetoric spread across the political spectrum, it became one of the few issues politicians all seemed to agree on. Ed Miliband pledged to 'tackle the scourge of tax avoidance', George Osborne said it was 'morally repugnant' and Nick Clegg promised to 'concentrate not just on the battle, but the war' against tax dodging.[21] In the glare of TV cameras, they all pledged to take action and clamp down on anyone avoiding tax in an 'aggressive' way.

So it's a bit mysterious that, despite political consensus and overwhelming public support, almost nothing has been done about it. It's an overwhelmingly massive problem and some signs suggest it's getting a whole lot worse.

When Cameron became prime minister in 2010, reports estimated that the UK lost up to £95bn every year in unpaid taxes. Four years later, that figure had risen to a mind-blowing £122bn.[22] That's £122,000,000,000 of government money lost every year! With that amount you could pay off the entire bill for MPs' expenses for a *whole millennium* and still have £9bn of loose change left over.[23] It's silly money.

Tax experts and campaigners have repeatedly suggested ways the government could crack down on the abuse, but ministers just don't seem to be listening. Around 16% of the money lost through tax dodging is done through methods that are still sanctioned by the government and considered legal.[24] But even illegal tax dodging (known as tax 'evasion') has been dealt with softly. For instance, between 2010 and 2015, authorities prosecuted just one out of 7,000 individuals who were named in a cache of leaked documents from a secretive Swiss bank.[25]

Cameron introduced new measures against tax abuse, but they were laughably weak. Critics said the regulations were 'wholly inadequate' and would not have stopped the likes of Google and Starbucks from aggressively dodging tax bills.[26] What's more, the new rules didn't include any penalties for firms that broke them. All in all, it was estimated that Cameron's new laws would stop less than 1% of tax avoidance.

So why have politicians backed off? As with the failure to reform the banks, part of the explanation for politicians' sluggish action on tax avoidance lies in their own financial affairs. Tax dodgers and MPs are not two separate groups, battling against each other – often they are the very same people. Some are doing it themselves; some are helping others to dodge tax; more still are just complicit in the culture. The public may want a crackdown on tax dodging, but if the lawmakers themselves are in on the act, don't expect a change any time soon.

Gisela Stuart may have questionable links to non-doms. But until 2010, members of the House of Lords were allowed to be non-doms *themselves*! And many took up the opportunity. No one knows quite how many non-dom lords there were, with estimates ranging from ten to a hundred.[27] But when it was eventually banned, five peers were so enamoured with their tax-dodging abilities, they decided to leave Parliament rather than give up their financial status. An unknown number of others quietly dropped it and carried on influencing Britain's tax laws in Parliament. They included Lord Paul and Lord Ashcroft – both major party donors, to Labour and the Conservatives respectively. In Ashcroft's case, this came after nearly a decade of refusing to confirm whether or not he was a non-dom, despite mounting speculation and pressure from the press.[28]

In his 2015 book *Call Me Dave*, Ashcroft even claims that David Cameron plotted with him to suppress the fact he was a tax exile, before he became prime minister. 'He was fully aware of my status as a so-called non dom,' Ashcroft writes. 'Indeed, we had a conversation about how we could delay revealing my tax arrangements until after the election.'[29]

Since giving up their non-dom status, both he and Lord Paul have used their position in Parliament to routinely quiz ministers over their tax policies. Ashcroft pointedly asked whether they 'expect citizens to organise their tax affairs in order to *maximise* tax payable,' and whether it is 'acceptable for one spouse in a marriage to be resident in the United Kingdom for tax purposes while the other is not'.[30] He went on to ask if the government applied 'any principles of acceptability to legal tax avoidance practices; and, if so, what are those principles'.[31] Meanwhile, Lord Paul has occasionally piped up to encourage the government to follow his ideas on business issues, such as 'lowering tax thresholds' for certain firms and claiming that 'the present taxation arrangements . . . are needlessly complicated.'

When politicians get cosy with tax avoidance, the problem is not just that votes may be swayed by conflicts of interest. It's more fundamental than that: it casts a shadow over their political standing. Can they really hope to understand and represent public opinion – not only over tax avoidance issues but anything to do with public money at all? Does it compromise their integrity?

'We don't just collect tax, we decide how it's spent,' says Margaret Hodge, who famously battled with Google and other corporations over their avoidance schemes. 'I think being a tax avoider and pretending to be a public servant – either in the Commons or the Lords – is a pretty difficult position to hold. You can't do it.'

'Income can be rolled up tax free'

Guernsey's main harbour is a quaint, picture-postcard setting. Sparkling blue waters highlight the crumbling fairytale castle that juts out into the sea. But this idyllic island is also harbouring thousands of the world's biggest tax dodgers.

Based in a small office two minutes' walk inland, it was here that one Westminster politician helped run a particularly candid offshore avoidance scheme.[32]

Until it was sold in 2015, Ardel Holdings was headed by a group of directors that included Lord Razzall, a top Lib Dem peer and the party's former treasurer.[33] Razzall has had an illustrious career and is known as 'one of the liveliest figures in politics'.[34] But when it comes to tax avoidance, he seems to have one rule for himself and another rule for everyone else.

In Parliament he's urged the government to take action on the issue. He once raised concerns about companies like Starbucks, et al., in the House of Lords, saying: 'They seem to do significant business in the UK but pay very little tax. What progress has been made in that area?'[35]

But his own offshore company, Ardel Holdings, had a more relaxed attitude, which it spelled out shamelessly. 'Capital gains and income can be rolled up tax free in Guernsey, thereby maximising the potential pension available on retirement,' it explained. 'By transferring assets into a single premium insurance bond, capital gains and income tax can be reduced, deferred or avoided entirely.'[36]

Ardel boasted about the benefits of its services:

- 'A tax free source of funds in the UK for resident non-domiciled individuals;'
- 'Assets can be efficiently passed to the next generation free from capital gains tax;'
- 'No UK reporting requirements;'
- 'Gains are subject to income tax on an arising basis at the appropriate rate. This can be avoided;'
- 'Funds are held in a safe offshore environment.'[37]

While other schemes might argue that they merely facilitate 'sensible tax planning', Ardel left no doubt that its services are specifically designed to cut the tax bills of the super rich. In a note to financial advisers, a document on its website said: 'Given that the highest rate of tax is now 50%, it is more important than ever that you and your clients are fully aware of these vehicles.'[38]

The firm also explained how it could navigate legal loopholes. For instance, one Ardel brochure appeared to tell clients how to avoid arousing the suspicions of UK authorities: 'Care must be taken to avoid the Inland Revenue claiming that the transfer into the trust and out of the trust are connected,' it said. 'A sensible amount of time should elapse between stages.'[39]

Another document said: 'An important feature [of the scheme] is that assets transferred to [the scheme] immediately cease to be part of the transferor's estate for inheritance tax purposes . . . but it is vital to understand that the purpose for setting up the scheme must be for legitimate retirement planning – HMRC will not accept them as death bed planning vehicles for the sole purpose of avoiding IHT [inheritance tax].'[40]

In the House of Lords, it may look like Lord Razzall is on the side of those who want to tackle tax avoidance, but his business history tells a different story.[41]

Dodge City

There are hundreds of politicians in Westminster, so perhaps it's unsurprising that one or two are linked to tax avoidance. But the truth is that Westminster's love affair with tax avoidance is endemic. Cases like Lord Razzall and Gisela Stuart may be among the most striking examples, but they represent the tip of a pretty enormous iceberg.

A few years back, I wrote an investigation for the *Guardian* that exposed sixty-eight MPs and peers who had business links to tax havens.[42] Twenty-seven were Conservatives, seventeen were Labour, three were Lib Dem peers and another twenty-one were non-affiliated peers. In August that year, we contacted each of the sixty-eight politicians, asking them to explain themselves. We were frequently met with furious responses. Here's one of the many emails I got back:

Dear Mr Williams,

The arrogance of your email takes my breath away and quite apart from its inaccuracy I am astonished that you are so unaware that in August/September people tend to take holidays . . . I reserve my right not just to sue you but complain about you to the Press Commission. It might be timely that so-called 'investigative journalists' were scrutinised for their abuses.

As it happens, I have no connexion [sic] with In2Matrix (UK) Ltd but since January 2011 I have been a non-executive director of In2Matrix Services Group. I will pay my taxes on the relatively modest remuneration I receive but beyond that I have no shareholding.

Tomorrow we leave for Italy beyond email.

Peter Fraser.[43]

Another politician we reported, for having corporate links to a tax haven, was Lord Grabiner. He was a non-executive director for Arcadia Group, the retail empire which includes Topshop and Miss Selfridge. After emailing Grabiner, I was woken early the next morning with an angry call from Arcadia's chairman, Sir Philip Green. 'This is not a "link to a tax haven"! *OK?*' he growled angrily down the phone at me as I jumped out of bed. 'There is zero relevance to where this company is registered. All the directors, and the company, are UK taxpayers. End.'[44]

When we published the story, we named both men and – to nobody's surprise – they didn't sue. It's hard to deny there are tax haven links when your own company accounts show finance structures that pass through tax havens![45]

Yet more political tax haven links were uncovered with the release of the Panama Papers in April 2016, when 11 million secret documents were leaked. Among the files were the names of peers like Lord Flight and Lord Bilimoria (the founder of Cobra Beer) who had been connected to various tax haven companies. This friendly relationship with the offshore world extended right up to David Cameron, when it emerged that he had personal investment in his father's trust fund in Panama, which had never paid any tax.[46]

I need to point out here that it is – in theory – entirely possible to have tax haven links for legitimate reasons. If you own a shop in Panama, for instance, it's only natural to set up the company in Panama too. So operating offshore doesn't *necessarily* mean you're doing anything wrong, or even that you're avoiding any tax. But you might expect politicians to avoid association with tax havens like the plague. If you squirrel away your money offshore, then it can certainly give a bad impression.

The question you've got to ask is: if these companies *aren't* dodging taxes or benefitting from corporate secrecy, then why the hell are they registered in a tax haven in the first place? 'Places like the Caymans, there's no income tax, no corporation tax,' says Professor Prem Sikka. 'So what are these people doing there?'[47] Perhaps they just like the scenery.

My investigation in 2012 only told part of the story, because we relied almost entirely on the shoddy Register of Interests. When it was published I vowed to myself that one day I'd come back and do the same investigation again, better and more comprehensively. Now, armed with the mammoth list of companies I'd compiled with DueDil's data scientists, I started the long process again, to finally uncover the true scale of Westminster's cosiness with tax havens.[48]

There were still huge limitations, and I knew my analysis was always going to be very conservative. Tracking down details about foreign companies is a nightmare at the best of times, not least if they're stashed away in secretive offshore havens where even the most basic information can often be hidden away.

But trawling through the mass of documents I had traced, a picture slowly emerged. One by one, I added the politicians who have direct corporate links to a tax haven. The final score was more than has ever been estimated before: a grand total of ninety-nine.

Seven of these are Conservative MPs. The others are peers in the House of Lords. They include politicians who run firms based in tax havens themselves, and others with parent or subsidiary companies offshore.[49] They range from mining companies to investment vehicles; retail empires to lobbying firms – all running their operations via tax havens. The people behind these companies range from boring generic members of the Lords who nobody's heard of, right through to some of the most high-profile and influential people in Parliament.

Stanley Fink probably rates as Westminster's most notorious tax haven user. Apart from anything else, he's one of the few who actually admits to it. As a former Conservative Party treasurer and a member of the House of Lords audit committee, he is one of the party's most powerful and trusted people. But Fink has defiantly batted back allegations and controversies surrounding his tax affairs. When it emerged in 2015 that he had a secretive Swiss bank account with HSBC, rather than apologise he simply claimed: 'Everyone does tax avoidance at some level.' He added: 'What I did . . . was at the vanilla, bland, end of the spectrum.'[50]

Lord Fink is a large man with a cherubic playdough face. He made his fortune in the City where he earned a reputation as the 'godfather' of Britain's hedge fund industry. It's a sector that relies heavily on offshore vehicles. In fact, he once admitted: 'All of the industries I am involved in have to have some offshore entities . . . If you want to be a successful business and attract invisible earnings to the UK, you have to be based offshore.'[51]

And he's kept up his beliefs: company documents show that he runs several firms which operate via tax havens. These include Marex Spectron Group Limited, a global commodities broker, which owns several offshore subsidiaries and is itself owned by a firm in Jersey.[52] He is also a 'designated member' of a partnership known as ISAM (Europe) LLP, which is ultimately controlled via the Cayman Islands.[53]

Remember Lord Paul, the peer who gave up his non-dom status so he could stay in Parliament? He's still up to his neck in offshore business. Paul is the chairman of Caparo Group Limited, a £370-million-pound steel company.[54] It went into partial administration in late 2015, putting more than 1,800 jobs under threat in the West Midlands and south Wales.[55] But accounts reveal that the lord's own finances are carefully controlled: his business is owned by a firm in the British Virgin Islands tax haven, on behalf of a series of family trusts.[56]

Over in the Caribbean, Lord Paul is joined by another old chum, Lord Razzall. He is a director for Naia Limited, a privately-held, international drugs company. It says it is 'focusing on global drug development through novel approaches to funding'. These novel approaches include – you guessed it – registering the company offshore in the Cayman Islands.[57]

'Naia's operating structure includes a Cayman Island-based international management company and several holding companies that focus on development activities of like assets,' it says. 'This shared infrastructure and management team is expected to increase efficiency in drug development and decrease operating costs.'

Naia Limited would be well placed if it wanted to cut back on pesky 'operating costs' like, say . . . taxes. 'There are no direct taxes in the Cayman Islands,' the government there says. 'There is no income tax, company or corporation tax, inheritance tax, capital gains or gift tax. There are no property taxes or rates, and no controls on the foreign ownership of property and land.'[58]

In the House of Commons, two out of six Tory MPs who sit on the Treasury Select Committee have corporate links to tax havens.[59]

Jacob Rees-Mogg's Somerset Capital Management Limited has investment in a Cayman Islands firm called Somerset Capital Management (Cayman) Limited.[60] He's joined by newbie MP Chris Philp, who runs a company registered in Cyprus.[61] Philp says the offshore firm is 'not relevant to my role as a UK MP', and tells me: 'You are barking up the wrong tree.' But the Treasury Select Committee which he sits on was recently given evidence explicitly describing Cyprus as a tax haven.[62] Both MPs claim there is no tax advantage derived from the offshore firms.

Other MPs with tax haven links include Nadhim Zahawi, who co-founded the research firm YouGov, before becoming a Conservative MP and quickly rising within the party. He's been firmly on-message with the Tories' belief that people should pay their way in society and has described the welfare system as a 'trap' for the poor.[63] But records show he also works as a director at SThree plc, a mammoth recruitment firm which owns a series of offshore subsidiary firms in Switzerland, Luxembourg, the Netherlands and Singapore. In 2014, just 4% of its £200m gross profit went towards taxes.[64]

It's near-impossible to know exactly how these corporations use their offshore connections. There is no evidence that any have avoided tax in an inappropriate way – and there is certainly no suggestion they have acted illegally. But it is certainly striking that so many of these companies have such low tax bills, and it leaves the politicians with important questions to answer.

Whenever a politician is accused of having links to tax havens they always trot out the same old line: 'The company pays all the taxes due and is not involved in tax evasion.' Usually, this is true . . . if by 'all the taxes due' you mean 'all we are *legally* required to pay because of some handy loopholes we've found'. But the legal stuff can sometimes be just as aggressive and abusive. Even just by running a company via tax havens, politicians are still indirectly supporting a secretive offshore system that's responsible for letting the world's ultra-rich hide away at least £13tn.[65]

So, when the government claims to be fighting against tax havens and tax dodging, how can we believe them, when so many of their rank have offshore corporate links themselves? For many, this kind of thing is so ingrained in their culture and approach to business that they think the bad stuff is only what other people do. What they're involved with is just 'sensible tax planning', they reckon. It's just 'vanilla'. God knows what the raspberry ripple is like.

The vast majority of British business and individuals get by without channelling cash through these 'sunny places for shady people'.[66] In Westminster, however, the financial greed of the tax avoidance industry has become so normalised that politicians cannot see beyond it.

8

War

One of the twelve-year-old girls from al-Huda school was brave enough to speak out.

'Imagine. When the plane comes to strike,' she said. 'You can't hear it, you just feel the strike that falls on your head . . .

'Right now we are living in fear and in terror. Today I saw the plane and I was very afraid and terrified. The sound today was loud but the feeling I had was like that of all of the girls at school today: of course we are afraid . . . We just want the aggression to stop on schools. It is a shame for them to bomb kids, a shame for them to attack schools. Their kids study in Saudi Arabia in private universities and everywhere. Our kids are bombed.'[1]

Al-Huda school is in a small, rural village in the Hajjah governorate of Yemen. To the west is the tropical Red Sea coast. Travel north and you quickly arrive at the Saudi border.

Once upon a time, al-Huda was thriving with up to 700 pupils registered. 'Last year, when there was no war, students would come from the beginning,' the little girl said. 'They would be happy at school.'

But that all changed on 27 October 2015, when a huge missile struck a field just 100 metres away, causing devastation. Four children, aged between three and seventeen were injured in the airstrike, including a young boy who was hit by shrapnel while out playing football.

There was no possible justification. 'There were no weapons in the school,' the headteacher said. 'This is what is unjust and what hurts. If I had seen one weapon I would have said, that's it, that is the school's fate, and it deserves to be hit because it had weapons or fighters in it but this did not happen at all.'[2]

The attack on al-Huda was carried out by Saudi Arabia-led forces, as part of its crippling war against Yemen. But bombing the school was not a mistake. An Amnesty International report found that at least four other air strikes 'appear to have directly targeted schools'. Saudi Arabia was accused of war crimes.[3]

Elsewhere in Yemen, Saudi forces were brutalising the population. Just months earlier, military planes had swooped down over a refugee camp and bombed it, killing at least forty people and injuring two hundred more. 'One man came looking for his five children who were missing, and he was able to identify two of their corpses, but he couldn't find the others,' an eyewitness said. 'It was difficult to identify them. It is an inhumane situation, these are women and children who have nothing to do with war. In fact, they had tried to flee the war.'[4]

By January 2016, a UN investigation accused Saudi Arabia of violating international law, with 'widespread and systematic' attacks on civilian targets in Yemen.[5]

Making a killing

So where does Saudi Arabia get its deadly weapons and aeroplanes from? Look no further than the UK's very own BAE Systems, which has long been one of the biggest players in arming the Saudi dictatorship.[6]

BAE is the UK's biggest weapons manufacturer and is ranked number three globally.[7] Despite the airstrikes on refugee camps and schools in Yemen, the company has maintained its cosy relationship with the Saudis. It says it has 'a privileged position as a strategic supplier' to the country and has recently sold a range of Typhoon aircrafts.[8] In fact, since the bombing campaign in Yemen began, BAE and other British arms dealers have seen their combined sales to Saudi Arabia go up extortionately – now selling up to £1bn worth of military equipment every three months.[9]

BAE does not make moral judgements about murderous dictatorships. Just so long as they can sell them even more weapons. That's not my personal opinion: it's a fact. Ducking out of basic morality for the sake of a good business deal is company policy. Let me give you an example.

In early 2016, the Saudi government executed forty-seven people in a single, gruesome day. Amnesty International reacted, saying that the country has an 'utter disregard for human rights'.[10] But it didn't bother BAE's chairman, Sir Roger Carr. When asked, just days later, whether it was wrong to make millions selling weapons to the regime, he replied: 'We are not there to form judgements on individual countries . . . For us, this is a very important customer of which we have a very strong relationship.'[11]

The full history of BAE's special relationship with Saudi Arabia is a long story, involving a prince, a secret slush fund and the Serious Fraud Office. There's not time to get into all that now, but here's what you need to know:

Back in 1985, Margaret Thatcher's government signed an arms-for-oil deal with Saudi Arabia, which they named the Al Yamamah contract. At the prime minister's side was her chief foreign policy adviser, Charles Powell, who played a key role in sealing the deal. Afterwards, he also apparently became close friends with the secret 'fixer' at the heart of Al Yamamah.[12]

It was a record-breaker; the biggest export contract in UK history. It covered the supply and support of 220 military aircraft, naval vessels, shells, missiles, infrastructure and support services. And the prime contractor profiting from the deal? BAE Systems.[13]

Having worked next to Thatcher for years, Charles Powell was eventually rewarded with a peerage, joining the House of Lords in 2000. He styled himself as 'Lord Powell of Bayswater'. Now, he could vote on legislation and speak in Parliament for himself, rather than just advising. Meanwhile, his brother Jonathan had become Tony Blair's Chief of Staff at Downing Street. Together, they were quite the power couple. A foot in both camps and a finger in every pie.

However, in the years after Al Yamamah was signed, the deal became gradually mired in allegations of vast corruption and bribery.[14] When an investigation was launched, BAE hired none other than Charles Powell to act as its lobbyist. According to one comprehensive account of the scandal, Powell's job was to persuade the government to abandon the corruption inquiry. Blair's government caved to the pressure and did just that. They claimed the investigation had been scrapped because 'it would not be in the public interest'.[15] However, Powell later admitted discussing the investigation with 'senior government officials' and said it was 'perfectly possible' that these included his brother.[16]

Today, Lord Powell may be used to his place in the House of Lords, but he still loves the arms trade. So perhaps it's no surprise to learn that he's now an adviser to – you guessed it – BAE Systems.[17] The very company he helped to fund by brokering the Al Yamamah deal.[18] On top of that, he also has key advisory positions at other top arms companies, including Thales UK and Rolls-Royce.

Lord Powell is one of the great figures of the arms trade. A ghostly individual who knows every corner of the industry. Yet here he is, sitting right at the heart of British politics, in the House of Lords.

Lord Powell's nuclear options

If Lord Powell is so busy working in the arms trade, what does he get out of being a politician as well? After all, he hasn't shown much of an interest in politics recently. In the year 2014/15, he only bothered to turn up a handful of times. And although he claimed £1,800 in allowances for attending, he didn't make any speeches, ask any questions or contribute to any debates in the main chamber.[19] In fact, at the time of writing, Lord Powell has only spoken in Parliament on four occasions since 2006.[20]

Funnily enough, two of these four speeches were about nuclear weapons. In one of them (after drawing 'attention to my declaration of interests in the register') he went on to fiercely advocate renewal of Trident, Britain's nuclear submarine system, playing on the terrifying prospect of nuclear attack. He added: 'I do not entirely shy away from arguing that we should also preserve the deterrent for reasons of status.'

He said the nukes should be kept on submarines, rather than anywhere else: 'A submarine-based system provides the most effective form of deterrence with the smallest footprint.'

He added: 'I disagree with those who argue that the money spent on our nuclear deterrent could more cost-effectively be invested in conventional forces . . . I hope very much that the government will not weaken in their commitment to maintain continuous at-sea deterrence by building the number of boats required to achieve that and that there will not be pressure to abandon that position either by Treasury cheese-paring or by a need to appease those who oppose our nuclear deterrent altogether.'[21]

It was presumably just a sheer coincidence then that, when the government eventually did renew Trident, the companies that benefited most were the very ones that Lord Powell has had a long-term commercial relationship with. They are making the phenomenally expensive submarines that carry the missiles, under a scheme called Successor.

A statement on BAE's website explains: 'BAE Systems are the industrial lead for the Successor Programme and, alongside partners Rolls-Royce and Babcock, are designing a new generation of submarines to carry the UK's independent nuclear deterrent. They will replace the current Vanguard class, which was also designed and constructed at BAE Systems' site.'[22]

In the years that followed the decision, a series of vast contracts were given the green light by the government. The figures are mind-boggling. Two contracts worth £328m and £315m covered BAE's initial design phase, while a third £257m contract in 2015 covered the next phases of work to replace the subs.[23]

I mention Lord Powell's Trident speech to an MP. 'To have unelected people making these decisions in the first place is a gross anti-democratic measure,' she says. 'But then to have the information of the kind that you've just described I think just puts the whole institution into deep contempt.'

There's no evidence that Lord Powell technically broke any rules in his speech, or that he was actively representing BAE Systems at the time. So let's assume he was genuinely just airing his own personal views. There's still a problem: how can he *prove* that? Given his cosy links with BAE, his independence and integrity on the issue is partly a matter of trust. But why should the public believe him? What guarantee can he give that he's not being motivated and influenced by his commercial relationship with the arms trade?

If he can't give a guarantee, where does that leave his credibility and integrity as a member of the House of Lords? Why should we view him as anything more than a powerful business lobbyist?

'Is he speaking on nuclear weapons because he's interested in nuclear weapons . . . Or is he speaking on nuclear weapons because he's got a job with BAE? It could be cyclical,' one Westminster source wonders. 'The point is, if we want a democracy that is clearly not tainted and is clearly transparent and open and honest and clean, then to even have that question over you . . .'

'Merchant of death'

Who was he speaking for? Himself, the public, or BAE? The only person who could answer that question was Lord Powell himself. So, I tracked down his phone number and gave him a call.

Lord Powell is well spoken and straight-laced. So much so, he insists that his surname be pronounced 'Pole' (although his brother sticks with the standard 'Powell', to rhyme with 'trowel').[24] I approach with caution. At first I don't mention his Trident speech. Instead, I ask him about the relationship between his political life and his career in the arms trade.

'I don't regard myself as a politician,' he begins, defiantly. It's a strange comment coming from someone with a seat in Parliament. 'I regard myself nowadays very much more in the world of business.'

Do his business interests get in the way of politics?

'If I have to declare my interests before I say anything then it does sort of cast a bit of a shadow over what you're going to say,' he admits. 'You have to be very, very careful to declare all your interests, and I think probably my declaration of interests is likely to be the longest one in the whole Lords.' (It's not.)

Lord Powell has worked in the arms trade for so long that he doesn't think of it as controversial in the slightest. 'It's a bit of a hot potato,' I laugh stupidly, trying to meet him halfway.

'Well you may regard it as a hot potato. I don't think I do,' he says. 'But obviously it means you should not speak in any way which would appear to advance particular defence interests.'

After a few minutes of listening to Powell evangelise about the importance of avoiding conflicts of interest, I tell him that I've seen his Trident speech, which encouraged the government to continue funding for nuclear subs. 'What guarantee can people have that that is not you talking from a commercial point of view?' I ask.

But Powell bats the question away: 'I think you're rather stretching to make a point on that,' he says.[25]

I ask him again. 'I wonder whether you think that – the fact that those commercial interests do exist – means that the public cannot be absolutely 100% assured that you weren't speaking from a commercial point of view?'

'The answer is I think they can be,' he says stiffly. 'The idea that people are, or could be, suspected of being biased? No. I don't think so, any more than polytechnic lecturers are biased in favour of Marxism.'

Powell's message boils down to this: 'Trust me, I'm a lord'. But why should we trust him? I'm not saying he's lying about his financial influences. Maybe his work for the arms trade has absolutely no effect on his views about Trident. I can't prove what was going through his mind when he spoke. But neither can he, so it's all down to faith. We've got to just *trust* politicians to be honest. We've got to trust them not to corrupt Parliament with commercial interests. And if they don't have our trust, their credibility is zero.

Lord Powell doesn't think that this undermines his credibility, though. 'I honestly don't think it does,' he says. 'The interests are declared, open and above board.'

'But the fact alone that it's declared doesn't actually *stop* someone from still speaking commercially,' I point out.

'I think they would be pretty quickly discredited if they did that. I mean suppose I were to stand up in a debate on the recent strategic defence review and say "I declare an interest as an adviser to British Aerospace, and by the way I think it's going to be hugely to BAE's benefit to have eight more Type 26 Destroyers". I think people would look at me as if I was completely off my trolley!'

Lord Powell isn't trying to dodge the question – he just genuinely thinks I'm an idiot for even asking it. This time, though, he finally cracks. 'What guarantee can people have?' I ask again.

'They can't have a guarantee,' he says, grudgingly. 'But if they look at what I say, or anyone in a similar position says, I think they will find that they are perfectly respectable public policy views.'

And anyway, according to Powell, it doesn't even matter very much because peers aren't very powerful. 'There's no way in which an ordinary member of the House of Lords has any significant influence on anything,' he tells me. So that's alright then.

Forgetting the potential for conflicts of interest, I'm still not sure how comfortable outsiders would be knowing that one of the leading figures of Britain's arms trade sits in Parliament. Is this really the sort of person we want wielding power and influence in Westminster? Before I hang up, I ask Lord Powell if it's morally right for politicians like him to be profiting from the arms trade.

'I'm not sure how you think that politicians are profiting from the arms trade,' he says.

'In the sense that you're working for them,' I reply.

'. . . You call it the arms trade, I call it defence business,' Powell says defiantly. 'One sounds better than the other. No doubt you'll be using the phrase "merchant of death" next.' (Actually, I hadn't thought of that. But now, that gives me a great opportunity to quote him completely out of context in the subtitle for this section – cheers Lord P!)

'There are one or two big British defence companies in this country who are amongst our main exporters to the rest of the world, providing an enormous number of jobs and so on,' Powell continues. 'Of course there are crooks around and middlemen and so on, who benefit from some rather odd practices. But they're pretty rare these days, I believe. I don't encounter them anyway.'

'A clever way to channel bribes'

As you will have noticed by now, there's not much room for morals when politicians seek out extra jobs. They're not doing this work because of some personal crusade to save the world. They're doing it to make money. Never mind the collateral damage, it seems Britain's politicians will stop at nothing to line their pockets, just so long as it's legal.

One such person is Tory MP Sir Gerald Howarth, a silver-haired ex-banker who's been in Parliament since 1983. Howarth is known for his staunch conservatism and has built up a reputation as a defence specialist. At the moment, he's a member of Parliament's powerful National Security Strategy Committee.[26] And until 2012 he was a junior minister in the MOD, with responsibility for defence exports.

Howarth has another little project on the side. In 2013, he signed up to be a paid consultant to Blenheim Capital Services Ltd, earning himself a tidy £420 per hour.[27] It's a controversial business: it helps private arms companies deliver deals linked to weapon sales across the world. And some people would compare the services Blenheim provides to industrial-scale bribery, even though what it does is entirely legal.[28]

Let me explain. When big defence firms want to beat their rivals to win lucrative government contracts, they sometimes use a device known as 'offsetting'. It's an incredibly secretive practice. Very little is known about how this works, but it generally involves firms promising valuable investments or services as a way of sweetening potential arms deals.[29] For instance, if a British firm is competing with rivals to sell weapons to the Saudi government, they might entice them by offering something extra in return – perhaps a promise to use Saudi suppliers, investment in the country's own defence firms, or funding for a national project.

The Economist describes the offsetting industry as a 'murky world'. It says: 'Anti-corruption groups see them as a clever way to channel bribes. Even if many offset deals are clean, they are widely seen as a "dark art".'[30]

Regulators like the World Trade Organisation and the EU have tried to partially ban the practice.[31] But that hasn't stopped it. In fact, efforts to restrict offsetting in the Western world have merely encouraged defence companies to turn their attention to developing countries, where offsets are usually more prevalent. But the countries they sell to are often run by brutal authoritarian regimes.

Despite the controversy, the industry continues to bring in big money. An investigation by the *Financial Times* estimated the international offset market had grown to around $75bn in 2012:[32]

Offsets have become important to win international business . . . Many big companies have become fiercely competitive and sophisticated about their offerings.

Opponents see offsets akin to a bribe. They argue that necessity, quality and price should decide whether and what defence equipment a country buys. Offsets, they argue, increase the chance that a country buys equipment it does not need or decides to sign a contract that does not offer the best in quality and value. Beyond such fundamental issues, data and information on offsets remain almost completely secret.[33]

This is the industry Sir Gerald Howarth has chosen to work in.

Actually, he's had a cosy relationship with Blenheim Capital for a while. When he was a minister in charge of the UK's defence exports, he had 'official dealings' with the firm. Documents say this was 'in connection with Malaysia', a country with a terrible human rights record.

We know that Howarth sat alongside Blenheim's representatives in meetings with Malaysian government ministers.[34] But we can't say for sure what these meetings were about. However, two months into Howarth's government job, Blenheim announced a $5bn project with the Malaysian government. The deal covered financing and development for a defence and security technology centre, to offset hundreds of millions of dollars which were owed from arms deals.[35]

Company documents reveal a catalogue of other authoritarian regimes that Blenheim helps with their quest to buy weapons. 'The Company is expanding from countries such as the United Arab Emirates to countries such as the State of Kuwait, Malaysia, Kingdom of Bahrain, wider Middle East and North African region with opportunities now developing in Oman and Jordan.'[36]

The Economist notes that Blenheim is one of the more 'sophisticated outfits that structure complex deals'.[37] Nevertheless, you might think it's an inappropriate job for someone so high up in national security policy. The media and fellow politicians clearly disagree, though, because his role has rarely ever been noted.

Guns and rosettes

Let's not forget all the other parliamentarians who have their wages tied up in wars and weapons. Chief among them is Nicholas Soames, the Conservative MP for Mid Sussex and a former officer in the Hussars.[38] He is the grandson of Winston Churchill and looks as much; a large and hefty figure with a stately presence.

But while his grandad is celebrated for ending a war, Soames seems intent on starting new ones. It's curious that so many politicians seem this way inclined. Perhaps Soames has always been slightly in awe of his grandfather; keen to follow in his footsteps to battle. One story says that, when he was a kid, he asked Churchill: 'Grandpapa, is it true that you are the greatest man in the world?' Churchill turned to him and replied: 'Yes. Now bugger off.'[39]

Soames has been a keen advocate of military action throughout his career. He voted for the invasion of Iraq in 2003 and for continued action in Afghanistan.[40] When one MP dared to speak out against the Iraqi invasion, Soames criticised him for doing 'the best impression that I've heard of Neville Chamberlain in many, many years . . . He is an appeaser.'[41]

By happy coincidence, a company he now chairs has been a major beneficiary of both wars. Documents show that Soames is paid £611 an hour at AEGIS Defence Services Limited. The firm describes itself as 'a leading security and risk management company with project experience in over sixty countries.'[42]

According to American journalist Ann Hagedorn, AEGIS was one of the biggest financial winners of Iraq. 'By 2007, it likely had one of the biggest increases in profits since the beginning of the Iraq War,' she writes in her book, *The Invisible Soldiers*. 'In its first accounting year for the year ending December 31, 2003, its income was £542,000. By year's end 2006, its income had grown to £70.9m.'[43]

By the time Soames joined the board of directors in 2005, AEGIS had just signed a $1.3bn deal to protect US government agencies in Iraq.[44] The firm says it is 'one of the largest security contracts ever awarded.' These days, it brings in more than £168m a year, making some £13m in pre-tax profits.[45]

But just because he heads up a private military firm, that doesn't stop Sir Nicholas trying to influence defence policy in Parliament. Recently, he's made speeches, or asked questions, about Iraq, Iran, Syria, Gaza, Saudi Arabia, UK defence spending, counter-terrorism and the Army.[46]

★   ★   ★

Another Westminster arms trader I came across was Charles Guthrie (or to give him his full title: Field Marshal The Lord Charles Ronald Llewelyn Guthrie of Craigiebank GCB LVO OBE DL). These days, Guthrie is elderly and softly spoken, with wispy white hair. But he was once the head of the Army, and described as 'tougher than a rhino wearing body armour'.[47]

Guthrie has now been appointed to the House of Lords, but also earns $40,000 a year as a manager of Colt Defense, a US gun company registered in the tax haven of Delaware. Colt describes itself as 'one of the world's oldest and most renowned designers, developers and manufacturers of firearms'.[48] As well as selling guns to individuals for self-defence or 'recreational purposes', it also provides arms for a list of unnamed 'foreign military forces, global law enforcement and security agencies'. [49]

If you're not keen on America's gun culture then reading the company's official documents won't be very reassuring. One section on business risks warns: 'It is not always possible to deter misconduct by agents and employees and the precautions we take to detect and prevent this activity may not be effective in all cases.'[50]

Meanwhile, Colt's guns are advertised as being 'the closest you can get to an M4 [assault rifle] without enlisting'. A customer catalogue describes the speed with which one of its weapons can be deployed, saying: 'When every moment counts – don't think, just do.'[51]

The global arms and defence trade has wriggled its tentacles down the corridors of Westminster. In March 2014, *Time* magazine published an article titled 'Here Are the 5 Companies Making a Killing Off Wars Around the World'.[52] Incredibly, by the end of 2015, three of them had British politicians on their payroll:

- **General Dynamics:** US defence company. Lord Levene of Portsoken is the chair of its UK arm, which brings in more than £239m. Levene remains a member of the National Security Strategy Committee, alongside Gerald Howarth.[53]
- **BAE Systems:** As well as Lord Powell's advisory position, three peers each have at least £50,000 invested in the company.[54]
- **Lockheed Martin:** The world's biggest defence company, it has annual sales of more than $45bn. According to the Register of

Interests, Conservative peer Lord Patten worked as an adviser to the firm, as well as being non-executive director of its UK arm. He stepped down at the start of 2016.[55]

On top of that, another one of the companies on *Time* magazine's list has personal investment from a Westminster politician. It's a peculiar and depressing tale:

In the First World War, the anti-war poet Siegfried Sassoon wrote about the atrocities he saw and described the Army as being 'great at murder'.[56] Skip forward a couple of generations and his relation, James Sassoon, is a Conservative peer in the House of Lords. Records show he has tens of thousands of pounds invested in Raytheon, a giant arms manufacturer which makes bombs and missiles.[57] Raytheon says the deadly weapons it sells are specially designed for 'avoiding casualties'.[58] The makers of mustard gas should have thought of that line. Perhaps Siegfried would see the funny side, though.

Just like with banks and tax havens, it turns out that Parliament's financial interests are intrinsically tied up with the weapons industry. There's a very disconcerting link between the war*mongers* and the war *profiteers*: too often, the people who influence military affairs are the same ones who stand to gain.

I'm not suggesting individual corruption or deep level conspiracy. After all, it takes more than a few rich backbenchers to significantly change Britain's entire foreign policy. Rather, this is an issue about trust and integrity. If we can't be confident that our MPs are free from financial influence when debating war, then where does this leave the credibility of Parliament?

In the rest of this book, you might accuse me of being too puritanical. What does it matter if politicians allow pay cheques to sway their decisions occasionally? Here, though, it could literally be a matter of life and death.

Imagine this scenario. A parliamentary vote on whether to go to war is won by a single vote. Suddenly, every individual's financial interests *really do matter*. Could war have been avoided were it not for the influence of someone's commercial interests? In this situation, it's no use just writing your business affairs down on a piece of paper. We need a cast iron guarantee that none of those votes were cast with personal profits in mind.

There's another issue here, too: regardless of conflicts of interest, are we happy for our politicians to be profiting from this line of work? Is it *ethically* OK? I'm not just talking about your standard arms traders here. How about working for brutal foreign regimes and dictatorships?

Lord Inge is a prime example of this. Once a member of the Army's top brass, he went on to become an unpaid adviser for the repressive king and government of Bahrain.[59] He appears to have declared his position about a year before the Bahraini uprisings during the Arab Spring.[60]

The advisory role was just the latest move in a very cosy relationship between Lord Inge and the country's rulers. For instance, a year previously, Bahrain's Ministry of Information had wanted a seminar in the House of Lords.[61] The event was paid for by the Embassy of Bahrain, at a cost of £2,576 (paid to Parliament), and apparently 'focused on the King's efforts to promote democratic participation and his achievements in guaranteeing basic political and civic rights for women.'[62] In order to use the function room, Lord Inge agreed to act as a 'sponsor' for the event.[63]

The rhetoric in the seminar clearly worked. Afterwards, a *Telegraph* journalist who'd attended wrote critically about 'a group of Islamic radicals who are trying to overthrow the Bahraini government . . . one of our key allies in the Gulf region'. The journalist added: 'Equal opportunity and equality are the watch words for King Hamad's regime.'[64]

Two years later, however, the cruel reality could no longer be denied – Western media swung to the defence of protesters in Bahrain. At the height of the Arab Spring, the US had to call for 'restraint' from Bahrain's government as it savagely cracked down on pro-democracy rallies.[65] Even the *Telegraph* later described King Hamad's rule as 'brutal'.[66] Lord Inge, meanwhile, claims to have now retired from all his work. But his job as King Hamad's adviser is still listed on the Register of Interests.[67]

Alongside Lord Inge, working for another dictatorship, was the former head of the armed forces, David Richards – now known as The Lord Richards of Herstmonceux. Until November 2015, he provided 'strategic advice' for the king and government of Jordan.[68]

In interviews, Lord Richards has called Jordan a 'wonderful' country, which 'need[s] more help' from British forces.[69] Human Rights Watch describes the country a bit differently, though: 'Jordanian law criminalises speech deemed critical of the king, government officials, and institutions, as well as Islam,' it says, adding: 'Credible allegations of torture or other ill-treatment are routinely ignored.'[70]

The question of ethics is one we've avoided so far. But it's arguably just as important as the practical stuff, like the potential conflicts of interest. Never mind whether politicians are corrupting Westminster – are they corrupting *society*? None of the people mentioned in this chapter have broken any rules and their business affairs have largely been declared, as required. But perhaps that's a sign that the rules are too lax.

9

Corporate irresponsibility

How low are we prepared to let them go? Even if we accept politicians' arguments over second jobs, is there a point at which we say 'no'?

Some businesses make us wince. They go against our morals and principles so strongly that we can sniff them out in an instant. But saying 'no' is difficult because ethics are not an exact science. It's a matter of personal judgement.

'It's very difficult to put smell tests into formal regulation,' Jacob Rees-Mogg tells me. 'And it depends who's doing the smelling.' Plus, even if everyone agrees that a business is unethical, should that stop its director from becoming a politician?

How much responsibility should business leaders take for their companies? And what does it say about their own principles? These questions don't have easy answers. But one thing's for sure, if politicians want to look squeaky clean, they've picked the wrong businesses to work for.

Rees-Mogg gives a hypothetical case: 'If Marks & Spencer happen to buy T-shirts from a supplier in Bangladesh that used child labour, and an MP were a director of Marks & Spencer, should that MP resign? No, probably not. But it would be very embarrassing – both for that MP and for Marks & Spencer.'

As chance would have it though, this hypothetical example isn't far from reality.

Sweatshops and statesmen

When investigators went undercover in the Rosita and Megatex factories in northern Bangladesh, they witnessed a terrifying world.

'Corporal punishment is the norm,' they said. 'Workers arriving late are forced to stand at attention, with their arms at their sides, for at least four hours. They cannot talk, turn their head or go to the bathroom.' Other workers were beaten.[1]

In all, the two factories employed around 5,000 people in horrific, illegal sweatshop conditions. They were paid 'slave wages' of just 10p an hour.[2]

Under Chinese management, the factories were run 'like minimum security prisons'. A standard shift began promptly at 8 a.m. and stretched on for thirteen hours until 9 p.m. The workers did this six days a week, with another six-hour shift on their 'day off'. Their task was to make jumpers, and it was exhausting work: most knitters were on their feet throughout the day. Every lunch break was cut short after forty minutes, when security guards would blow their whistles and order them back to their workstations.

One wrong move, and they were fired. 'Our backs are close to the wall, and we live always in fear of losing our jobs,' one worker said. They even sacked people who dared to take time off to attend family funerals, telling one woman to 'submit her resignation and get out of the factory'.

By January 2012, a manager called Kamal Hossain started stalking a young woman who worked there, named Bina Khatun. He demanded that Bina have sex with him. Kamal threatened her, saying he would make her life a misery if she refused to submit. Eventually, Bina wrote to the factory's managing director:

'I rejected the offer and then Kamal propositioned me via telephone,' she explained. 'He asked me to go to Kohinoor's house after the factory work was over and proposed to spend a night with him like a husband–wife does. Considering my dignity and honour I disclosed this matter to my guardian.' She added: 'I would urge you look into the matter and give proper punishment to him.'

Bina got no reply, so instead decided to ask the Workers Welfare Association for help. But help did not come. After initially being told it would take two or three months to investigate her allegations, two supervisors later approached her and beat her. They threatened anyone who had witnessed Kamal's stalking to stay silent.[3]

*   *   *

The abuse and exploitation in these factories may have been thousands of miles away in Bangladesh, but a chain can be traced back directly to Parliament.

According to the report, published in 2012, the jumpers that Bina and her colleagues knitted in the two factories were made for some of the world's leading fashion chains. They included the UK high street store, BHS. Investigators suggested it was hard to believe that BHS didn't know about the illegal labour: 'It would seem impossible for Chinese management, Bangladeshi labor authorities and the labels to have all been unaware that 5,000 workers have been systematically cheated of their legal overtime wages for the last three years!'[4]

At this point, BHS was part of the £2bn retail giant, Arcadia Group Limited.[5] And Arcadia's non-executive chairman, at the time? Step forward Lord Anthony Grabiner.[6]

A combative character, heavy set with black thick-rimmed glasses, Grabiner made his name as a leading barrister, and now sits in the House of Lords. Recently, he's been enlisted to make a series of ethical judgements in high-profile cases. For instance, in 2011 he agreed to head up Rupert Murdoch's new ethics committee at News International, following the phone hacking revelations. He was reportedly paid £3,000 an hour for his services.[7]

More recently, Grabiner authored a major report into the Bank of England. But he came under fire for refusing to criticise a Bank official who failed to raise the alarm over market rigging.[8] As a specialist in commercial law, he's also represented a series of controversial clients in court, including Robert Maxwell, Mohammed al Fayed, Apple Computer Inc, and a range of banks, oil companies and insurance firms.[9] Speaking about his legal career, Grabiner has admitted: 'It's all grubby work,' adding: 'I get a turn-on from almost everything I do.'

For him, the goings-on in a Bangladeshi factory that supplies Arcadia must seem a world away. 'I've lived my entire life in a radius of three miles,' he once said.[10]

But under Grabiner's nose, Arcadia had a history of getting embroiled in exploitation scandals. In 2007, the firm was accused of selling products made with 'slave labour' in its Topshop stores. The clothes were apparently part of the outlet's Kate Moss range. Workers told *The Sunday Times* they had travelled to Mauritius from their homes in India, Sri Lanka and Bangladesh, with the promise of well-paid work. But when they got there they were paid as little as 22p, labouring for up to twelve hours a day.[11]

Channel 4's *Dispatches* made fresh allegations about Arcadia in 2010, after it uncovered shocking conditions in British factories supplying BHS and others. It said people were illegally employed, on half the minimum wage and working in dangerous factories.[12]

The company has pointed out: 'We do not own or operate factories ourselves and Arcadia Group is rarely dominant in an individual factory.'[13] It adds: 'Our ethical trading work is wide ranging, multi-layered and involves different stakeholders.' Yet Arcadia is conspicuously missing from the membership list at the Ethical Trading Initiative, a collection of high street retailers who work together to improve conditions.[14]

Lord Grabiner is not the only peer who's been involved with controversial fashion brands. In 2015, the Scottish entrepreneur Michelle Mone was appointed to the House of Lords. She made her fortune from the Ultimo bra company, which she founded in 1996 while still in her twenties. The business sourced its products from factories in China, but Mone told everyone that the Chinese workers were treated well. At one point, she even travelled out to assess the conditions and proudly claimed: 'There is no child labour.' She added: 'There are no ridiculous hours. The food is good and the pay is great.' During her visit, Mone even stayed in a workers' dorm, which she said was 'brilliant like a Travel Inn'.[15]

But when the Scottish *Daily Record* investigated in more detail, they found a bleaker reality. The 'great' pay turned out to be as little as £1 a day. The 'brilliant' dorms were sweltering and cramped, with eight or more women squeezed in each room. And the reasonable hours involved just one short holiday each year during the Chinese New Year.[16]

Mone's brand is now said to be worth £20m.[17] But shortly before joining Parliament she severed all links with the firm; a statement said she had 'no involvement in Ultimo either as a shareholder or as a director'. Meanwhile, the government has stuck resolutely behind the baroness, saying: 'She is more than qualified to help entrepreneurs from deprived backgrounds to turn a good idea into a flourishing business.'[18]

These textile barons make millions for themselves, but fail to stop their companies being linked with dangerous and exploitative work practices. It's difficult to know how much responsibility we should lay with them; there is obviously no suggestion that they've knowingly allowed these things to happen. But are we happy to welcome them into Parliament, to design laws and make ethical judgements that could affect millions of people?

Here's another one:

In his autobiography, David Alliance admits he has made 'a decent living', adding that his 'greatest glory' was being appointed as a peer in the House of Lords. He is a non-executive director at N Brown Group and has boasted about controlling 'the biggest textile company in the Western world'.

But an ITV documentary in 2014, which exposed abuse and child labour in various Bangladeshi factories, also highlighted dangerous conditions at Vase Apparel, a facility used by N Brown. Secret filming inside the grubby building showed that fire escapes were padlocked shut, even though factory fires have claimed the lives of hundreds of garment workers in recent years. Lord Alliance's company admitted the factory conditions were 'illegal and morally reprehensible', adding that it was 'shocked and disappointed' that it had sourced clothes from the factory.[19]

In another case, Lord Jay of Ewelme spent nine years as non-executive director of Associated British Foods plc.[20] By the time he resigned in December 2015, he was on at least £71,000, with the business group bringing in nearly £13bn a year.[21] One of the group's chief businesses is Primark, the popular high street brand.

Primark was one of the main retailers associated with perhaps the worst garment factory accident in history.[22] More than a thousand workers were killed when a structurally unsafe factory, called Rana Plaza, collapsed in 2013.[23] Primark has since said it was the first brand to admit 'clearly and unambiguously that it had an independent third-party supplier factory in the Rana Plaza building'. The chain had sourced clothes from the New Wave Bottoms facility on the second floor of the factory, and later paid out millions of pounds in compensation.[24]

Gang rape and gold

My old friend, Lord Charles Powell of Bayswater, had already accused me of portraying him as a 'merchant of death', because of his work for the arms trade. But it wasn't until later that I found out about Barrick Gold. As scandals go, this company has been embroiled in just about the most horrific cases imaginable.

Barrick is a Canadian firm, reported to be the world's biggest gold mining business. Lord Powell joined its high-profile International Advisory Board in 2000, when the company was selling $1.3bn of gold a year.[25] By 2014, Barrick's annual gold sales had risen to more than $10bn.[26] But getting your hands on the yellow metal can be a dirty business.

Hidden in a remote region of Papua New Guinea's tropical highlands lies the Porgera gold mine. A vast rocky dent, etched in the side of rainforest hills, the site sprawls for miles. Though it was ignored by the government for years, it has now become a key part of the country's economy. Porgera accounts for an astonishing 12% of Papua New Guinea's total exports, having produced more than 16 million ounces of gold since 1990.

Barrick Gold acquired the mine in 2006, describing it as 'a valuable part of our portfolio'.[27] But Porgera already had a reputation for controversy and violence – it is said that extrajudicial killings were carried out against illegal miners who were caught trespassing by security staff. However, the new owners promised: 'We conduct our business with the highest ethical standards and in accordance with all applicable laws, rules and regulations.'[28]

The violence around Porgera did not stop, though. Barrick took some steps to discipline security staff, but it wasn't enough. When Human Rights Watch spent three weeks in the area, talking to locals, it uncovered allegations of abuse, violent attacks, excessive force and even gang rape by security personnel working at the mine. One gang rape apparently took place in 2008, with a spate of five more alleged incidents over the following two years. A graphic report was published in 2011:

Some of the women interviewed by Human Rights Watch described scenes of true brutality. One woman told how she was gang raped by six guards after one of them kicked her in the face and shattered her teeth. Another said she and three other women were raped by ten security personnel, one of whom forced her to swallow a used condom that he had used while raping two other victims.

Several women said that after arresting them for illegal mining on the waste dumps, guards gave them a 'choice' of submitting to gang rape or going to prison to face fines and possible jail time. But in some of those cases the women said that guards raped them even after they pleaded with their assailants to take them to jail.[29]

In another case, a fifteen-year-old boy claimed he was handcuffed by security guards, who then threatened to set an attack dog on him.

While Lord Powell was on its International Advisory Board, Barrick Gold made 'glaring failures', such as not monitoring the conduct of its security staff. Human Rights Watch said it was worse than just simple oversight. The company, it said, has a 'history of angrily dismissing human rights and environmental concerns', adding: 'Too often, Barrick has responded with dismissive hostility.'[30]

When Amnesty International made separate human rights allegations about Porgera in 2009, Barrick responded by merely questioning the research's 'adequacy and objectivity'. Human Rights Watch later wrote: 'Far from addressing the very serious human rights abuses that took place during the evictions, the company's initial response refused even to concede basic contextual elements that were obviously true.'[31]

In 2011, the company conceded that the 'ongoing challenges' at the Porgera mine 'underscored the critical importance of ensuring our practices on the ground live up to our policy commitments'.[32] But Barrick's scandals have had precisely zero implications for Lord Powell. Maintaining his place in the House of Lords, his advisory work for the gold firm goes unquestioned.

When I asked him about Barrick, Lord Powell admitted he has 'only a broad knowledge of the matters alleged in the Human Rights Watch 2011 report'. But he claimed the company has 'high ethical standards' and addressed the failures, adding that he wasn't involved in the day-to-day running of the business. 'I have no misgivings about serving on its Advisory Board and don't believe any other fair-minded person, whether a member of the House of Lords or not, would have reservations either,' he said.[33]

Climate change and credibility

It's late 2015 and I'm on my way to meet the leader of the Green Party, Natalie Bennett. We're meeting in a juice bar.

Bennett is a curious figure. With a coarse Australian twang to her accent, she is militantly friendly. Bennett came to mainstream attention at the General Election after appearing in the Leaders' Debate with David Cameron and Ed Miliband. In person, she manages to appear both boldly confident and sheepishly awkward at the same time. But her views on business ethics are firmly held: for her, environmental responsibility is key.

'The place where this starts for me was my first ever interview on *Newsnight*, which was on climate change with Peter Lilley,' she tells me as we sit down.

A Tory politician since 1983, Peter Lilley has long been the scourge of the Green Party. He has criticised steps to tackle climate change and downplayed environmental concerns. And he was one of only three MPs to vote against the Climate Change Act.[34] But Lilley has also been paid lucrative wages from not-so-environmentally-friendly businesses. They include a stint as non-executive director of Tethys Petroleum, where Lilley was non-executive director until November 2014.[35] It goes into countries like Kazakhstan (an 'abusive dictatorship' with appalling human rights records) and extracts oil and gas.[36] All the while, the firm is registered offshore in the Cayman Islands.[37]

'It was really difficult, knowing that he was a director of an oil company with very significant income levels,' Bennett says. '*Private Eye* had just done a whole exposé on it.

'At what point do you say "hang on a minute, you're making [lots of money] from this industry that you're then acting as an advocate for"? It's really tough to know, because you're there talking about the issues . . . You've only got three minutes.

'I didn't raise the oil company directorship because it's like, if I do that then we don't get a chance to discuss the actual issue. But this *is* an issue, and it *should* be discussed.'

Bennett claims: 'That night, Lilley threw a strop when he was shown the preview video and threatened to not go on. And I can imagine that if the BBC said "we're going to introduce him as the director of an oil company", he'd just walk away.'

Lilley is not just a random backbencher. He's a former minister and now sits on the Environmental Audit Committee. Until 2015, he was also part of Parliament's Energy and Climate Change Committee.[38] But he's long come under heavy criticism for his business interests. The Green Party's Caroline Lucas has claimed: 'He is likely to be far more concerned with the short-term profits of the dinosaur polluting fossil fuel barons than tackling the huge threat posed by climate change.'[39]

Environmental campaigners may not like what Tethys Petroleum does, but should that mean Peter Lilley shouldn't have worked there?

He agrees to talk and invites me into his stately office, upstairs in the House of Commons. I wanted to know if he saw any cut-off point. His work at Tethys had already associated him with environmental concerns, tax havens and dictatorships. Are there *any* companies which are *so* ethically dubious that MPs should avoid them?

He pauses to think. 'I personally would not get involved in a lobbying company,' Lilley says after a while. But that's just a personal thing. He's got no problem with MPs getting involved in whatever corporations they fancy, just so long as it's within the official rules and laws. He doesn't want politicians to be held up to a higher standard than other people. 'If it's wrong for MPs to do it, it's wrong for anybody to do it. If it's right for anybody to do it, it's right for MPs to be involved,' he says. 'Business is about trying to do things that are mutually advantageous.'

So he sees nothing wrong with working for an oil firm. And as for people who criticise him for working under a dictatorship? They just don't understand business, he says. 'I don't think they're principled, I just think they're absurd.'

He flat out denies that his business interests damage his political credibility in any way. 'If you've got no answer to my arguments, then my motives are pretty irrelevant,' he says bluntly. 'The idea that the green lobby tried to promote was that somehow I was being paid to say these things . . . Attempts were made to discredit me. They don't seem to have had much impact.'

But Caroline Lucas tells me: 'One gets the impression that this is something that he does believe – that he does think that climate change has been massively over-stated and measures to address it are damaging. That could be a sincerely held belief, but the fact that he has concrete, significant financial interests in fossil fuels, means that you can't take what he says simply as a reflection of his own beliefs. You can't help but think there is a vested interest behind what he is saying.'

Lilley is quick to reject the criticism. 'She's ill-informed,' he says. 'One can't help feeling that she's trying to discredit me because she can't refute my arguments. And she can't . . . She's just discrediting herself – not me.'

However, even as we talk, Lilley reveals yet more ammunition for critics of his business affairs. He discusses the background of his work for Tethys, which he says 'was only operating in Central Asia'. Astonishingly, it turns out that Tethys appears to have benefitted from his own actions as a government minister.

It's a pure coincidence, but when I was Secretary of State for Trade and Industry, the Soviet Union had broken up and we'd [the government] taken the strategic view that Kazakhstan – who were then a basket case, with a 1,000% inflation and hideous debts – had potential. So we wooed Kazakhstan, and President Nazarbayev came over and had meetings with the prime minister and his whole government, and so on. And as a result, British industry became one of the principal investors in, and trade partners with Kazakstan. Or disproportionately. No, that was just a coincidence . . . So when I got a chance to go on this board [Tethy's] . . . I did.

. . . Subsequently, the government said to me 'you're the only person in a British business involved in Uzbekistan, would you be Britain's co-chairman of the trade council UBTIC – the Uzbek-British Trade and Industry Council,' which I didn't particularly want to do because it was unpaid and time-consuming. But it was to promote trade between Britain and Uzbekistan. So I agreed to do that for a couple of years . . . So there was a direct link there between Britain's interest and my company interest.

Toxic waste and Tories

In 2009, the toxic waste scandal in West Africa should have been all over the newspapers. But much of the coverage was suppressed, thanks to bullish lawyers acting for Trafigura, a London-based oil trader. When BBC *Newsnight* tried to cover the story, it was threatened with legal action and accused of not doing 'responsible journalism'. A 'super-injunction' not only prevented the *Guardian* from reporting parliamentary proceedings, but also banned the paper from saying who was gagging it, or why.

It had been a few years since 31,000 people were mysteriously poisoned in Ivory Coast. But details didn't emerge for a while, thanks to a huge alleged cover-up. The story is shocking.

Trafigura had been looking for a cheap way to dispose of 'slop tanks' full of waste, created by a chemical process to remove impurities from Mexican oil. In a bid to save money, officials decided to pass it on to a 'waste disposal company' in Africa known simply as 'Tommy'. Eventually, the waste ended up dumped on open ground near a city in Ivory Coast.[40]

Publicly, Trafigura always claimed the waste was 'absolutely not dangerous'.[41] But in September 2009, the *Guardian* got hold of a stash of internal emails sent prior to the incident.[42] They revealed that the firm knew the stuff was 'hazardous' all along. Plus, Trafigura officials knew that the operation they'd planned was 'banned by most countries'.[43]

Journalists were forced to battle against lawyers in a bid to expose the story and, after months of libel threats, they finally won. The scandal has now been well documented; victims were eventually offered around $46m in compensation.[44]

But what is less well known is that a Conservative politician was working for Trafigura at the time. Lord Strathclyde had a senior position in the firm: non-executive director at the company's hedge-fund arm. His salary was not disclosed.[45]

He finally quit the job after the internal emails were published in September 2009 – four months after the initial allegations were raised by the BBC.[46] Strathclyde claimed he had always planned to step down from the role 'in preparation for the forthcoming General Election'. But he added: 'I've read today's stories about Trafigura with concern and I am making inquiries about the situation.'[47]

When the General Election came, Strathclyde was appointed leader of the House of Lords and chancellor of the Duchy of Lancaster. His new role meant he was now in David Cameron's inner circle, attending cabinet meetings.

Then, when he left again in early 2013, it took just three months before he was back working for his old flame, Trafigura. This time, he accepted a more senior role as non-executive director.[48] He had simply taken three gap-years out of his controversial business career, for a stint in government.

Clearly, he was unfazed by the toxic waste scandal. 'Trafigura has learned from that episode and has reviewed its policies and put changes in place to ensure that something like that does not happen again,' he said. No further questions.

In Westminster, the ethical standards of your business affairs don't matter much. Business *is* the ethic. As long as you duck out of the picture while you're in the cabinet, it doesn't matter what corporate controversies you're associated with.

While we may find it repugnant that politicians have become associated with such extraordinary controversies, there's nothing in the rule book against it. And the logic I kept hearing from politicians says that, if it's not explicitly banned, then it must be OK. Scandals might cause minor embarrassment for a few days, but there is no real redress. Short of strangling a kitten on camera, peers are free to do just about anything without fear of being kicked out. MPs, meanwhile, do run the risk of being voted out at the next elections, but those in safe seats have little to worry about. Besides, there are plenty of businesses out there with questionable ethics, and scandals are quickly forgotten. Come election day we'll just be talking about the latest silly gaffe instead.

In theory, political leaders can kick MPs out of their party – but not out of Parliament. And with every vote counting, they will only do this in extreme cases where they have little choice. So it doesn't worry most politicians. 'I don't think there ought to be occupations that are regarded as not acceptable,' one senior politician tells me. 'But I don't think people who have those occupations – for example, brothel keepers – are appointed!'

Business ethics simply don't register. The media will soon move on to something else and parties won't pick a fight with their own people. So Parliament is open for business as usual: politicians are free to place money over morals.

PART THREE:

Politics for sale

Lobbying: the insiders

> Commercial lobbyists acting for particular, narrow interests bend our system
> of government to their will to such an extent that it can be said to no longer
> serve the interests of the wider public. Certain players in society through
> their paid lobbyists, are drowning out everyone else. Viewed from this
> angle, lobbying appears as a corrupting force that undermines democracy.
>
> Tamasin Cave and Andy Rowell, *A Quiet Word*[1]

Battle scars

I'm on my way to meet a politician who got caught out. Badly.

Lobbying scandals come and go in Westminster; but this one was
a corker. In 2010, a string of senior MPs were snared in an investigation by *The Sunday Times* and Channel 4's *Dispatches* programme.
Undercover reporters posed as executives from a US lobbying
company and told politicians they were recruiting.

The results were devastating, with MPs offering political favours
in exchange for thousands of pounds a day. Former ministers
Stephen Byers, Patricia Hewitt, Geoff Hoon and Richard Caborn
were all reported to parliamentary authorities after the story broke,
along with Conservative Sir John Butterfill and Labour backbencher
Adam Ingram. Secret footage showed Byers describing himself as a
'cab for hire' and Hewitt claiming that, for the right price, she
could get clients a key seat on a government advisory board.
Meanwhile, Hoon was filmed saying he wanted to turn his political
experience into 'something that frankly makes money'. He implied
he could disclose sensitive information from the Ministry of Defence
to a paying client.[2] The sorry affair became known as the Cash For
Influence scandal.

For those involved, the wounds are still fresh. All of them have avoided the public eye ever since. But I wanted to understand the mindset that motivated them and find out how Parliament has moved on since the scandal. Were these just a few rogue MPs, or was it part of a culture that excused politicians who are paid to lobby?

Eventually, one of the Cash For Influence gang agrees to talk to me on condition that I don't identify them.[3] 'The biggest problem I've got is that the moment I say anything publicly, someone will say "well, he would say that because he got caught out",' he explains. Reluctantly, I agree not to name him (and I may have also changed their gender). So from now on, let's just call him 'Gary'.

'I don't want this to simply turn into yet another opportunity for *The Sunday Times* or the *Mail* or whatever to have a go at me,' he says. 'I'd want to be sure about the context you are using it. If it was, you know, "Gary thinks *The Sunday Times* are a bunch of miserable ratbags" – which he probably does . . .'

The setting seems weirdly appropriate for an anonymous interview: we're sitting in a completely stark, dull room without any hint of personality. Gary is stony-faced and talks in an abrupt, no-nonsense kind of way. It's clear from the off that he's not in the mood for apologising for the scandal. In fact, he actually says: 'I didn't really believe that I had anything to apologise for.' During our hour-long discussion, he doesn't admit doing *anything* wrong – apart from falling for the undercover sting in the first place. Everyone is to blame but himself.

'I still feel slightly disappointed that I wasn't able to get this across,' Gary says. 'The journalist who was conducting the interview knew what she was doing. And I didn't.' He says this as if it somehow justifies or excuses what he said in the secret recording. 'Obviously looking back on it, I shouldn't have fallen into the trap.'

Gary goes on to defend the comments that cost him his job: 'In the glare of publicity it wasn't a very happy thing to say. But at the same time, in a private conversation, I'm not sure.'

He suggests there is 'a positive case' to be made for politicians having a cosy relationship with big business and corporate lobbyists, claiming there is a national benefit to allowing corporations to pay political insiders for insights. 'Business needs that kind of expertise, that kind of knowledge and understanding,' he says. 'How decisions are taken, what factors are influential and so on . . . I think is valuable expertise that is to the benefit of the UK . . . Maybe I'm naïve, but I can't see that there is such a problem.'

Instead, it's the political system that has got it wrong. Life is too hard for politicians, he says. First he criticises the 'reluctance of successive governments to actually make sure that MPs are paid properly'. Then he says he feels 'desperately sorry' for colleagues who have been caught out in other financial scandals.

He even tries to excuse his part in the lobbying scandal by claiming that it's hard for MPs to earn enough money. He reckons they need to take whatever work they can get, or else face the prospect of unemployment when they leave politics. It's desperate stuff and, no matter how hard I try to empathise, I just can't.

'It is not easy for politicians to get jobs in businesses,' he says. 'The idea of revolving doors and cosy relationships. I think you'll find – if you really checked – that the number of MPs and even former ministers who actually have proper jobs after they leave Parliament, I would say is quite the fingers of one hand. It's not very many. Most of the ones I keep in touch with are pretty much unemployed, in one way and another.'

'Is that because they're unemployable?' I ask, bewildered.

'I think so . . . I think actually UK companies are nervous, I think that's the real reason.'

I'm going to interrupt Gary's rant here to point out that he's talking rubbish. In fact, his claim that former MPs are unemployable is so blatantly untrue that it's even disproved by the CVs of the very MPs who were exposed in the Cash For Influence sting. Here's what some of those poor, 'unemployed' folks are up to nowadays:

- **Stephen Byers**
  Byers landed a gig as non-executive chairman of ACWA, a multi-national water company which boasts clients including Kelloggs and Coca-Cola.[4] The business is owned via the tax haven of Cyprus and brings in more than £6.8m a year. Despite this, under Byers' watch, ACWA keeps making hefty financial losses in the UK.[5] He said he wanted to be a 'cab for hire'; I wonder if anyone feels like they've been taken for a ride yet?

- **Patricia Hewitt**

  A few years after leaving Parliament in disgrace, she finally got the lobby-ing job she'd apparently been looking for. Hewitt became a senior adviser to FTI, a powerful political consultancy which operates in Westminster. Announcing her appointment, the company proudly reeled off a long list of other jobs she held: 'Currently a Director of EuroTunnel Group, a member of the global advisory board for technology firm, Sutherland Global Services and Chair of the UK India Business Council.'[6]

- **Geoff Hoon**

  Kicked out of Parliament for appearing to suggest he could give clients confidential information about defence and security,[7] Hoon went on to a top job at a defence company, AugustaWestland.[8] As chance would have it, Hoon had approved a £1bn government deal with this very same firm while he was defence secretary, a few years earlier.[9] In his new job he was called to give evidence at the trial of two former AugustaWestland executives who were accused of bribery.[10]

- **Richard Caborn**

  Caborn became a strategic adviser to Sheffield's Advanced Manufacturing Research Centre.[11] By happy coincidence, it was Caborn who apparently helped set up the research centre when he was a minister, by securing £6m of government funding.[12] His high-profile role has even brought him back to the heart of Westminster, giving evidence to Westminster committees.[13]

Unemployed? I reckon they're doing OK. And these are the MPs who left in disgrace! For the others, getting a lucrative job after quit-ting Parliament would surely be a piece of cake.

But even if MPs really *are* underpaid – and even if they *did* find it tough to get jobs afterwards – does that excuse bad behaviour? It's not the sort of argument you'd expect to hear from an elected repre-sentative: 'either increase our wages, or we'll be forced to accept dodgy money'. Blaming the lobbying scandal on anything other than MPs' own greed is deeply cynical, because it implies that sinking to the depths of near-corruption is inevitable human nature that can only be avoided with a system of carrots and sticks.[14]

Gary is clearly a lost cause in the mission to clean up politics. But has Parliament changed since the scandal which caught him out? Gary reckons it has, but not in the way we might hope: 'This took place before Leveson [the enquiry into journalism ethics] and before the kind of fightback by politicians against the media.' He thinks authorities were 'afraid' to give the impression of a cosy relation in Parliament if they did not rule against the MPs caught out in the sting.

The implication is that authorities have now become more, not less, forgiving of those embroiled in lobbying scandals. Politicians are now standing up to meddling journalists who expose their wrongdoing. Certainly, the scandal that lost Gary his seat in Parliament has not stopped other politicians taking fat pay cheques to join lobby shops. The lobbyists weren't going down without a fight.

The politicians fight back

Skip forward to January 2015. Sir Malcolm Rifkind walked into a blank Mayfair office to meet two consultants from a Hong Kong communications company, PMR. The former foreign secretary didn't know it at the time, but the company was bogus. The consultants were in fact a fresh set of undercover reporters, from the *Telegraph* and Channel 4. Secretly, they filmed the whole rendezvous on hidden cameras, aiming to expose a fresh lobbying scandal.

They told Rifkind that PMR had been highly successful overseas. The company was now looking to hire an influential British politician as an adviser, to help them get a foot in the door in European markets. Would Rifkind work for them?

Sitting back in his chair, the MP seemed relaxed about the idea. 'You'd be surprised how much free time I have,' he said. 'I am self-employed, so nobody pays me a salary. I have to earn my income. But when I'm not doing something, I can do what I like.'

Rifkind told the consultants he could write to ministers to get information and 'wouldn't name who was asking'. For payment, he said that £60–80,000 'sounds reasonable'.[15] The job certainly seemed to interest him. Subsequently, he explained that he wanted 'to have the standard of living that my professional background would normally entitle me to have'.[16]

When the story broke in early 2015, it was billed as a new Cash For Influence scandal. Rifkind quickly quit as chairman of Parliament's Intelligence and Security group and said he would not stand as an MP in the forthcoming election. Meanwhile, Jack Straw – who had also been caught by the sting – suspended himself from the parliamentary Labour Party. The media had a field day. 'David Cameron once said that lobbying was the next great Westminster scandal waiting to happen. But it already has and nothing much has been done to arrest it,' the *Telegraph* said.[17]

As the news rocked Parliament, it seemed for a moment like something might finally be done to stop MPs cashing in from lobbying companies.

But jump forward to September of that year and the tables had turned. A report by Kathryn Hudson, the parliamentary commissioner for standards, inexplicably cleared Straw and Rifkind of any wrongdoing and attacked the journalists instead. The media had supposedly 'distorted the truth and misled the public as to what had actually taken place'.

But many rejected the verdict. 'If you believe that, you'll believe anything,' one ex-MP tells me. The *Telegraph* responded to the inquiry boldly: 'The sorry tale of Sir Malcolm and Mr Straw and the standards committee's shameful response prove beyond doubt that MPs cannot be trusted to regulate themselves over lobbying.'[18] Indeed, reports revealed that Rifkind and Hudson had an interesting personal history: in 2012, the MP had been part of a five-person panel that recommended Hudson to the position of parliamentary commissioner for standards.[19]

The truth is, Straw and Rifkind did not *technically* break any rules because they didn't formally agree to lobby. The inquiry cleared them because it believed the pair didn't intend to back up their words with actions. But does that give them a clear bill of health? 'It still doesn't alter what they said,' one Labour MP tells me. 'They said enough to condemn themselves.'

Above all, the scandal proved how easy it would be for a sitting MP to earn money on the side through lobbying, if they so chose. 'It seems one of the most egregious cases of people out to prostitute their inside knowledge,' the MP says. 'They should have been punished.' But my Labour source suggests the authorities may have approached the case sympathetically because there was no pre-existing antagonism with the two men. 'Jack Straw – for reasons I don't understand – is regarded as a good bloke,' he explains.

Parliament's decision to not only clear the pair, but also attack the press for daring to expose lobbying, marked a significant turning point. In Gary's case, politicians were on the defensive over lobbying, beaten and battered. An MP hit by scandal would be obliterated. But now, Jack Straw and Malcolm Rifkind had put up a fight – and they seemed to have won.

Exactly a week after the report came out clearing the pair, I'm sitting in a stately drawing room in Somerset House waiting to meet Malcolm Rifkind. He appears at the doorway, leans in and flashes a mischievous grin at me. He's pretty chuffed to have been 'cleared'.

It's mid-afternoon and he's just come out of a lecture he was giving to the military's top brass in nearby King's College London. 'I'm doing now essentially what I was doing before I ceased being an MP,' he explains, 'with the exception obviously of the parliamentary side of it.' (Maybe that was always part of the problem – being an MP was just one job of many.)

Rifkind was once one of the Tories' most respected figures and, although he comes across as pleasant enough, he asserts his authority and control over our conversation with a forceful charm. I begin explaining what my book is about, but he has no time for it and interrupts. 'OK, let's get into the Q&A,' he snaps. So we do. But it's mainly just 'A', because I can't get a word in.

His attitude echoes the same things I'd heard Gary say: defending himself and blaming other people for the scandal. Most of the time, he just lashes out at the undercover journalists. If you're a fan of *The Thick of It*, Rifkind is a bit of a Steve Fleming type character. You can imagine him turning on one of these audacious reporters, steam coming out of his ears, and snarling: 'I'm going to take you down! I'm going to take you down to Funky Town!' Rifkind phrases it differently, though:

'As in any profession, there are decent people; there are indecent people. There are journalists with ethical standards and there are journalists with none,' he says. 'I was unfortunate enough to be in the presence of people who were the shits.

'. . . It's quite unscrupulous and it's shitty. It's not serious journalism, it's disgraceful.'

I try likening his case to previous lobbying scandals, but Rifkind isn't having any of it. 'I rest on the commissioner's own conclusion that there was distortion [in the journalism],' he says. 'Not a single sentence of the discussions I had with these buggers was about cash for access.'

The inquiry which cleared Rifkind acknowledged that he made some 'silly' remarks and 'errors of judgement', but it said there was no evidence 'that Sir Malcolm had done anything which could be considered a breach of the rules on lobbying.'[20] Rifkind takes this to be a clean bill of health, resting in the fact that he didn't technically break the Code of Conduct – and he doesn't see why anyone would still be concerned about what he did.

The thing is, most of us don't know the ins and outs of Parliament's rule book. But what the public *is* really good at, however, is sniffing out an odious politician when it sees one. The regulations on lobbying are often way too relaxed, so merely sticking to the rules does not necessarily exonerate the likes of Malcolm Rifkind and Jack Straw. As one key insider tells me: 'It is probably true that they did not break the rules – and therefore we have got a problem with the rules.'[21]

Just to prove that the rules don't go far enough, a subsequent review by Ofcom later ruled that the pair *did* seek to 'exploit their experience and connections' after all. And, contrary to Parliament's own inquiry, it said the media 'did not give a misleading impression of their conduct'.[22] Malcolm Rifkind, it seemed, was prepared to compromise his credibility for the sake of sniffing out a lucrative job. One MP tells me: 'I assumed that he was already vastly rich. Maybe he is, and maybe he's just greedy.'

But the former foreign secretary genuinely seems to think he did nothing wrong. It's not just that he's bitter – he comes across as someone in a state of denial. Why would anyone possibly still be angry at him? After all, lobbying isn't much of a problem in Westminster, he says. 'I don't think it's widespread at all, because I think most MPs are people who've got their own standards and don't wish to be involved in that kind of lobbying.'

But the records suggest otherwise.

The new lobbyists

'I just wondered if I could have a chat about, sort of . . . what kind of things you can offer?'

I was on the phone to a lobbying company, but I wasn't using my real name. I was undercover, posing as 'David', a freelance consultant looking to buy political influence in Westminster.

My cover story was simple: one of my clients was an expanding company in the financial services sector, I told them. Without any political network at the moment, they were willing to pay big bucks to get the ear of government ministers for their commercial advantage. David's job was to sound out the lobbyist and report back.

I approached a firm called Nudge Factory and said I didn't want to hear wishy-washy comments. I needed to gather cold hard facts about what Nudge Factory could offer them. What had these lobbyists already done? Do they operate at the highest level of politics? Can they fix meetings with ministers?

This was no 'fishing expedition', though. There was good reason to phone Nudge Factory undercover. You see, one of its directors is Paul Scully, the Conservative MP for Sutton and Cheam. On the Register of Interests, he describes his role at Nudge Factory as 'unpaid and informal', but he also has a direct financial stake in it, as he owns 40% of the business.[23] Scully is one of a sizeable stock of parliamentarians linked to lobbying companies.

But judging by his official declarations, you might be mistaken for not realising that. When I checked the Register of Interests, Scully had described Nudge Factory as merely 'a corporate affairs consultancy', and there was no mention of the company's clients. Plus, it wasn't listed on Westminster's official register of lobbyists.[24] So what exactly was this business? Nudge Factory's website gave a bit more detail, but it was still fairly vague:

Our team have specialist knowledge developed through working at the heart of government on individuals, issues and the legislative process. That in-depth knowledge twinned with wide trusted relationships with players in Westminster and Whitehall makes the team at Nudge Factory a formidable force in helping our clients to engage in effective communication and dialogue with the decision makers that really matter.[25]

What level are we talking here? Lots of people can claim to have 'relationships with players in Westminster', but are they top government ministers or junior aides? And has Nudge Factory ever actually influenced government policy on behalf of paying clients? Given that an MP was involved with running the company, the answers to these questions were vital. Most importantly, who were the clients?

In less than ten minutes on the phone, Paul Scully's lobby firm tells me they can fix meetings with MPs, for my paying client.

'They'd like their say,' I explain. 'Do you help people out with things like that? Is it kind of getting meetings with ministers and things like that?'

'Yeah, definitely,' the reply comes. 'Those are exactly the sort of things that we do. Try and get issues on the policy agenda; push them up to higher profile. We'd get clients into – you know – meet with important people, important ministers or their parliamentary secretaries or civil servants, or whoever would be the appropriate decision maker in that regard. Yeah, that's the kind of stuff we do.'[26]

It's a good start, but I want detail. In my cover story, my client won't go with Nudge Factory unless they know it has a strong track record of high-level lobbying. So brashly I ask the man on the other end of the phone to give me 'examples of where you've had that kind of policy success, which I might be able to report back'.

He obliges. Nudge Factory lobbied for a client in the housing market, he tells me. 'Working on behalf of a client to re-classify a sort of specific form of housing, to make it more beneficial for developers.' He explains: 'To do that we've met with ministers and so on, to get them to sort of have our client present their case to say why they thought this change should be made . . . what the benefits are for the government essentially.'

Then he gives me another example: 'Lobbying on behalf of another client for sort of tax issues.' He says this was 'related to a certain industry, in terms of how they're being taxed or not being taxed . . .'

'Yeah, I see,' I say. 'And you had success with that?'

'Yes, we– yes. So far, yeah.'

That example involved lobbying ministers too, he says. 'Meeting with people at the Treasury, or civil servants, ministers. Yeah, that kind of thing, to get it on the agenda . . . Pushing our clients' voice to be heard.'

So Nudge Factory could help my financial services client 'if they wanted to talk to MPs or whatever?' I ask. 'That probably wouldn't be a problem?'

'No, no. Absolutely,' he says.

Why I didn't leave it there, I don't know. But I went back for more. I wanted to speak to the manager to find out more details and ask about Paul Scully's personal involvement. That wasn't going to happen, though.

I phoned back a few days later and got the manager, Ahzaz Chowdhury, who co-founded the company with Scully.[27]

'Would you be able to drop me an email?' Chowdhury asked me, cooly. 'It's just I need to do a couple of checks, because . . . you would be aware, this industry . . . it's notorious for sting operations with the press.'

My heart jumped out of my throat. I'd been found out! What do I *do*?

I did what anyone would do in this situation – laugh like a crazed maniac. 'Ahahahaha!' I spluttered. 'Right! Yeah, yeah, yeah!'

He gave me his email address and hung up.

I didn't email back. Obviously.

Hush hush

Paul Scully is far from the only politician in Westminster with a position at a private lobby firm. Lots of insiders I spoke to during my research for this book claimed that parliamentarians don't do lobbying any more. And if any did, it was only one or two. Some even claimed it was illegal for MPs to have jobs in lobbying. But they were wrong.

At least eight politicians work for – or are directors of – companies registered on the official lobby register. Far, far more (including

Scully) have positions at unregistered firms.[28] Part of the difficulty with transparency in this area is that there's no single clear definition of what 'lobbying' is. At the most liberal definition it could include anything where people are using political knowledge, insight or contacts to further the interests of a paying client. So, potentially that could include all manner of advisory and consultancy positions.

A rough-cut analysis of data from DueDil and the Register of Interests brings up just under 600 positions held by MPs and peers which fit loosely in this definition. This isn't a scientific reflection of the scale of lobbying in Parliament (not all 'strategic consultants' will advise on political issues, and so on). Rather, it highlights how common consultancy and public relations work is among politicians – and how difficult it is, therefore, to separate the full-on lobbyists from the harmless majority. That's why vagueness about Paul Scully's firm leaves the door open to confusion.

For twenty years, up until May 2015, MPs were required to hand in copies of their work contracts to the Parliamentary Commissioner, if their job involved 'the provision of services in his capacity as a Member of Parliament'. These were available for journalists and the public to read. But this requirement was scrapped at the 2015 General Election, so job contracts are now a strictly private affair – even when MPs are being paid to advise on political issues. Parliament's standards watchdog confirmed: 'They don't have to deposit contracts with us now.'[29]

This means the public now has no right to view the roles and responsibilities that their representatives have agreed to take for private companies – beyond the tiny scraps of information included in the Register of Interests.

A few of the old contracts still float around, upstairs in the Parliamentary Archives. But even these give little substantive detail about the jobs. For instance, documents filed by Peter Lilley for a position on an advisory council includes a line saying that the MP 'will offer advice from time to time'.[30] Another MP's contract talks about 'advice on Parliamentary matters'.[31]

Among Parliament's array of current lobbyists is Tory MP, Bob Neill. According to his declaration of interests, Neill is a non-executive director of Cratus Communications Limited, a registered lobbying company. He's paid up to £417 per hour.[32]

In 2015, Cratus lobbied for a number of clients with interests in the property market. They included Gleeson Strategic Land, which is part of an £81m business group specialising in land development and urban regeneration. 'We are widely recognised for our specialist expertise in identifying new opportunities and successfully managing them through the planning system,' the company says.[33] Also in 2015, Cratus lobbied for Lend Lease, another development firm, which describes itself as an 'international property and infrastructure group'.[34]

Although Bob Neill has declared his directorship with the lobbying company, he appears not to have mentioned the clients.[35] But that hasn't stopped him talking about urban development in Parliament – despite Cratus's work for property firms. Around the time Gleeson was on the lobby shop's books, in November 2015, he asked the government to 'look at particular changes to the planning regime for brownfield land'. He explained that changes would accelerate the process for developers.[36]

The same year, he also quizzed Labour over rent control policies, which he claimed 'would drive up rents and choke off investment in the sector'.[37] And in January 2016, he called on the government to ensure that businesses would not 'lose out on the uplift in value' that comes from the granting of housing permission.[38] On none of these occasions did he draw attention to his entry on the Register of Interests, or mention Cratus's clients in the land development sector.

Let me be clear, I am not suggesting that Neill or Cratus are corrupt. It would be completely wrong to suggest he was being paid to make these interventions in Parliament. Quite simply, there is no evidence to support that claim. But that doesn't alter the potential for a huge conflict of interest.

The situation is compounded by Neill's own lack of transparency. Since he had not mentioned Cratus's clients in either the Register of Interests or the Commons debates themselves, I sent him an email, politely asking for a full list of the firm's clients.

Dear Bob,

I'm writing a book about politicians' financial interests.

I noticed that you are a non-executive director at a lobbying company called Cratus Communications – which is included in your declarations for Parliament.

> For transparency, I wondered if you might be happy to provide me
> with a list of Cratus's past and present clients, as they do not appear to
> be included on your Register of Interests?
> Best regards,
> Martin [39]

No reply. I waited a couple of days and emailed again. 'I haven't heard back yet, but would be very grateful for your response,' I said.[40]

Still no reply. It seems that you and I do not have the right to be told this information.

With smaller consultancies, there is often so little information available publicly that we *rely* on MPs to provide us the details. Without the right information, it's often hard to even know whether it's a proper lobbying firm or not. But for many of these people, silence is the name of the game.

When I questioned them about their consultancies, only a few politicians responded. Wes Streeting, a newbie Labour MP, was one who did. He runs a consultancy business – Wes Streeting Associates Limited – but has not mentioned it in his declarations.[41] He told me: 'I set up the company when I effectively went self-employed in case it became a long-term thing. As it happens, because of the short-term nature of my freelance work, I instead registered as a sole trader and am winding the company up.'

It doesn't sound like a terribly scary company – there are no big business clients. Streeting said: 'I haven't done any consultancy since the election, but when I was freelance I did some campaigns consultancy work for the British Youth Council, TeenTech, Magic Breakfast and, for Progress, editorial support.'[42] Hardly the kind of top level lobbying we should be worried about, but without transparency on the Register of Interests it could have been anyone's guess what his company was up to.

Other MPs were not so forthcoming. None less so than Michelle Thomson, the MP for Edinburgh West. She was elected in 2015 as part of the SNP's new cohort, but she was soon forced out of the party – becoming an independent – after her property deals became the subject of a police investigation.[43]

According to her declarations, Thomson has shares in an eponymous consultancy firm. But although she doesn't admit it on the

Register, she is also the company's sole director, meaning that she has an active role in running it.[44] Exactly what type of consultancy the business does is anyone's guess, though. Over the course of three months, I contacted Thomson four times asking for a list of her clients. There was no reply.

It was a similar story with others. Lord Boyce, who was once 'First Sea Lord' in the Navy, now runs a small business called MCB Advisory Services Limited. When I emailed Boyce asking why he'd not declared this, he didn't reply. Mysteriously however, the company was quietly added to the Register the very same day.[45]

Lord Stevens of Kirkwhelpington was another one. The former head of the Metropolitan Police, he's held a series of high-powered public positions, recently becoming a senior international security adviser for David Cameron. But Stevens also heads up Quest Global Limited, which specialises in 'strategic intelligence'.[46]

One of the firm's main services is 'strategy for sporting organisations'. And that includes lobbying. 'Political lobbying is one of the most important, yet complex challenges for sporting organisations,' it says. 'With extensive political experience, and staff members from national and international political backgrounds, Quest provides guidance on political networking and navigating to ensure client organisations can efficiently achieve their strategic objectives.'

By now, it will come as no surprise to find out that my request for a list of Stevens's clients was met with silence.[47]

Lobbyists, it seems, have a lot to keep silent about. 'There are quite a few directors of lobbying companies who are working peers,' a Labour MP tells me. 'The lobbying companies may be working for all kinds of clients, but [the peers] don't declare who their clients are. So therefore you could have Lord X happily in the House of Lords doing all sorts of things. He declares that he is employed by a lobbying company, but you don't know who the clients are.'[48]

It was becoming clear to me that politicians are still flirting with lobbying as much as ever. Some are even prepared to compromise their own credibility for the sake of a quick buck. Now, I wanted to get inside the lobbying industry itself.

Lobbying: taking the bait

Before I meet Charlie, I imagine him to be the embodiment of sleaze.[1] The archetypal political lobbyist: perhaps in a pinstriped suit, puffing on a fat cigar and swigging champagne. He would sneak around Westminster like a corporate ninja, using dark arts and bundles of cash to secretly manipulate the government.

He gives me instructions to meet him at a bar on Gutter Lane, in the heart of London. The address alone seems to conjure up the impression that I'm venturing into some murky underworld. When I get there, I buy a pint and wait.

When he arrives, though, Charlie is not what I'd been expecting. For a start, he's young; still in his twenties. Sharply dressed and bursting with self-confidence, he looks more like a new recruit at a slick City firm than a high-powered consultant at one of the leading lobby groups in town. Charlie is the kind of person you feel was probably born wearing a suit and tie. The kind of person who is unable to have a normal conversation which doesn't consist entirely of business jargon.

As I slurp my cheapo larger, Charlie beckons a waitress and orders an espresso and a bottle of San Pellegrino. 'Now then,' he says. 'What do you want to know?'

Very quickly it becomes clear to me that the lobbying industry is a world away from what it once was. It may be just as poisonous and corrupting as ever before, but now it has an air of legitimacy about it. Charlie is the living embodiment of a quiet 'reputation management' exercise that has been taking place over the last few years.

Back in the 1990s, the reputation of lobbying hit rock-bottom. The era was defined by the fall of Westminster's most successful political fixer, Ian Greer. A slippery character with a wide teddy-bear face, Greer found himself at the centre of an almighty sleaze scandal, first exposed by the *Guardian* newspaper in 1994. Two Conservative MPs were alleged to have taken money from Greer in exchange for tabling questions in Parliament, on behalf of Mohamed al-Fayed, the owner of Harrods.[2] Greer told al-Fayed: 'You need to rent an MP just like you rent a London taxi.'[3] (Sound familiar?)

The affair became known as the Cash For Questions scandal and it ruined Greer's business. Not only that, it weakened the government and made lobbying the dirtiest word in Whitehall for years to come.

For those who criticise lobbying, Greer represented everything there is to hate about it. Alongside his political manoeuvring for multinational business clients like Coca-Cola and British Airways, he also worked for Slobodan Milošević, the murderous Serbian president who was later prosecuted for genocide and war crimes.[4] Reports said Greer's firm was indirectly hired to 'communicate the Serbian message'.[5]

It was part of a grand tradition in the lobbying industry of putting money before morals. Top consultancies have frequently tried to influence governments for a plethora of horrendous causes. Indeed, not long after this episode, another Westminster lobby shop reportedly helped orchestrate a campaign for the release of General Pinochet, the Chilean military dictator.[6] Lord Chadlington (another lobbyist) explained the industry's rationale: 'We're in it for money.'[7]

It's hard to shake off a reputation for being amoral when all the evidence clearly points in the same direction. But it used to be more obvious. In Greer's time, it was easy to realise that lobbying was a scourge on democracy, mired in sleaze and secrecy. Indeed, in his 2002 book *The Best Democracy Money Can Buy*, the investigative journalist Greg Palast describes going undercover to expose lobbyists, saying that he had to act like a 'scuzz-ball, sleaze-o-"consultant" on the take . . . *just like them*.'[8]

Something has changed since those days. Not the lobbying itself – that's much the same as ever (minus most of the illegal bribery). But there is now a veil of professional respectability and 'brand management' to the industry. By 2014, veteran lobbyist Lionel Zetter was leading the charge to rebrand his industry. He wrote a book for fellow insiders, which moaned about campaigners and journalists, who always 'insist that lobbyists are secretive, and that we are somehow ashamed of what we do'.

'The actual term lobbying is sometimes shunned by practitioners and clients alike. The press has tried to associate the term with sleaze,' he wrote. 'I feel, however, that the industry needs to reclaim the title.' Zetter went on to claim that journalists have continually tried to shine a light on lobbying partly because 'they may be jealous of the influence that lobbyists can and do deploy', and because lobbyists' salaries have 'added to the resentment' among cash-strapped journalists.[9]

So lobbying was given a makeover.

'Nobody calls themselves lobbyists any more,' says Labour MP Paul Flynn, who has long campaigned against the industry. 'They're always "public affairs consultants", and so on. And they have lovely people working for them.' But Flynn still criticises the practice: 'It's there to pervert the legislation – and not on the basis of the merit of the case, but on the basis of the greed of the person who's making the case.'

However much spin lobbyists want to put on their industry, it doesn't change the fundamentals. Corporate lobbying exists so that big, powerful businesses can exert huge, disproportionate levels of influence over the government. In doing so, it corrupts democracy to its core.

Other organisations with less money don't get a look-in. 'When you have groups of students who can't pay for lobbyists . . . they find it very difficult to get their message across,' Charlie admits. 'They don't have the money to pay for the services that we can offer. Some views are over-represented.'

But he adds: 'It's not my problem. It's not the problem of a lobbyist. If they can pay us, fine.'

The question is, how open is Parliament to the influence of lobbyists? The rules on this are predictably sparse. Officially, MPs are perfectly entitled to meet lobbyists and take their advice. Although there are certain rules about declaring gifts, they are completely within their rights to accept an invitation for dinner with a corporate representative. The main restriction is simply that MPs are banned from being *paid* to speak or vote in Parliament. In other words, it's not illegal for politicians to schmooze with them (or even work for them) – just so long as their political decisions are not for sale. But that distinction can often be blurry.

'You have backbenchers who are willing to put in [parliamentary] questions,' Charlie says, as we drink in the Gutter Lane bar. 'They'll do it for people who they have an affinity with.' He describes parliamentary questions as 'a tool for lobbyists', adding: 'It happens often, but it's impossible to track.'

'We can get them talking; get them opportunities to build friendships, so that when I say "hey, I would quite like there to be a question asked on the floor of the House on this subject", it can happen,' he says. 'Just this week we secured five questions to be asked by an MP on the floor of the House. Obviously that means that the government has to respond to that within ten working days.'

'Is that MP paid?' I ask, mindful of Ian Greer's Cash For Questions scandal.

But Charlie says he's not allowed to pay them. 'What's in it for them is that usually they get support from the business,' he says. 'Yes, there are greedy politicians, just like there are greedy people. I mean, they are human.

'Some of them want to be wined and dined, some of them want to be speakers at your receptions, some of them want you to make a big thing about them and the fact that they want a photo opportunity.'

I've agreed not to identify Charlie (which isn't his real name), or the powerful lobby shop he works for. And under the cover of anonymity, he starts to spill the beans on his trade, boasting about the incredible influence he has over Parliament.

Every day I'm trying to get a meeting with someone in the Treasury. Just today I was prepping a client for meeting with the prime minister on Monday . . . Quite often something that I have written will make it into legislation.

. . . Sometimes we might need a politician to speak on our behalf in Parliament. We might want to get some influence in the Parliament policy agenda. Sometimes we try to force certain politicians' or certain ministers' hands by saying to them: 'Look, we know this is your position. This is ours . . . And we're kind of forcing your hand because, actually, we might do something like pull all of our investment from the UK'.

The only issue that comes with lobbying is that politicians' integrity can sometimes be questioned by it. And that is the problem of the politician, not the lobbyist.

Charlie even claims that he successfully lobbied all of the main political parties to include a specific key line in their election manifestos in 2015. He did this on behalf of a client: a large, financial services corporation which was paying big money for political influence. Every party he lobbied apparently agreed to do it – adding the company's message into their official policy pledges.

'Part of my job for the election was getting the manifestos to say certain things,' he explains. 'It was about lobbying the parties and saying: ". . . Hey David Cameron, you should be including this as part of your manifesto, and this is why." '

'Nobody knows that,' he adds.

Charlie tells me the line that was included and – lo and behold – when I check later, there it is! A small subtle policy pledge, allegedly dreamed up by a huge financial corporation. It was written in every one of the main parties' election manifestos.

I check with a well-placed source: 'Can you imagine that sort of thing happening quite easily?' But my source nods: 'Oh yeah, yeah. All the time.'

Another insider agrees: 'If you can keep them happy by putting a line in that's not going to actually piss anyone off, then why wouldn't you? It's all just part of political management.'

It's all too easy to attack the lobbying industry, though. The real problem is that it *actually works*. Let's be honest, it's hardly a surprise that big companies try to influence politicians. Indeed, there's nothing inherently wrong about trying to get your voice heard. Instead, what we should be concerned about is that politicians take the bait.

In the old days it was easy to see why they did: cases like the Ian Greer scandal suggest lobbyists were keen to dangle wads of cash in front of MPs. These days, that kind of thing seems to have all but disappeared. And yet the lobbying industry has grown exponentially – so they must be doing something right.

Before he became prime minister, David Cameron promised to crack down on lobbying. 'We all know how it works,' he said. 'The lunches, the hospitality, the quiet word in your ear, the ex-ministers and ex-advisers for hire, helping big business find the right way to get its way.

'Today it is a £2bn industry that has a huge presence in Parliament.

The Hansard Society has estimated that some MPs are approached over 100 times a week by lobbyists. I believe that secret corporate lobbying, like the expenses scandal, goes to the heart of why people are so fed up with politics. It arouses people's worst fears and suspicions about how our political system works.'[10]

The company accounts of these lobby firms tell a revealing story. By analysing the changing fortunes of the UK's biggest consultancies, we can see precisely how they – in fact – thrived under Cameron's governments.

For this experiment, let's use the official Register of Lobbyists. The biggest firms on this list will have all filed full financial accounts with Companies House, so we can see how much money they're making. There are twenty-six of them who have done this since the start of Cameron's premiership in 2010. These documents will therefore paint a picture of how successful Britain's top lobbyists have been during this period.

Back in 2010, they reported a combined total income of £7.3bn, making a profit of £1.8bn. Not bad. Jump forward five years, however, and these same companies had increased their turnover by almost 50%. In 2014, they brought in a whopping £10.8bn, on which they made £2.4bn profits.[11]

Yet even this represents just a fraction of the UK's lobbying industry. As the campaign group Spinwatch has pointed out, the official lobby register that we're using here only lists a small proportion of consultancies. 'The UK's register was built expressly to keep the vast majority of the government's interactions with lobbyists secret,' Spinwatch says.[12]

These figures can't be seen as a precise measure of the industry's growth. However, it does suggest that lobbying is on the rise, becoming more fruitful and profitable. Between them, the consultancies represent some of the biggest names in business: Google, Facebook, Associated British Foods, FirstGroup, British Gas. The list goes on. These companies are prepared to pump big bucks into lobbying for one reason only – it gets results.

I ask Charlie if it feels like his industry is on the move. 'I would argue that we're growing,' he replies. 'We are becoming an increasingly important part of the political process.

'The lobbying industry is changing, it's evolving . . . We don't look like the lobbying industry we were five or ten years ago, because we're not the same industry. We're offering more, we're doing more.'

We've seen how lobbying has penetrated Westminster politics. Now let's look at why politicians have been so receptive to it. If there are no (or very few) illegal cash bribes any more, is personal financial greed still part of the explanation?

There is going to be no straightforward answer here; different politicians engage with lobbyists for any number of reasons. And you'll never clean up the system altogether. On the whole, though, there are two main factors at play: personal incentives and systematic necessity.

Incentives

'An astute minister struggling on around £90,000 a year can rack up future earnings at a rate many, many times that,' *Private Eye* wrote. 'The government's revolving door police can always be relied on to look the other way.'[13]

This so-called 'revolving door' between government and the private sector has been the subject of much discussion over the years, although nothing substantial has been done to improve things. A cosy relationship between the two worlds has allowed scores of public officials to cash in on their knowledge of government and then jog off to big businesses, who pay them handsomely for their useful government experience.

Recently much of the criticism over this has been directed at non-elected officials. The most notable case was Dave Hartnett. He was the UK's top taxman at HMRC, before dancing happily over to Deloitte – an accountancy firm embroiled in a tax avoidance controversy over its handling of Vodafone and Starbucks accounts.[14] At the time, the Public Accounts Committee's chair, Margaret Hodge, reacted saying: 'Doesn't it make you sick? It is terrible when people's individual greed means they lose all sense of what's right.'[15]

When I spoke to Hodge myself, she pointed out how wide-ranging the issue is: 'The revolving door is both ways,' she said. 'We had cases of people coming in from the tax world, helping the government write laws, and then going out and exploiting tax avoidance. But it isn't just tax – it happens in energy, it happens in transport and in defence procurement.'

The revolving door is perhaps most sickening when it's MPs themselves who are involved. Elected representatives using prized political insights to help them cash in on lucrative commercial jobs. One MP described the situation to me, saying: 'You can be a health minister one day, and working for Bupa the next.'

It's often thanks to lobbyists that MPs are able to establish such cosy relationships with big business in the first place. MPs know that if they do favours for them, they might be rewarded for their efforts. With the prospect of hard cash out of the question, they can still be rewarded with a cushty job offer. And time and again, they have successfully landed top jobs with the very companies they assisted in Westminster.

When I ask Charlie if this is part of what makes lobbyists attractive to politicians, he's in no doubt. 'Absolutely,' he says. 'It's human nature for you to plan ahead.'

Of course, on a case-by-case basis, it's impossible to know whether they had this in mind when they first accepted the lobbyists' bait. Are they literally thinking 'there might be a future job in this for me'? What's certain is that politicians are unashamed to translate the expertise they honed in Parliament into a commercial asset. One ex-MP I speak to accuses former colleagues of 'acting in the interests of corporations, and even foreign states, in the full knowledge and expectation that when your political career ends in tears, they will be tears of laughter and joy as you count your money.'

Examples of the revolving door in action are not hard to find. Take former Tory MP Mark Simmonds, for example. Since leaving his role as Africa minister in summer 2014, he's bagged no fewer than ten jobs. They include several with direct links to African affairs, and some with companies he'd personally dealt with while in government.[16] Each new position was approved by Westminster's very own toothless watchdog, the Advisory Committee on Business Appointments (ACOBA).[17]

Simmonds's new jobs include being non-executive director of African Potash, a mining and fertiliser business in the Republic of the

Congo. Announcing the appointment, the company said Simmonds would bring 'a wealth of business and political contacts, which will support African Potash'. The chairman added: 'His significant political experience, particularly within Africa, will be invaluable.'[18]

He also became a senior strategic adviser to the International Hospitals Group, a UK firm which has been involved with at least eleven hospitals in Africa.[19] He'd already chummed up with the company while in government: documents say he met them 'in order to gain a greater understanding of the skills that organisation has'. Simmonds went further still, by plugging the company in a ministerial speech that encouraged investment in Africa. He told his audience that he'd 'witnessed a new hospital project rising from the ground courtesy of International Hospitals Group', and suggested that the African economy 'offers huge potential for British investors'.[20]

Mark Simmonds is not alone in this practice. Former ministers have racked up scores of appointments linked to their previous work without any criticism from Westminster authorities. In fact, over the last five years, the ACOBA watchdog has approved each and every one of the roughly five hundred appointments it has considered.[21] What's more, its chairperson has even admitted: 'We have no remit or resources to police the advice we give.'[22]

Some politicians get jobs working for the lobby firms themselves. As my contact, Charlie, explains: 'Most lobbyists have ambitions to go into Parliament – or some sort of political office – and vice versa.'[23] The two worlds are constantly colliding.

Recent cases include the former secretary of state for energy and climate change, Ed Davey. When he lost his seat in 2015, he went off to join MHP Communications. He had connections with the firm already: MHP acted as lobbyists for EDF Energy, who Davey 'had dealings with as a minister'.[24] But ACOBA didn't think there was a problem. It simply warned Davey not to personally lobby the government for two years – and not to draw on 'any privileged information available to him as a minister' – and then set him on his way.

Even with ACOBA's restriction in place, when MHP's chief executive announced Davey's appointment he was able to speak candidly about the benefits of employing a former energy minister. 'Ed's unique insight into the energy sector will be particularly valuable to the companies we work with in that industry. His knowledge of the top-level workings of Britain's political system will also prove immensely useful to a range of our clients and to MHP itself.'[25]

Other politicians don't have to even go through the toothless ACOBA watchdog. Ministers are duty bound to get ACOBA's permission for any job they get within two years of leaving office. But, of course, if you're just over that time threshold, you avoid the risk of bad publicity. That's what happened to Paul Burstow.[26] He was a Lib Dem health minister in the coalition government until 2012 and then stayed on as a backbencher until 2015. By the time he left Parliament, three years had passed since being a minister, so he didn't need to worry about the watchdog. Like Ed Davey, Burstow also ran off to a job with MHP Communications.[27] It's all one big happy family there!

Working with the firm's health sector team, the former health minister can expect to deal with the likes of Astellas Pharma, Merck & Co and AbbVie – all huge multinational pharmaceutical companies who have been clients of the firm.[28]

Yet again, it turns out that Burstow had already developed a special relationship with MHP while he was in government. Before a party conference, one of the firm's lobbyists gave him advice on how to sell social care reforms to the public. Afterwards they boasted about their success, saying that Burstow 'followed it [the advice], at least to some degree'.[29] The company also heaped praise on him, calling him 'genuinely knowledgeable and passionate' about his work in the Department of Health.[30]

It can hardly have been a surprise, therefore, when Burstow got the call offering him a job. A move like this might normally cause controversy but, because ACOBA didn't have to publish a report about Burstow, the news slipped under the radar and was only reported by trade publications like *PR Week*.

When I questioned him about it, Burstow defended his appointment. He claimed the advice he'd been given by MHP as a minister was just 'rhetorical'. He added: 'I didn't work for MHP before entering Parliament or before entering the department and I have no plans to stand for election again, so this is not so much a revolving door.'[31]

Selling your political experience to money-making corporations has become standard procedure in Westminster. A *Mirror* investigation in

2016 found that at least twenty-five former ministers from Cameron's coalition government had gone off to work for the very sectors they used to regulate. One MP reacted to the news, saying: 'It used to be that a ministerial post was the pinnacle of any career. Now it seems to be a stepping stone to retirement riches.'[32]

These cases included Steve Webb, who had been the government's pensions minister, before running off to work for . . . a pension company, Royal London. ACOBA noted that, while in government, Webb had 'met regularly with pension companies including Royal London, although he stated that this was only "on occasion".'[33] Like all the others, Webb's appointment was approved.

But you get the sense that, deep down, some of these politicians think it's all a bit shabby. They know it's not really cool to cash in on their government experience, working for a lobbying firm. But they don't want to feel bad about themselves while they're banking the money.

Accepting a role at registered lobbyists Westbourne Communications in 2015, the former home secretary Jacqui Smith said, apropos of nothing: 'There's nothing shady about me bringing my political experience and commitment to the political process to work at Westbourne . . . People say I've gone over to the dark side but everything I've seen so far has been pretty open.'[34]

In 2015, Westbourne lobbied for clients including BAM Nuttall Ltd (a scandal-hit construction firm which blacklisted workers),[35] HS2 Ltd (the controversial and shambolic £42.6bn railway dismissed by critics as a vanity project), and the private taxi firm Uber (accused of everything from providing unsafe services with drivers allegedly involved in abductions, to using a tax haven and bullying its critics).[36][37] No, Jacqui, you're definitely not on the dark side.

The steady flow of politicos leaving Parliament to join lobby shops doesn't stop at MPs and peers. Scores of political aides, researchers and civil servants have also joined the dark side. There, they can use their inside knowledge, friends and influence to push forward the demands of rich clients.

Take Blue Rubicon, for instance, a £26m lobbying firm based in London, it has a host of friendly, cuddly clients like HSBC, Coca-Cola, Tesco, McDonald's, Heathrow Airport and Ebay.[38] These companies want top-level influence and insight into politics, which is lucky because Blue Rubicon's staff list reads like a who's who of Parliament drop-outs. From Alan Johnson's adviser and a Downing Street bod, to one of Grant Shapps's aides and David Cameron's interns. All of them went on to join Blue Rubicon to help influence the government, working under Emma Haselhurst – one of the firm's directors who also happens to be the daughter of a prominent Tory MP, Sir Alan Haselhurst.[39]

Together, they form a powerful army that can trample over democratic politics. For instance, when concerns grew over the state of the UK's gambling industry, the government eventually took notice and started cobbling together some tighter regulations. But the sector's biggest player, William Hill, didn't like the way things were going. 'William Hill was concerned to ensure that its contribution to the UK as a provider of safe well-regulated betting and gaming was *better understood* by policy-makers and parliamentarians,' Blue Rubicon explains on its website.

The solution was simple: lobby Parliament to make sure any new regulations wouldn't damage profits. Consultants scuttled off to charm 'all the key political and policy audiences that matter to the company'. They called for 'a balanced approach to regulation that recognised the huge contribution that the bookmaking industry makes to the UK'. And their efforts paid off. 'Feedback showed that it was taken very seriously by politicians preparing for a new government.'[40]

Another time, Blue Rubicon was called on by BAE Systems.[41] God knows what sparked the guilt trip, but apparently bosses at the arms company one day decided to embed an 'ethical culture' into their business (while still selling tanks and missiles to tyrants, of course). It was a tall order, but Blue Rubicon felt they were up to the job. Their mission: to 'demonstrate [BAE's] coherent approach to ethical behaviour and commitment to communicating and embedding it throughout the company.' Sadly the solution had nothing to do with trying to stop kids from being bombed. Instead they settled for an 'internal communications campaign'. This, they said, would 'launch, explain, educate and embed' BAE Systems' first ever global code of conduct. Quite how BAE got to this stage *without* a global code of conduct already is another story.

*   *   *

Some politicians may not get a job from the lobbyists, but they can still enjoy lots of enticing treats. There is nothing in the rules that says MPs can't be spoiled rotten by private firms – just so long as they make their parliamentary decisions independently. Money and gifts cannot direct their parliamentary affairs, but being wined and dined might help to nudge them in the right direction.

Here's one case of an MP being treated well by private companies. Philip Davies has long been a champion of the gambling industry, having once been a bookmaker himself. The MP sat on the influential Culture, Media and Sport Committee for nine years, during which time it recommended that laws should be relaxed over fixed-odds betting terminals. The machines are controversial – known to be the 'crack cocaine' of gambling – but they also bring in £1.7bn every year for the companies that run them. Separately, Davies has also called for tax cuts for the industry and mocked proposals for stricter regulation of gambling adverts.

But Davies has been the recipient of hospitality from these firms – including some that he did not declare. On one occasion, Ladbrokes paid for the MP to go to the Cheltenham festival, a trip worth £870. Six months later, he was quizzing Ladbrokes' chief executive in a committee meeting, but didn't mention the gift he'd had.[42]

In 2016, *The Times* also alleged that Ladbrokes had given the MP 'extremely favourable' treatment on his personal betting account. The paper said Davies had restrictions placed on his account, but had them lifted after writing to one of the company's directors. An insider said the move was 'almost unheard of', because it 'would effectively allow a punter to make money from them indefinitely'. Davies accused *The Times* of a 'personal slur' and said his gambling activities had never influenced his parliamentary work.[43]

Necessities

There's another side to this, too: a completely separate reason why politicians listen to lobbyists, which has nothing to do with greed at all. But it's worth mentioning because it's linked in an unexpected way to other issues around MPs' personal finances.

It's this: sometimes they *have* to listen to lobbyists.

Lots of people in Parliament know that lobbying is a corrupting force. Some of them genuinely wish the industry didn't exist. But for the time being, they need to cooperate with them because they've got no other choice.

'When you get to a debate, we just simply don't know very much about most areas,' a senior Labour adviser admits to me. 'So you get organisations that come along and say "look, here's an amendment, here's a briefing on what this does and how it will help". Basically, they are the experts . . . The fact of the matter is you have no other resource.

'Otherwise, we would not have a bloody clue about the issue. We'd have no idea. Should we support the government, should we not support the government? Should we whatever?'

The adviser adds: 'It's not a promise of "we'll give you a bottle of champagne if you do it". It's literally a promise of "you'll understand what you're talking about and not look like a prick in the debate". It's the promise of doing your job effectively, because we don't have the resources to do our jobs particularly effectively. And it's only if you're using outside groups that we can do it.'[44]

This is the paradox of Parliament's money. While millions of pounds are flowing into the pockets of fat cat politicians, there is actually a distinct lack of funding for genuine political work. Insiders have stories about having to pay for fact-finding missions out of their own wages because there was no other way to cover it. After the experience, they vow to never pay again, instead getting a private firm or lobbying company with interests in the area to foot the bill.

'We don't want to spend much on our politics. "We need to reduce the cost", and all that bollocks,' the Labour aide says. 'Actually, what it means is we're far more reliant on outside groups.'

So the strange thing is that, in order to crack down on the influence of lobbyists, we might actually need to put more money into the system.

New beginnings?

When I said goodbye to Charlie at the London bar, I left with a slight glimmer of hope. Although his loud-mouthed confidence hadn't wavered throughout our conversation, he said something that made me think the lobbying industry might just be taken down a few pegs.

He'd told me about a client of his – a big, highly controversial financial client. It was less than a fortnight after Jeremy Corbyn was first elected Labour leader and Charlie was clearly puzzling over how to present his client to the party's new team. 'They are completely under fire by this new opposition,' he had told me.

'With a really hard-left Labour bloc . . . we now have to respond to the fact that they're going to be pressing this agenda in Parliament through parliamentary debates. Every amendment they can put forward, we're going to have to find a way of opposing. So, for us, it means we're going to have to make more friends to make sure that there are people fighting our corner in Parliament.'

Later, I Googled to see if anyone else was predicting a breakup between Labour and the lobbyists, thanks to Corbyn's new leadership. And they were. A *Buzzfeed* article proclaimed excitedly: 'Jeremy Corbyn's New Politics Is Bad News For Lobbyists'.[45] And an article by *Spinwatch* said: 'The UK's commercial lobbyists are in a huff because, for once (in the last 20 years, at least), they don't have privileged access to the new Labour leader.'[46]

Maybe there was hope for cleaner politics. Maybe lobbyists' stranglehold on Parliament could be knocked away after all.

I waited. After a few weeks, I phoned Charlie back to see how it was going. Was Corbyn kicking out the lobbyists from Labour's offices?

Charlie is more relaxed than I'd hoped.

'If you have clients who are targets of Corbyn's cabinet – so, for example, if you're working for big finance companies or big technology companies – you're going to find it harder to have a conversation with Labour's team,' he says. 'Otherwise, it hasn't really changed a great deal.'

'So it's not like he's come in and the whole industry's been disrupted?' I ask.

'Oh God no. Actually, Corbyn is such a quiet person. He could have come in and said "this is Labour's position, this is what we're pursuing", and we could have seen lots of significant action. But what we're seeing more of, actually, is the SNP being more disruptive than him . . . We're seeing questions that we would have expected Labour to put out.'

But when Charlie says the SNP are being disruptive, he doesn't mean they're anti-lobbying. On the contrary, he loves them because they're so willing to talk to him.

'These people are fantastic,' he says. 'The Scottish National Party MPs are the most receptive, open, transparent MPs that I've come across in a long time.'

But I feel he's giving the word 'transparent' an Orwellian twist. 'In terms of being prepared to meet *you*?' I ask.

'Yeah, being prepared to meet,' he says. 'They're fantastic people. All I can do is praise them for the way they do business really.'

The SNP score ten out of ten on the lobbyists' fan list, then.

Just before I hang up, I suddenly get a stark reminder of how ruthless lobbying can be. We're talking a couple of days after the devastating terror attacks that hit Paris in November 2015. For lobbyists, that meant business.

'This is a political incident as much as it is a human crisis,' Charlie says coldly. 'The reaction politically is going to impact our clients.'

He goes on: 'They might be reviewing whether or not they want to invest in that area, or what the impact is going to be financially . . . Anything like this is going to have immediate effects on the business.'

While Charlie was jumping in to push forward corporate agendas, France was still reeling in horror. As I checked the news, the death count reached 130 and the country was on a heightened state of alert. The lobbying industry, it seemed, knew no boundaries.

I2

Institutional corruption

When is corruption not corrupt? When the establishment says it isn't.[1]

Nick Cohen, 2013

My mate Gordon would make a great lord. He's clever and sharp-witted; principled but not dogmatic. He's one of the most down-to-earth, honest and intellectual people I know. Gordon is everything a member of the House of Lords should be. Plus, I can imagine him looking smug in one of those posh ermine robes.

So one day I asked him: 'Why don't you apply to become a member of the House of Lords? The application is easy!'

The House of Lords claims to be a 'forum of independent expertise'.[2] The idea is to bring people together from all walks of life who can offer insight, knowledge and experience. And that's why Gordon would be such a good lord. Since graduating from university he's worked as a support worker, helping people with learning disabilities through their day-to-day lives. It's a rewarding job, but the cuts to social care budgets mean resources are scarce, pay is low and the work is often challenging. He's on the front line, with first-hand experience of many pressing issues that Parliament makes decisions about.

However, in the House of Lords, their idea of 'expertise' is not based on real life experience, or even intelligence. Although most peers come from the political world, the recruitment of non-party political extras is largely based on professional and commercial success. They specifically look for 'major achievements' and a record of 'significant' successes. The result? It's crammed full of business tycoons. There's little room for ordinary people.

Everyone knows that the Lords is not democratic – and that's bad enough. But the situation is actually far worse than this. There's been no attempt to make it representative. If you come from a non-political background, you stand far more chance of getting in if you have significant professional or business interests. For 'merit' read 'high flying career'; and for 'success' read 'wealth'.

Recent appointments include a millionaire businesswoman, a financier, a City banker and a company chief executive. Even if you believe this is the sort of 'expertise' we need our representatives to have, these people are not always so useful in practice. As one peer admits, 'the role of experts can be overstated'.[3] Some are so caught up with their business affairs that they only show up once in a blue moon, while others find themselves joining debates which have nothing to do with their specialism.

There is a more fundamental problem, too: this setup is not just bad for diversity, it also means that peers are more likely to have conflicts of interest. The system is *specifically designed* to put business leaders in a position of political power. So instead of having a group of politicians, it often looks more like a high-powered corporate lobby group.

It's all very well complaining about the influence of lobbyists in the House of Commons. But there's no need for them in the House of Lords. The peers themselves are the country's top business representatives, there to put forward their agendas.

What the Lords really needed, I thought, was a twenty-nine-year-old support worker from Chester to join their ranks. That would shake things up a bit. So I was pleased as punch when Gordon agreed to apply. Realistically – without the vast business history that many lords boast – we knew he didn't stand a chance. But we wanted to play with the system.

The application process is surprisingly simple. You just have to fill out a short form saying how you fit the requirements and send it off with a CV and a couple of references. But most of the requirements allude to grandiose statements of professional success, rather than the ability to represent the public. Gordon was honest, though. Asked about his 'record of significant achievement', he wrote simply: 'As a support worker for people with learning disabilities, I don't measure the quality of my work in terms of "major successes". It's about helping people get through their lives on a day-by-day basis.'

Application complete, he posted it to the Lords Appointments Commission. A silence followed. He wasn't going to be getting his peerage any time soon.

The reality is that most ordinary members of the public simply don't stand a chance of getting in. I tell Pete Mills at Unlock Democracy about Gordon's application. 'My impression is that he won't get very far,' he says. 'These things are generally oriented at the great and the good. There are very few people in the Lords who are just the best nurse in the country, or whatever.

'A lot of people who might want to contribute to the legislative process are potentially put off by the fact that you have to essentially become an aristocrat.' He adds that the House of Lords looks for new peers with personal achievements, 'but personal achievement in the field of making money.'

Peer pressure

Gordon's application reflected a bigger problem with Parliament. Filling the House of Lords with top business leaders means that political power is placed straight into the hands of corporate interests.

Peers don't have to be *individually* corrupt to bring undue influence from the private sector. The whole system is corrupt: wealthy figures are *invited* to influence public policy.

In the House of Commons, there are simple solutions that could clean things up. Whether any changes will actually take place is another matter, of course, but in theory it's perfectly easy. Tightening regulations on lobbying could completely reform MPs' relationship with commercial firms. If we wanted to do that, it would only take a few tweaks to the rule book.

But in the House of Lords, these problems are built into the very core of the institution. High fliers are told to keep their lucrative careers and help design new laws in their spare time. Potential conflicts of interest are not just tolerated, they are actively embraced. Peers are not appointed *despite* their business affairs, but *because* of them. A researcher for the Electoral Reform Society, Jessica Garland, tells me: 'It's rare to find any lords that don't have some sort of business interests.'

This doesn't just create the possibility of specific conflicts of interest, which can be neatly labelled and condemned. Outside interests influence the whole underlying ideology and mindset that runs through the House.

Perhaps the influence of outside interests wouldn't be such a problem if peers at least came from a more diverse range of backgrounds. But – from the outside, at least – it looks strikingly like a club for the establishment.

An analysis by academics at UCL found that 43% of peers had a professional background in banking, finance or business. And almost 20% had a background in law. That compares to 9% from the voluntary sector, 7% from trade unions, 6% from medicine and healthcare and just 1% from manual and skilled trades.[4]

On the government benches in the Lords, diversity is even more lacking. About a third of Conservative peers count banking, finance or business as their *primary* profession – compared to 0% manual labour, 0% from the police and 0% from the voluntary sector.[5]

The UCL academics said there were 'large numbers of peers with backgrounds in banking and finance or business and commerce (plus further peers with other private sector backgrounds). If anything these backgrounds are downplayed as many with part-time directorships will not be counted.' They added that there was 'a general under-representation of more junior jobs'.

Separate research also shows that half of all peers went to private school – compared with just 7% of the UK public.[6]

With so many high-ranking figures holding significant commercial interests, it's hard to know how the House of Lords can avoid being anything other than a mouthpiece for society's most privileged.

Dr Dean Machin, a political scientist, argues that having so many peers with similar business interests will inevitably affect the angle from which issues are approached. 'It just does affect the kind of decisions that are made,' he says. 'It may not be that members of the House of Lords are deliberately corrupt, but they are biased because of their interests and experiences and who they know. They're more likely to weigh certain types of considerations as significant.

'It's not that the Lords will say "right, I'm going to make sure this law favours my interests and my friends' interests". It's just that, in effect, that's how it operates because of the way they think,' he says.

'That's a significant problem because that's about the quality of the decisions and laws that come out of our democracy.'

This is not an abstract threat: the effects have been felt by peers themselves.

One ice-cold January morning, I meet Baroness Joyce Quin in the House of Lords. Friendly and softly-spoken, Quin is in a minority of peers who want to see the institution drastically reformed. I follow her lead as she darts up the stairs and into one of the building's enormous draughty halls. We sit down at an old oak table as she tries to remember instances of inappropriate bias that have happened here.

'I remember when we were discussing the sell-off of the forestry estate,' she says. 'There were some landowners here who were obviously hoping to benefit.'[7]

'Was it quite obvious that they were hoping to benefit?' I ask.

'Yeah, I think so. But I'm not saying they didn't declare they were interested – I think they probably did.' They did it despite the transparency, Quin suggests, shamelessly trying to twist the law for their own financial gain.

Quin takes a strong stand against conflicts of interest, which is refreshing. But I worry that, like many peers, she's blissfully ignorant of any real details. 'I've got a feeling I'm not always aware of what people's financial background might be when they're speaking,' she admits. 'I don't feel I've got enough information to back it up.'

But some insiders know the whole thing is rotten. 'The fact lords declare an interest in the Register but can still speak and vote on an issue they have a direct interest in is disgraceful,' one peer tells me. Another says: 'I have heard peers speak on matters for which they should have declared an interest, and haven't. And that brings the whole thing into disrepute.'[8]

What Quin is certain about, however, is that it's misleading for peers to downplay their power. It's something I'd been arguing about with lords and baronesses for months. Remember, Lord Powell of Bayswater said that being a peer 'doesn't have actually very much power'. And Lord Flight downplayed his personal influence, saying: 'I'm participating in discussions, but if you look at the reality of it, it's that most of the legislation is constructed by the Treasury.'

Baroness Quin has a different take on it, though. 'There is a lot of influencing behind the scenes going on here,' she says. 'There is a certain amount of power, a certain amount of ability to make life difficult for ministers.'

> [Peers] have got more power than an opposition backbencher in the House of Commons, I would say . . . If you are keen on something, you want to try and get an amendment passed, you can go to quite a cross-section of people and get support for that.
> You as an individual (working with others, but as an individual) you can very often alter the shape of legislation . . . We're not just a talking shop: we hold ministers to account, and we do change legislation.

In the House of Commons, most MPs can see clearly the power that peers hold. One tells me: 'A lot of the decisions about laws aren't made by elected legislators at all. It's shaped very often in the Lords.'

'With my commercial hat on . . .'

Plenty of peers are happy to gloss over Baroness Quin's concerns about the influence of financial interests. They condemn any proper criminal corruption, but play along with the House of Lords' built-in links with the private sector.

One such man is Clive Soley, a former probation officer who climbed the ranks of the Labour Party before joining the House of Lords in 2005. 'I do think at times we're a bit over-precious,' he says, casually. 'I don't want to see people having *lots* of business interests, but to have a business interest or two is justifiable . . . As long as you've got your interests registered, I don't have a problem.'

And he's one to know. Lord Soley used to be paid as campaign director for Future Heathrow, a group calling for the expansion of Britain's largest airport. Soley describes it as a 'coalition' of businesses, trade unions and interest groups – including three airline operators.

'I was literally leading the campaign and I was speaking in public,' he tells me. 'It was a paid job with a proper contract and the contributions were from predominantly BA [British Airways], but also all the other groups.'

The fact that he was also a peer in the House of Lords didn't seem to bother him. So – with pay cheques backed by the £7bn airline company – Soley campaigned for Heathrow to be expanded, until quitting the job in 2010.[9]

During this time, he frequently spoke on the subject in the House of Lords. It was fully declared and no rules were broken. But that didn't alter the fact: he was being *paid* to campaign on this issue by big business. On one occasion he called on a government minister to back the airport's expansion, saying: 'The runways are operating at more than 98 per cent full . . . Does the minister agree that modern-isation and expansion at Heathrow is in the national as well as the local interest?'[10]

Soley says that he had already campaigned for Heathrow expansion before getting the job, so the money didn't make a difference to his views. But did the money compromise his integrity? And did it make him speak out more often than he would have done otherwise?

'It was difficult,' he admits. 'I did speak on Heathrow a number of times in the House, but I was always careful.' He adds: 'I didn't see it as just a conventional business interest. It wasn't as though I was a chairman of an energy company and arguing for fracking or some-thing. It was different to that.'

A scan through the pages of Hansard (which documents everything that's said in Parliament) sheds some light on how relaxed peers are with pursuing business interests in the House of Lords. Here are some common phrases you will come across. They don't all suggest a conflict of interest; but they paint a picture of Parliament being treated like a focus group for big business. These have all been squeaked out by their lordships in the last few years:

- 'I admit to being professionally involved . . .'
- 'I was thinking, with my commercial hat on . . .'
- 'I speak as a humble landlord . . .'
- 'I speak as a businessman and as somebody who has employed many people through several business ventures . . .'
- 'Wearing a hat as a banker I would add . . .'
- 'As a businessman who is chairman of several companies, I feel that . . .'
- 'Speaking personally as a banker . . .'

And, as if to admit the problem:

- 'As a businessman, I have no other frame of reference . . .'

Like it or loathe it, this is the way the House of Lords works. To change it would require more than a new set of rules; the entire structure would need reform. But that's unlikely to happen any time soon. 'The problem is you need cross-party agreement,' one insider says. 'There's not the hunger for it to happen.'

A Tory peer tells me: 'A great majority of members of this House – and of the Commons and the public – think that the Lords does need further reform. The problem is, agreeing exactly what the reforms should be.

'If you ask the man in the street, "does the House of Lords need reform?", they would say "yes it does". But it's not, I think, going to determine the way they vote.'

So the House of Lords looks set to continue inviting business insiders to join its ranks. For them, Parliament will remain a side-project to their day jobs; their commitment to real politics often questionable.

'If the vote is scheduled after the dinner break for the House of Lords, some will just go home,' one source says. 'Even if their disappearing will change the result of the vote against their interest, against their stated preference. Going home after dinner is more important to them, to some extent, than voting.'

A lot of peers are 'just hopeless', the source says. 'Self-important, inexpert, not committed, don't turn up.'

But at least most of them are not *criminally* corrupt. They're just ageing business leaders who have wound up in a political institution that's more concerned with prestige than accountability. However, that 'accolade' cannot be said for all the peers. There are some crooks hidden in the woodwork.

13

Cash for peerages

Seth Thévoz is a young political historian at Oxford University. But a few years back he was looking for a job in Parliament. He applied for a position working for a Conservative peer and was invited for an interview.

A smartly dressed chap with thick-rimmed glasses and a received accent, Seth would have fitted in well at the House of Lords. But the interview didn't go quite how he'd expected. As the meeting progressed, the peer started bragging.

'He was very upfront, very much showing off,' he tells me. 'Something he casually mentioned, while boasting about his great wealth, was that he clearly suggested that he'd bought his peerage.'

Buying a peerage is illegal. It's top-scale corruption: you're literally paying your way into Parliament. 'I thought this was a rather bizarre thing for someone to boast to someone they'd only met three minutes ago,' Seth says.

'I should say that – lest I be thought of as somebody who has sour grapes – I was actually offered the job. I decided it's probably a good idea to not take a job with somebody who's just admitted to a criminal act to you in the interview. So I made my excuses and said "no thanks".

'But it did stick in the mind . . .'

This Conservative peer is still in the House of Lords today, Seth says.[1] A criminal in their midst. He can't be convicted because it's impossible for Seth to actually *prove* what he heard him say that day. There was no recording and no paper trail which could categorically confirm the facts.

Rumours about 'cash for peerages' had flown around Westminster for decades before this. Everyone knew the allegations: rich tycoons agreeing to make big donations to political parties so they would then be 'rewarded' with a seat in Parliament. For the right price, they could influence politics and add the word 'Lord' or 'Baroness' to their name. But there was never any rock-solid evidence to prove these stories. This anecdote was just another piece of gossip that would slowly be forgotten.

But a few years later, Seth remembered his encounter and started work on an ambitious project. What if he could prove it using statistics?

He wouldn't just study this single rogue lord, he would study them all. He wanted to show there was an undeniable link between the appointments of politicians and the money they dished out.

Together with two other academics, he set to work on an exhaustive study, tallying large political donations with the appointment of peers in the House of Lords. It was titled: *Is There a Market for Peerages? Can Donations Buy You a British Peerage? A Study in the Link Between Party Political Funding and Peerage Nominations, 2005–14.*[2]

'We knew that there was a huge amount of material there, but the question is really whether you can viably prove it,' Seth explains. 'There's no paper trail because people aren't stupid enough to breach [corruption laws]. But there are indications that they leave in plain sight. And actually, if anyone tots up all this stuff, you can find some very, very interesting things.'

What they discovered was groundbreaking. For the first time, the academics were able to say, without doubt, that the 'relationship between donations and nominations [to the House of Lords] has been found to be significant.' Their figures were 'wholly in keeping with the theory that lifetime appointments to Britain's Upper House are being sold to wealthy donors.'

The findings couldn't prove that any specific individuals were guilty of corruption. Rather, they revealed a massive overarching statistical correlation between money and peerages.

The research paper was leaked to the *Observer*, which named some of the many lords and baronesses who had donated huge sums to their party before being awarded peerages. This included donations from their families, unions and companies. Again, the newspaper was at pains to stress that this did not *prove* any of them were individually corrupt or had done anything wrong. 'Correlation is not the same as causation,' it said. 'And even if it is proved that a peerage came as a reward for a donation, there is nothing necessarily criminal in that.'[3]

Here are some of the names the *Observer* listed, with the donation values as they were at the time:[4]

Lord Michael Farmer
Donated £7.3m to the Conservatives
Became a peer in 2014

Lord Stanley Fink
Donated £3.2m to the Conservatives
Became a peer in 2011

Lord William Haughey
Donated £1.5m to Labour
Became a peer in 2013

Lord Gulam Noon
Donated £1.1m to Labour
Became a peer in 2011

Lord Rumi Verjee
Donated £1.4m to the Lib Dems
Became a peer in 2013

Lord James Palumbo of Southwark
Donated £1m to the Lib Dems
Became a peer in 2013

According to the findings, the chances of these guys getting a seat in the House of Lords would have been astonishingly small, were it not for their donations. Here's what the statistics showed:

It is of course perfectly possible that it is pure coincidence that 'big donors' are disproportionately likely to be nominated for peerages. However, the odds of it being pure coincidence are roughly the same as those of entering Britain's National Lottery five consecutive times, and winning the jackpot on each occasion. Whilst coincidence is theoretically possible, this explanation does stretch the limits of credulity.[5]

This might sound hyperbolic but, if anything, this analysis is fairly conservative. 'The only possible correction that can come up from any of this – because we were so exhaustive – is it's far worse than we ever realised,' Seth says. 'There's no way of being absolutely precise when there are so many imponderables. So we were very, very cautious at every stage.'

However, when the findings were published in March 2015, the response from Parliament was total silence. Here was statistical evidence that correlated with claims of endemic corruption at the top of British politics, and the authorities did nothing.[6]

'After publication, we had one peer's spouse who gave me a very angry, threatening phone call,' Seth recalls. 'But other than that, we just had a sort of stone silence from the twenty-eight people named.'

Maundy Gregory

Seth's new statistical evidence followed nearly a hundred years of conspiracy and cover-up. We may never know the truth about all that's happened over the decades.

It started back in 1918, when a mysterious figure named Maundy Gregory was hired by the prime minister as a peerage tout. His job was to find rich men who wanted an extra dose of power and privilege. Secretly, he began to broker deals with them: they would pump money into the Liberal Party and be rewarded with a position in Parliament.

Gregory was a suave, monocled hustler who crawled into dark corners of the British establishment. A former theatre producer, his corruption contract with the government brought in a small fortune. A peerage could be touted for about £50,000.[7] With his share of the money, Gregory bought a nightclub in Mayfair and a luxury hotel in Surrey, reportedly of ill-repute. It's said that, for years, he knew all the shady secrets of dozens of society figures.[8]

Insiders knew that the House of Lords was being sold off to the highest bidders, but they did nothing about it. In 1919, an MP called Victor Grayson threatened to expose Gregory, saying that the peerage trade 'can be traced right down to 10 Downing Street and to a monocled dandy with offices in Whitehall. I know this man, and one day I will name him.'

But Grayson was silenced. In 1920, he was beaten up on the Strand. A few days later he got a mysterious message calling him to a Leicester Square hotel and was never seen again.[9]

In 1925, the Sale of Honours Act was passed, which outlawed Gregory's business – but he carried on regardless, helped by quirks in the law.[10] By now, he had ditched the Liberals and had built strong connections with the Conservative Party. Eventually, in 1933, he was arrested after offering to sell a baronetcy to a straight-laced naval officer who went straight to the police. But, despite his downfall, the details of Gregory's corruption have been shrouded in secrecy ever since.

One account of his arrest says that the then Conservative leader, Stanley Baldwin, urged him to flee the country, rather than face prosecution. Baldwin was apparently worried about what secrets might spill out to the public. Before his trial, a senior MP visited Gregory, promising that when he got out of prison he'd be discreetly handed a car, a pension and a house in France.[11] He was shuffled away and quietly cast into the realm of political legend.

'Nearly a century of falsehood and fantasy has obscured the reality of Maundy Gregory's life,' one historian wrote.[12]

The Blair rich project

Maundy Gregory may have been sidelined, but politics was still for sale. Rumours that seats in the House of Lords were being sold to big donors continued. One account of the 1990s claimed that the Conservative government 'operated a lucrative peerages-for-loans system – the 'loans' being written off once the ermine was handed over.'[13]

On very rare occasions, those behind the corruption let slip. In 1998, Francis Pym – a Tory politician who chaired the Political Honours Scrutiny Committee – admitted that political donors were favoured as new peers. Pym said it showed a candidate's commitment to public life, by putting his 'money where his mouth is'.[14]

Largely, however, the sale of peerages was kept hushed up. The journalist Matthew d'Ancona has written about how the deals could be done subtly, without leaving a paper trail that would incriminate those involved. 'Political life requires a steady flow of euphemism and code, and senior politicians often need the cover of plausible deniability,' he explains. 'The recipient of the gong cannot be seen to have bought it; the fixer cannot be seen to have sold it. Once the nudge and the wink are replaced by an open sale, it cannot proceed.'[15]

By 2006, the messy affair had resurfaced again, in all its scandalous glory. It emerged that Tony Blair's Labour Party was asking wealthy individuals to give loans, rather than normal donations. Technically, this didn't make much sense for the party – loans are a liability that usually need to be paid back. But the great advantage was that loans could be made secretly, whereas donations had to be publicly declared. This meant that if Labour decided to award any of the lenders with a peerage, the embarrassing financial dealings would be neatly hidden from the press. Those giving the money were clear that they regarded it as a 'soft loan', which they expected would never be repaid.[16] Effectively, they were just secret donations, and subsequent investigations found there was a 'deliberate attempt to stretch the loophole'.[17]

Authorities got wind of what was going on when four of the lenders – Gulam Noon, Barry Townsley, Chai Patel and David Garrard – were nominated for the House of Lords. Details of their loans eventually spilled out into the public domain.[18]

Eventually, in March 2006, there was enough evidence to raise significant concerns that peerages were being sold. The SNP politician, Angus MacNeil, lodged a formal complaint with Scotland Yard and it looked as if the whole system might finally come crumbling down. But it didn't.

Ten years on, I caught up with MacNeil, who is still just as outraged by the scandal as ever. He says the police were 'reluctant' to investigate the allegations at first and seemed disinterested. 'I went and actually looked at the law,' he says. 'There's basically three paragraphs: "don't buy honours, don't sell honours, and if you do, we'll jail you for up to two years". And I thought "right . . . let's go with it".'

Despite the police's initial reluctance, a sixteen-month investigation ensued with scores of witnesses being interviewed. Key political figures were arrested, questioned, bailed, questioned again, bailed again. The line of inquiry went to the very highest levels of politics: for the first time in British history, a sitting prime minister was interviewed by police. Detectives quizzed Blair for around two hours in Downing Street.[19]

But after everything: nothing. Scotland Yard had amassed a treasure trove of evidence, with hundreds of witness statements, audio recordings, transcripts and documents. Together they filled 165 boxes, which are now gathering dust in the back rooms of a police building in London.[20] But ultimately the investigation came to nothing. Not a single person was prosecuted.

For Angus MacNeil, the police probe went far further than he could ever have expected, but he was left disappointed. 'They said there wasn't a high enough possibility of a successful conviction, which is interesting because they didn't say there was *no* probability,' he says.

'I've seen some of the interviews,' MacNeil adds. 'There were some very, very nervous characters there, who I think under the pressure of a courtroom might have been saying something quite different.

'The idea of the House of Lords (I don't really agree with it), but it's a chamber of the great and the good. But this is the great and the good and the rich. That's a real problem, when you have rich people, by virtue of their wealth, finding themselves in a law-making position.'

Forgotten, but not fixed

Much like the array of lobbying scandals, the controversy over Cash for Peerages has quietly slipped into the background. It's become old news. But what has actually happened since the police investigation?

'Nothing has changed in the last decade,' says MacNeil. 'Nothing at all.'

Since no one was charged, any peers who *did* use donations to buy their place in the Lords are almost certainly still there. Parliament is still just as plagued by corruption as it ever was. 'You can still pay to become a member of the House of Lords,' Labour's Paul Flynn tells me. 'If you pay enough, you'll get there. And we still call ourselves a democracy!'

Indeed, the columnist Yasmin Alibhai-Brown once claimed on telly: 'I know three people who bought their peerages . . . The institution is rotten.'[21]

But with the police investigation now behind them, the gang is set to stay safely where they are. 'There's nothing you can really do about it, because you can't get rid of them,' MacNeil says. 'They're there by virtue of their connections and their pals. And sometimes by their *money*, their connections and their pals.'

Inside, peers don't like to talk about it much. Either because they don't know the details, or because the issue is a little too close to home. They also have to be careful what they say: if they've got solid evidence of corruption, they can't be seen to be covering it up. Instead, they refer to it in vague, veiled terms.

'It's been going on a long time,' one Labour lord tells me.

Why is he so sure that it still goes on? 'You get to know, let me put it that way,' he says.

'We've got Labour peers in here who've made big donations to the Labour party. Whether they've been made peers because they did that, nobody will be able to tell you that.' But he adds: 'Where there's a will there's always a way.'

It's a similar story from a top-ranking Conservative peer: 'There are people who have been big donors, and I think that the parties' gratitude to such people has been a factor in their appointment. There are certainly people who – if one's quite candid – you think there can't be many other qualifications that they had, other than the fact that they've given money.'

Some are keen to downplay the scale of corruption: 'I've known a number of these lords who've given money,' Lord Soley tells me. 'One of them's just died – Lord Noon. Noon was a very generous contributor, but he's also done an awful lot of bloody good work. So would we say "well you can't come in just because you've given money"?'

Soley admits the system needs reform, but adds: 'I would have no problem with putting forward someone like the late Lord Noon and saying "this guy ought to be in the House of Lords". I don't think we should say no just because they've given money.'

But other insiders have a stronger opinion. 'It's literally selling democracy,' one says.

Ironically, Scotland Yard's investigation may have actually *increased* the risk of further corruption. By concluding that there was insufficient evidence, the police sent out a clear message to any shady political movers considering selling peerages: just make sure you don't leave a paper trail. 'It wouldn't be very difficult to do,' MacNeil says, imagining a likely scenario:

> I will play tennis with you, we'll have a wee mention or something. I'll give you a million pounds. You know that we can't write anything down, we could both end up in jail. That's why I'm not writing anything down. But, you know, you're a good bloke and it was a good serve there and a good volley and a rally. And I tell you what, let's have a drink afterwards, a gin and tonic. But I would really think you're the sort of person who could be going to the House of Lords, you certainly have the skills and abilities and—

'Wooah! What happens next?' MacNeil says. 'He suddenly wants to give a million just so he really remembers the guy. It's far too opaque.'

Besides which, Scotland Yard are unlikely to have the political clout to go sniffing around in Parliament again any time soon. 'The police have got weaker and the political parties have got bolder,' he says.

So the mystery never ends. A decade on from the police investigation, there's still a whitewash from the authorities. Using the Freedom of Information Act, I requested copies of internal documents related to the scandal from several corners of government. All my requests were refused.

The Cabinet Office told me they couldn't provide any documents about Cash for Peerages because the 'relevant information could be contained in numerous files held by various teams.' It would take them too long to find the right things, they said.[22]

The reply I got from the Attorney General's Office was stranger. 'We do hold some information,' it said, but added: 'The balance of public interest favours withholding this information.'[23]

I fired an email back. How could they justify the secrecy over these crucial documents? 'They relate to allegations of criminal corruption at the top of British politics,' I wrote. 'To downplay the public interest in disclosure is, frankly, ridiculous.'

But they stuck to their guns and flatly refused to release the files. 'The public interest in maintaining the exemption outweighs the public interest in disclosure.'[24]

Seeing that I wasn't going to get anywhere with the government,

I turned to Scotland Yard. Could they provide copies of any internal documents relating to the Cash for Peerages scandal?

A response hit my inbox in February 2016. 'I have decided to refuse your request as it has been deemed a "Vexatious Request",' it said. 'There is no requirement for a public interest test.'

The email continued: '[Scotland Yard] can confirm that it holds the requested information. The Cash for Honours investigation was a considerable investigation and as such accumulated a significant amount of material as evidence . . . This would be a huge undertaking, and one for which the MPS does not have the time or resources to accede to, especially in this current financial climate with shrinking budgets and workforce.'[25]

So that was that. Nothing. The police did not even allow my request to be narrowed down, so that it covered fewer documents. Access to their stash of information had been firmly denied. And if the authorities think the truth is too much for you, then we really have got a problem.

The whitewash from authorities over this century-old corruption scandal seemed in fitting with Parliament's whole attitude to financial interests. Whether it's investments, outside interests, lobbying or this: it's a world we're not welcome in.

The full facts about Cash for Peerages may be hidden from us, but all that does is bolster the impression that Parliament acts with self-interest. The failure to fix the problem creates 'a quiet seething and contempt amongst the people', MacNeil says. 'Most people know it's wrong. Most people feel it's suspect and certainly most people don't have any respect for it. That's not a healthy way to run a society.'

PART FOUR:

Justifying it

14

Millionaire mindset

The more I ventured into the world of MPs' private wealth, the more I kept returning to the same question: how do they justify it to themselves? There seemed to be a unique culture that surrounded Parliament's financial impropriety. A collective attitude that excused – or at least overlooked – greed and excess.

It reminded me of Lloyd George's government in 1911 and the fuss they made when salaries were introduced for MPs. The establishment's efforts to block the £400 wage was marked by elitist preservation; a desire to protect their exclusive club from the masses. That may have been over a century ago, but it is this same sense of entitlement which now lurks behind Parliament's financial controversies. Today, quiet figures haunt the corridors of Westminster, preaching a familiar message: the superior minds of wealthy elites should not be diluted by an uneducated rabble of ordinary people.

Rich people are better

Before I've even had a chance to pull a notebook from my bag, Tory MP Andrew Bridgen has already slipped in the fact he's a 'self-made millionaire'. I've joined him while he eats lunch in one of the many cafes dotted around Parliament, and he tucks straight in, spreading a chunk of bread with thick layers of butter.

'I used to earn a million pounds a year before I came here,' he says proudly, looking up from his food. 'So I took a 94% pay cut to be an MP.

'If anyone on the doorstep says you're only doing this for the money, it makes me laugh.'

Andrew Bridgen is the kind of bloke who seems like a permanent feature of whatever room he's in. He's a 'head screwed on, sit down, no nonsense' kind of guy – and I get the sense he's more sure of himself than I'm sure about anything in the world. His whole person-ality seems to centre around his wealth and professional success. With his sharp suit he even wears golden cufflinks in the shape of Parliament's portcullis emblem.

Despite already having millions in the bank, Bridgen has been one of the very few politicians to *publicly* demand higher wages for MPs. It's won him many friends in Westminster. 'The number of colleagues who came up to me and said "that was brilliant, I wish I could support you but I can't",' he tells me. 'Labour MPs came to me and said "we're glad to have you as our shop steward negotiating with the public".'

Bridgen thinks that the public must, surely, want 'successful' people to be in Parliament. And by 'successful', he means *financially* successful. He spells this theory out bluntly: 'Surely [the public] want successful people?' he says. 'Successful people tend to have earned some money.'

There's lots of reasons why rich people might make better MPs than poor people, Bridgen reckons. '[If you're rich] you're not bought out by the government,' he says. 'You don't have to be a minister, do you? You're not necessarily on the greasy pole, are you? Cos, you know, is it going to change my life financially whether I'm on an MP's salary or the prime minister's salary? The money wouldn't change my life.' He adds: 'Also, London's not a place you want to be if you haven't got some money.'

If, like Bridgen, you think that rich people tend to be better at politics, the next step is to design a system that actively encourages them to join Parliament. A system which allows them to keep the money rolling in while they're there. That means high salaries and the freedom to take extra outside work for private companies. Otherwise, the 'successful' people will ditch Parliament and get a job in the City.

If there aren't enough of these people to fill the seats of the House of Commons, Bridgen worries that the place will be overrun by 'people who were MPs because they would actually, in the real world, never earn that sort of money'. His comments bear a striking likeness to the MP in 1911, who said he was 'afraid of this House being flooded by the failures of society'.[1]

He's not the only politician who holds this controversial view; it's prevalent in Westminster. On one occasion, a Tory grandee warned that banning second jobs might leave membership of the Commons confined to 'the inheritors of substantial fortunes or to those with rich spouses, or to obsessive crackpots or those who are unemployable anywhere else.'[2]

More recently, in early 2016, Sir Alan Duncan defended David Cameron's tax affairs, saying that his critics just 'hate anyone who's even got a hint of wealth in their life'. His view seemed to be that 'non-wealthy' people were 'low achievers'. Duncan said: 'We risk seeing a House of Commons which is stuffed full of low achievers, who hate enterprise, hate people who look after their own family and who know absolutely nothing about the outside world.'

Another MP still, Peter Lilley, tells me: 'They [the public] don't want Parliament crammed full of people who . . . couldn't earn seventy grand a year outside Parliament.'

One of the funny aspects of this argument is that many of those who espouse it are actually living proof that they're wrong. 'You were prepared to do it,' I say to Bridgen, pointing out that he took a massive pay cut to become an MP. Doesn't that disprove the theory that rich businessmen will be put off unless they can still earn loads?

'Yeah,' he shrugs, 'but if you take it to extremes, where it was going will be so far off the mark you'll be losing a lot of people.'

In fact, a recent official report found there was no evidence to suggest wage levels had hindered diversity among MPs.[3] In his best-selling book, *The Establishment*, the political commentator Owen Jones also points out that high wages can actually have a perverse effect on MPs' work ethic. 'MPs have become corporate politicians, envious of the hyper-wealthy elite they helped create,' he writes. 'MPs now see their role not as a vocation, a duty or a service – but, rather, as just another upper-middle-class career option that is not being remunerated as well as other comparable professions.'[4]

People from well-paid professions have not been put off entering politics. And the statistics confirm it. For instance, between 1979 and 2010, the number of solicitors sitting in the Commons increased by 66%.[5] Business professionals increased by 13%, while the number of doctors has remained roughly the same.

Instead, the opposite has occurred. There has been a stark decline in MPs coming from jobs which are traditionally paid more modestly, like manual workers and schoolteachers.[6] It's rarely talked about, but representation of the less-well-off half of society is now one of Westminster's biggest diversity problems, and appears to actually be getting worse. So if MPs like Bridgen really *do* care about class diversity in Parliament, they'd be better off focusing on increasing access for poorer people, not worrying about well-off businessmen.

Incidentally, it's curious that MPs' wages is the sole issue for which right-wing politicians are prepared to abandon their free-market principles. In any other scenario, Conservatives would normally encourage economic competition, which they say creates 'efficiency'. They say that wages should be controlled by market forces, rather than allowing unions or regulators to set them 'artificially'. It's based around an idea economists call 'market-clearing': employers should pay enough to attract and retain a decent workforce – but they shouldn't have to *exceed* this amount. It's supply and demand, they say.

Right-wing MPs put this theory into practice in other sectors. Indeed, a Tory minister recently said that changes to public sector pay aimed to 'address recruitment and retention pressures', explaining: 'There should not be an expectation that every worker will receive a 1% award.'[7]

Yet raising MPs' wages would also be 'artificial' because there is no market demand for it. There is no evidence that higher salaries are needed to continue attracting good MPs from diverse backgrounds – so boosting pay regardless would seem to be at odds with free-market ideas.

Of course, how much value we should attach to those ideas in the first place is another question. But it seems MPs like Bridgen are willing to make exceptions to their political beliefs when it comes to their own salaries.

'I would like MPs to be considered as a profession,' Bridgen tells me. 'Respected; looked upon a little more kindly than we are . . . MPs' pay is not really very high. I know people aren't going to want to hear that, but for the *calibre* of people I think you would like to have.'[8]

In fairness to Bridgen – whatever you may think of his views on MPs' wages – he clearly did not become an MP for the money. 'I'll be honest, when I took a 94% pay cut, my wife left me,' he laughs. 'We flushed that one out!'

But now that he's in politics, he's fighting for more money. MPs *deserve* more, he seems to suggest. And Parliament should help him maintain his lifestyle. It's as if politicians are downtrodden and desperate. At one point he even compares wealthy businessmen who take pay cuts to become MPs – like he did – to benefit claimants having their tax credits cut. It seems a crude analogy, coming from a multimillionaire:

> If [a politician] had been earning more money than an MP's salary before they came here, they and their dependents probably have a lifestyle. Everyone can live on £10 a week more, can't they? But you try and live on £10 a week less than you've had coming in. It's not easy is it? At whatever level. Otherwise you wouldn't have this hoo-hah about tax credits, would we?[9]

Like many MPs, Bridgen does not accept that Parliament has a problem with privilege and entitlement. Instead, he simply says that the public will never be satisfied with politicians, no matter what they do. 'I hate that word. "Entitlement" – that's the worst word in the world. I hate that word. It's what my ex-wife uses on me!' he says. 'As someone who went to a bog-standard comprehensive and was born in poverty, I don't really like the word entitlement.'

Family values

'Do you know what it's about?' said Tory MP, Anthony Steen. 'Jealousy.'

It was 2009 and Steen had just been exposed for claiming nearly £88,000 on expenses for services, including caring for five hundred trees at his countryside mansion in Devon. The press was up in arms.

'I have got a very, very large house,' he said, rebuffing the criticism furiously. 'Some people say it looks like Balmoral, but it's a merchant house of the nineteenth century. It's not particularly attractive, it just does me nicely and it's got room to actually plant a few trees.'

He added: 'What right does the public have to interfere with my private life? None. Do you know what this reminds me of? An episode of *Coronation Street*.'[10]

Later, Steen claimed he got 'tied up in media hysteria' and denied his reputation had been 'tarnished' by the revelations over his expenses.[11] The media, he suggested, were too quick to label politicians as 'greedy' and 'posh'.

That's certainly the impression you get from the press. Just Google 'posh politicians' and you'll see what I mean. Recent articles include headlines like: 'How politics got "posh" again' (*Daily Telegraph*); 'Here are some of Britain's poshest politicians' (*Independent*); 'A posh politician's guide to keeping it real' (*Guardian*); 'Why today's politicians are too posh (and I don't just mean the Tories)' (*Daily Mail*); 'Is the UK Parliament too posh?' (BBC).[12] And so on. We all know that the press can often be sensationalist, but actually there is a serious point behind the headlines: politics *is* dominated by rich people.

The public might be more sympathetic over MPs' earnings if all the money had a positive effect on politics. If higher wages and moonlighting really *did* translate into diversity and a better democracy, they might be justified. But many of Britain's political leaders still come from families with a history of big business and wealth.

For them, making millions is totally normal; part of their upbringing. So could family expectations go some way to explaining Parliament's attitudes to money?

'It comes across as an air of entitlement,' one of Parliament's new MPs tells me. 'But what it is, is a phenomenal self-confidence – cos a lot of these kids were brought up and told that they're going to inherit the earth. It is literally bred into them. You don't get that amongst ordinary people. Working class kids might aspire to be pop stars, but they don't aspire to run the world. Which is a shame.'

When he first became prime minister in 2010, David Cameron's top team were branded a 'cabinet of millionaires' by the press. 'David Cameron's coalition Government may have adopted "fairness" as one of its defining slogans,' one newspaper said, 'but his team of Ministers has been drawn almost exclusively from the ranks of the financial elite – leading to accusations that politics is once again becoming the preserve of the wealthy.'[13]

Out of twenty-nine ministers, twenty-three were estimated to be worth at least a million each. Together they were thought to have around £60m in the bank.[14] And much of that wealth was inherited.

Lord Strathclyde was declared the richest among them, with an estimated £9.6m.[15] Full name, Thomas Galloway Dunlop du Roy de Blicquy Galbraith, his investments include a hefty stake in his family's estate management company, Auchendrane Estates, which was originally set up in 1945. He's also reported to have a £2m house in Westminster.[16]

The leader of the House of Commons was another one the press pointed to: aristocratic baronet, Sir George Young.[17] The son of a diplomat, he inherited his title when he was eighteen and became known in Westminster as the 'bicycling baronet'.[18]

Cameron's closest adviser, Oliver Letwin, was also said to be worth £1.6m, with homes in London and Somerset.[19] Letwin's background was not dissimilar to those of his aristocratic colleagues. His parents lived, for a time, in the leafy Hampstead area of London and were members of the Carlyle Club fine dining society.[20] They sent Letwin to Eton College and Cambridge University, which impressed the future minister so much that he later said he would rather 'go out in the streets and beg' than send his children to a state comprehensive.[21]

His American-born mother, Shirley, was friends with the free-market economist Friedrich Hayek, who argued that businesses should have free rein over the economy without being regulated.[22] This love of making money clearly rubbed off on Letwin, who went on to write a book that is genuinely titled *Privatising The World*.[23]

Others in Cameron's first cabinet included Iain Duncan Smith, the former work and pensions secretary, whose wealth is partly thanks to his wife, Betsy. The couple apparently live rent-free in a sixteenth-century Tudor mansion, worth £2m, on a large country estate in Buckinghamshire. Betsy's father, who styles himself as 'The 5th Baron Cottesloe', gave them use of the aristocratic house in 2001.[24] One report claimed it 'appears to be tied up in a series of complex family trusts'.[25]

★   ★   ★

After all the talk of diversity and meritocracy, did things improve after the General Election in 2015? Not a bit. Most millionaires kept their bottoms firmly on the bench. They were even joined by a few fresh faces who shared their love of lucre. Newcomers included Amber Rudd (who went on to become Home Secretary in 2016), whose family moved in high social circles. Her parents knew each other at Oxford University and her father, Tony, became a successful stockbroker. Rudd's mother, Ethne, was a magistrate who also had an influential position in the Kensington Society, playing a key role behind the scenes in plans for the Princess Diana Memorial Garden.[26] Like her mother, the future Tory minister enjoyed a privileged education at Cheltenham Ladies' College, one of the country's most prestigious private schools, where fees are now nearly £12,500 per term.[27]

Research by the Sutton Trust charity after the 2015 election confirmed the cabinet's disproportionate privilege. It found that half of them went to private schools, and half also went to Oxbridge. The charity said the figures highlighted a huge problem with diversity in Parliament, with poorer people too often excluded. 'Parliament and Government should represent society,' a spokesman said. 'The best people should be able to become ministers, regardless of social background.'[28]

The point is that when the likes of Andrew Bridgen complain that wealthy people are put off entering politics, they are simply wrong. The diversity problem is the exact opposite: it's actually people from poorer backgrounds who are under-represented. (And it would hardly be surprising if that had some practial impact on the way politics is conducted). When the Conservatives came to office in 2010, dominance of wealthy individuals extended right up to the two most powerful figures in government: David Cameron and his chancellor, George Osborne. The pair had a true dedication to money instilled into them from an early age.

As a kid, George Osborne learned the ropes about finance from the family firm, Osborne & Little. 'It's been a part of my family for the whole of my life,' he once said. 'It's given me a strong understanding of what's involved in running a business – the risks, the hard work and the commitment.'[29]

Osborne & Little was set up in the 1960s by his father and uncle,

Sir Peter Osborne and Anthony Little, and became one of the go-to places for luxury fabrics. Based in London with a branch in Connecticut, USA, the business is now owned by a handful of investors, including the chancellor and his parents. But archived files reveal that the firm's past shareholders include several based in tax havens in Guernsey, Jersey and the Isle of Man.[30]

By 2004, the company had teamed up with a secretive offshore firm in the British Virgin Islands. Together, they got planning permission to redevelop Osborne & Little's London headquarters into flats. The site was then sold to the offshore firm for more than £6m, allowing it to potentially dodge huge tax bills.[31]

Embarrassingly for the chancellor, before he left office it emerged that the family business had not paid any UK corporation tax for the past seven years. Despite this, private shareholders (including Osborne) had still been treated to a £335,000 payout that was divided between them. In the year to March 2015, the company made £722,000 profits on a £34m revenue.[32]

In 2016, Osborne was forced to claim he currently has 'no offshore interests'. However, questions still remain over a family trust fund, of which Osborne was a beneficiary. The details of the fund have been kept private.[33]

It has also emerged that his uncle, James, invested in a notorious tax avoidance scheme, known as Ingenious Film Partners 2.[34] His name was among a mass of prominent millionaires involved in the tax-dodging operation, including celebrities like Bob Geldof, Anne Robinson and Victoria Beckham. When the scheme was finally shut down, authorities said it was 'good news for the vast majority of taxpayers who do not try to avoid paying their fair share of tax'.[35]

David Cameron can trace his family's wealth back for generations. His great-great-grandfather, Emile Levita, came to Britain in the 1850s as an immigrant from Germany. He worked in the City and became extremely well off, eventually becoming the head of the Chartered Bank of India, Australia and China. Based in London, Levita also owned a grouse moor in Wales and began the family tradition of sending the boys to Eton.[36] Levita's eldest son, Arthur, married a cousin of the Royal Family, meaning that Cameron is related to the Queen.

Another of Cameron's great-great-grandfathers was also a wealthy banker, Sir Ewen Cameron. He worked for the Hong Kong and Shanghai Banking Corporation.[37] In fact, a line of high-level City figures continued right down the family tree to Cameron. Both of his grandfathers were stockbrokers, and one was also awarded the title of High Sheriff of Berkshire. As one account says, his family history is 'drenched in money'.[38]

Cameron himself was born in the London Clinic, a private hospital favoured by the Royal Family.[39] He grew up in a Grade II listed building in the Berkshire Downs decorated with antiques and paintings. These included two eighteenth-century pictures that later sold for more than £1m. Those who knew him as a teenager have told tales of croquet and caviar. When he was later accused by government colleagues of being born with a silver spoon in his mouth, Cameron apparently replied: 'No, I was born with two.'[40]

His father, Ian, was a City man who specialised in offshore investment funds. When Margaret Thatcher made changes to financial regulations in 1979, he realised he could use the opportunity to help companies channel huge sums of money through tax havens like Panama and Geneva. He quit his job as a stockbroker and headed up a series of asset management firms, making a fortune for the family.[41] When he died in 2010, Cameron's father left £2.74m in his will, from which the prime minister was given £300,000.[42] An extra £200,000 was gifted to him by his mother the following year, allowing the potential to avoid £80,000 worth of inheritance tax.[43]

Before he became prime minister, Cameron rejected claims he was worth £30m, but refused to clarify how much money was in the family. A more realistic analysis in 2012 estimated his net worth to be closer to £4m. Together with his wife, Samantha, the couple make nearly £100,000 a year by renting out their home in Notting Hill, and own a second house in Oxfordshire.[44] Just before he took office, they sold around £30,000 of shares held in one of the offshore funds set up by his father in Panama.[45]

The media's assessment of Cameron? 'Swimming in cash and cossetted by privilege.'[46]

With a government packed full of millionaires from high-class families, it's easy to imagine that cultural norms might slip over into Parliament. It's not to say that wealth leads to greed. Rather, the high wages and cosy business links are not thought of as controversial in their circles.

For them, the expectation of wealth is not seen as a 'sense of entitlement' – it's just standard procedure. Making lots of money is what they know best.

Gang mentality

Power does strange things to people at the best of times. Chuck them in a lavishly decorated, 200-year-old building and start calling them 'honourable', and you're in for some trouble. So perhaps it's unsurprising that politicians might imagine themselves as the Chosen Ones.

Of course, the peers are quite *literally* the chosen ones as the House of Lords is still entirely unelected! There are even ninety-two places still reserved for peers chosen by *birthright*! Although the nobility no longer have instant access to a seat, all they have to do is join a short register of fellow hereditary peers. Then, when one of the ninety-two dies, the noblemen on the list can exclusively apply for the position.[1] In an embarrassing nod to democracy, existing peers vote for their favourite hereditary peer. There are often so few votes cast that in 2015 one peer got his seat despite only having a total of seven votes.[2] The *Independent* has described these as 'the world's most elitist elections'.[3] But it allows Parliament to top up with blue-blooded earls and dukes, whose families have for centuries owned half the country; an expectation of power and wealth literally bred into them.

In the House of Commons, though, you might expect them to have shaken off any sense of entitlement these days. After all, they're merely representatives of the public who are there to work for us. But you only need to be in the building for five minutes to realise that elitism is contagious. One MP spells out the problem clearly:

> There is something about the way Westminster is organised: the door-men in their black and white suits, and the way doors open before you even knew you wanted to walk through them. It does reek of privilege. And although it would be very hard to draw a causal connection between that and any particular mindset or actions of the people who

inhabit this place, I think it must have an impact. I think there is a
sense of people here being insulated from the rules that govern everybody else.

In order to understand the mindset, we first need to understand the
kind of lifestyle that comes with being a politician. People often
describe Westminster as a 'bubble', but it's so much more than that.
The grandeur and privilege are woven into the very fabric of the
buildings and the culture sneaks inside you like a bad virus. If you're
not already part of an elite when you become an MP, you will be by
the time you leave.

Even the most 'anti-establishment' politicians in British politics
buy into the culture here. To a certain extent, they have to. Whether
it's Jeremy Corbyn, the Green Party's Caroline Lucas, the young
SNP politician Mhairi Black, or UKIP's sole MP, Douglas Carswell.
They may claim to be offering radical ideas, but in order to function
properly in Westminster they *have* to accept the elitism and pompos-
ities that surround them. It's almost part of the job description. They
have to mingle with the establishment in order to make political
negotiations; they have to call each other 'honourable'. And, of
course, they have to accept the £75,000 salary.

Inevitably, too, most of them will snugly nestle down into the
broader lifestyle here – the subsidised bars, the Westminster gossip,
the very status and spirit of the House. And with little time or desire
to ever step outside of this insular political hub, it quickly becomes
your life.

Obviously, that doesn't mean you're *greedy*. Becoming institutionalised doesn't make you a bad person. But the Westminster machine
breeds homogeneity; a kind of herd mentality. Once you're
entrenched in it you become part of a collective way of thinking.
That's why the expenses scandal scarred so many MPs from across the
political spectrum: if everyone else is on the fiddle, why shouldn't
you be too? You're a bird in a flock – all travelling the same way, but
without any individual responsibility or leadership. Westminster will
get under your skin and change you.

'You become middle class when you're here,' Margaret Hodge
tells me. 'Some of us were born into that middle class; others
become it.

'You're part of the establishment here . . . All the stuff in the House is so ruddy establishment! Everything! Everything! The way we work, the language we use, the way we do business.'

Don't underestimate the psychological impact of suddenly becoming one of Britain's selected politicians, chosen by thousands of people to help run the country. It can go to your head. Being in Parliament is a thrill for most MPs – and it can also be a daily justification for egotism. The power and status is electrifying.

'When you've got that mandate from the people . . . that made me feel empowered,' Andrew Bridgen says. 'It has its rewards that aren't necessarily monetary.'

Another politician tells me: 'To be a Member of Parliament is a great honour. So you do feel very proud of that and very flattered by it. People who are elected by the people, who represent them in the nation's Parliament, ought to be treated with honour and respect. And I regret that they're not treated more with honour and respect.'

A third admits: '[Parliament] does encourage a lack of humility among some members.'

Dr Julian Huppert, a Lib Dem who lost his seat in the 2015 election, describes the institution he left behind as one that tries to 'suck people in'. The problem is that once you've been sucked in, the status and privileges you've come to expect from Parliament can start to spill out into a broader sense of entitlement. The grandeur becomes not only your surroundings, but also your *own* culture and lifestyle. 'Some people do feel very entitled,' Huppert tells me, as he recalls overhearing a senior Tory bragging about exploiting his status to get theatre tickets ('I just ring them and tell them who I am').

Margaret Hodge agrees: 'People think their position imbues them with an entitlement,' she says. 'Not everybody, of course, but for a lot of people.'

When I mention the pomposity of the House of Lords to one of the SNP's new crew, he just snorts with laughter. 'Oh, don't get me started,' he says. 'It's a very badly produced pantomime, actually. I tell you, they ought to bring in Danny Boyle or somebody to do the sound and lights for the state opening of Parliament. I mean the costumes are good – they've spent a lot on costumes. And the sets are good. But the sound and lights are terrible! Just absurd really.'

Toffs and plebs?

Westminster's most famous 'snobs' are quick to deny it. So quick, in fact, that you get the impression there's something to hide.

For a time, Westminster's number one 'snob' was Andrew Mitchell, the former Tory minister who resigned in the wake of the so-called Plebgate scandal. He called a policeman a 'fucking pleb' after getting in an argument while trying to leave Downing Street. 'Best you learn your fucking place,' he reportedly told the officer. 'You don't run this fucking government.'[4]

When the story broke, the *Telegraph* wrote: 'We can all agree that Andrew Mitchell is a snob and a twit,' while the *Independent* blamed his 'privileged upbringing' for his undoing.[5]

Belligerent and pompous, Mitchell was said to enjoy the perks of power. He apparently ordered everyone in his department to address him as 'Secretary of State', and liked to use a coffee cup with the words 'Secretary of State for International Development' inscribed on it. One backbench MP has claimed that Mitchell once tried to take his seat in a restaurant because 'he was the minister and I was just a backbencher'.[6]

But when I ask him about Plebgate, the response is quick and to-the-point. 'I shan't tell you anything about it,' he snaps.

Mitchell is no longer a minister, but remains a highly influential MP in the Conservative Party. At his office, I notice the day's schedule on a whiteboard, which seems to include a meeting with George Osborne. It's spacious and bathed in sunlight, with an impressive view of Big Ben. Adding a nice touch, he's decorated the room with photographs of himself.

He's an old-fashioned politician. Mitchell sits behind a huge oak desk without a computer in sight. Instead, as we talk, he dips his fountain pen into an inkwell and starts signing papers. When I ask him questions his attention seems to mostly remain on writing his signature, glancing up only occasionally with the look of a smug owl.

If you find it hard to warm to politicians at the best of times, Andrew Mitchell is not your man.

He's not in the mood for talking about privilege or entitlement. When I mention the word 'pleb', he refuses to budge, saying only: 'I don't really have anything to add to what I've said before.'

And as to whether there's a sense of entitlement in Parliament? 'No. I think it's a sort of ludicrous Wodehousian conceit,' he says, explaining: 'Politicians have always been vilified by the media.'

But if the media makes sweeping statements about politicians, Mitchell is doing the exact same thing. It's perhaps fair to argue that snobbery in Westminster is exaggerated by the press. But his utter denial of any snobbery *at all* makes it hard to take him seriously.

I ask him again: 'You don't think that exists in Parliament now?'

'If it did, it doesn't any more,' he says firmly. There seems little point in arguing.

Another 'Tory toff', Jacob Rees-Mogg, is considered so posh that it's made him a minor celebrity. With his love for Latin, he's become the butt of frequent jokes on *Have I Got News For You* and once featured in an interview with Ali G. It's thought that Rees-Mogg has never been seen in public without a suit and tie, and he's been attached to his briefcase since his schooldays at Eton.[7] He also holds the record for using the longest word ever recorded in the House of Commons ('floccinaucinihilipilification'). The late parliamentary sketch writer, Simon Hoggart, described him as 'the ultimate toff, the nob's nob'.[8]

And he's every bit as posh in real life. But when I join him for a drink in the House of Commons tea room, the Tory MP knocks away any suggestion that he's out of touch with ordinary people, in typical flowery language.

'Do I think I'm the Ordinary Joe? No, because I don't believe in the Ordinary Joe as a concept,' he says. 'Not because I think I'm a grand panjandrum.'

'I think the appearance of the disconnect between the electorate and the elected is always important. But I also think that it is always like this,' he says. 'It's hard to think of a legislature in the world where there isn't a feeling that those who are elected are not like the people they represent.

'You certainly wouldn't want a Parliament that was made up of entirely people like me. The truth is, most of them aren't like me. But because probably thirty years ago they were *all* exactly like me, that's still the image of Parliament.'

Rees-Mogg doesn't try to downplay the privilege in Westminster. Instead, he makes an interesting argument defending Parliament's grandeur. 'I think there *should* be something grand about democracy,' he says. 'It ought to be something we're proud of. And, therefore, having a grand building and a certain pomp and circumstance is a legitimate expression not of the Members of Parliament, but of our belief in the system.'

He goes on: 'I'm going to sound very pompous. Why not? I think I'm mainly entitled to things on behalf of my constituents. So I am entitled to get answers from ministers or public bodies that I write to.' Though he admits: 'Sometimes, this gets elided into a feeling that the MPs, of themselves, have these privileges.'

But Rees-Mogg's 'pomposity' does not impress all of his fellow MPs. One even suggests that Parliament is so ridiculously grand and outdated that it's time to close the whole thing down and set up base elsewhere. Somewhere that won't breed a sense of entitlement so easily. 'Turn the Houses of Parliament into a museum,' the MP suggests. 'You could leave Jacob Rees-Mogg in charge as the curator.'

Another politician supports that idea. 'They could do "MPs through the ages",' she suggests. 'He'd have to change the costume; he wouldn't have to change the accent or anything.'

It seems they're on to a winner: 'What a brilliant idea!' Rees-Mogg says, when I tell him. 'I like that.'

Pomp and circumstance

The daily grind in Westminster is a little more refined than most jobs.

To start with, fine food and wine come cheap. Inexplicably, Parliament believes that running an 'operating loss on catering facilities is *inevitable*'. So MPs' food and drink is part-funded by us taxpayers.[9] Under David Cameron's coalition government, the House of Commons alone managed to fork out more than £23m of subsidies to fund MPs' bars and restaurants.[10] And with near-exclusive access to a wide selection of drinking holes and restaurants, politicians are spoilt for choice.

Fancy something nice? You can pop over to the Strangers' Dining Room, which recently had a £200,000 refurbishment.[11] A starters course of Mull of Kintyre cheese mousse with piccalilli vegetables, followed by seared venison loin for mains, comes at £24.25.[12] Or, if you're counting the pennies, you could just get some 95p mushroom soup from the Terrace Cafeteria.[13] Failing that, you can hang out in the 'sinfully comfortable' Pugin Room with its 'champagne-rich atmosphere'.[14] There's a similar range in the Lords, with everything from a £2.75 risotto all the way to a £37 Brixham Dover sole. A bottle of House of Lords vintage champagne (with 'hints of honey and cinnamon') comes in at a cool £59.50.[15] And that's even with the subsidy.

In his guidebook for new MPs, Paul Flynn writes: 'There is a persuasive army of people bent on bloating the bodies and dulling the senses of Members with fine food and drink.' He adds: 'It's possible to go through the whole day, from a breakfast seminar with Danish pastries to afternoon and evening receptions with wine and finger food, accepting the hospitality of those who seek your company.'[16]

Meanwhile, the subsidised alcohol fuels a notoriously boozy life-style among many. 'You'll see them in Strangers' Bar every night just getting pissed and waiting to vote,' a former ministerial aide tells me. 'A lot of politics is done around drink. I'm not a huge drinker myself, but working in Westminster you find yourself having to be in the bars every night.' In fact, a survey by Alcohol Concern in 2013 found that more than a quarter of MPs acknowledge that there is an unhealthy drinking culture in Parliament.[17]

In their exclusive bars, politicians can get a pint for nearly 90p less than the London average, thanks to subsidies.[18] While everyone else was struggling with higher prices during the financial downturn, a private committee sat behind closed doors in Westminster and decided to freeze the price of their own drinks for two years. By 2015, they had agreed to push prices up by a tiny 0.5%, but also elected to use taxpayer funds to replace their cutlery because it had become 'worn'.[19] And we can all agree: there's nothing more aggra-vating than a worn spoon.

Then there's the art. In other workplaces, you're lucky if there's anything to spruce up the office at all. But politicians enjoy privileged access to around 8,500 works of art that adorn the building, including many which are not available for public view.[20] Since 2000, the five most expensive new paintings to have been acquired have all been worth at least £80,000, with one costing some £270,000.[21]

If you get a top job in business, you might get your mugshot on the company's website. But in Westminster, you can get a full painted portrait – intended to hang on the walls of Parliament till the end of time. In 2010, Russian artist Sergei Pavlenko was commissioned to paint a group portrait of the House of Lords at a cost of £45,000.[22] And individual MPs in top jobs can expect their very own picture, often costing tens of thousands of pounds. Speaker John Bercow's set the public back £37,000. Rebuffing criticisms, a statement said that 'no alternative to a painting in oil on canvas was considered', claiming that a simple photograph 'would not have been appropriate'.[23]

As you'd expect, the pomp surrounding peers is on a whole other level. 'There is a climate around the House of Lords which kind of favours grandiloquence,' one baroness tells me. 'Partly the ridiculous use of titles. There is an atmosphere which, if you're not careful, can mean that you get a bit cut off from reality.'

Before they are appointed, new members toddle off to Ede & Ravenscroft on Chancery Lane, which is reputedly the oldest tailor's in the world. Here they enter an episode of *Mr Benn* as they're fitted out with a wardrobe for egotism. An ancient ceremonial robe in red, white and gold, topped off with a black cocked hat.[24] The Lord Speaker, meanwhile, has his ceremonial gear provided courtesy of the taxpayer at a cost of £6,122.[25] Then, when peers arrive in Parliament, the doorkeepers are expected to have learned their names.[26]

Once elevated to this position, who can blame them for wanting the moon on a stick? Peers demand the highest levels of service and expect Parliament to provide for them. One lord even wrote a message to authorities in the House of Lords begging: 'I'd like an office in the palace so I don't have to keep running across the road in all weathers.'[27]

A group of them run a Refreshments Committee that fields formal letters of complaint from fellow peers when the subsidised fine dining doesn't meet their high standards. The correspondence was originally kept private, but authorities agreed to release parts of it under the Freedom of Information Act.

In one hand-scrawled letter, two pages long, a lord vented his fury after having to wait too long for a sandwich. He said the delay was 'not acceptable'. Another peer objected to a 'rather basic' £60-a-head banquet, while a third fired off a list of grievances that included a 'cheese creme brûlée which wasn't very cheesy' and a fish meal that had 'a hard crust on top'. He added: 'If there is a new chef, he'll (if it is a he) have to buck his ideas up.'[28] Meanwhile, some people are just miffed by the prices: '£58 for a bottle of Champagne is a scandal,' one lord complained.[29]

It's not just about value for money. Peers have also complained that staff members don't speak to them with enough respect. 'The tone of staff has changed from helpful to regulating headmistress,' one lord said. Another said she found staff were 'ignorant' and 'have a bad attitude'.

Clearly, some politicians have little sympathy for the minions who work around them. For instance, one demanded that staff 'listen and consider how to act'.[30]

But the contrast between their own working conditions and those of parliamentary staff sometimes makes the place seem like an off-cut from *Downton Abbey*. MPs and peers may be surrounded by luxury, yet the rooms and corridors which house them are teeming with an unhappy, underpaid workforce, who labour away behind the scenes with little thanks. A report in 2015 even claimed that dozens of staff, including up to thirty-nine caterers, were on controversial zero-hours contracts, without the guarantee of work or the chance to get redundancy pay if they were sacked.[31]

In an official survey of House of Lords staff – released under the Freedom of Information Act – only 30% said they were paid fairly. The internal report found that just two thirds of staff felt proud to work in Parliament. And almost half claimed that allegations of discrimination and unfair treatment were dealt with badly by managers.[32]

Those who responded to the survey sent a clear message about Westminster's inequalities. 'This is a workplace, not a club,' said one. Another added: 'Shut some of the restaurants and charge members non-subsidised prices in outlets which are aimed at staff.'[33]

'It is an embarrassment how much is available to members,' a third said. 'This is a 21st century workplace. Maintaining fine dining is an own-goal in terms of reputation. Media coverage of this often distracts from the work of the House of Lords, and is quite frankly an embarrassment.'[34]

They complained about the stark contrast between people's pay. 'It is grossly unfair,' said one staffer. 'The junior staff (who have been here years longer than some senior staff) get a pittance . . . And we're supposed to be grateful for that. It is indefensible.'[35]

They demanded 'a complete and utter end to the sycophantic behaviour of the management towards the Peers', saying that staff were 'treated like a placeholder: a warm body to welcome the Peers, but not actually allowed to make any choices or decisions for themselves. Suggestions are immediately knocked down or ignored, morale is incredibly low.'[36]

One staff member simply wrote: 'I can barely afford to either pay my current travel costs or move closer to London. I cannot even save money for the future.'[37]

All the while, our 'honourable' MPs sit back, take a sip of their discount beers and moan that their salaries aren't high enough. So insular is Westminster's culture that politicians can be blinded by it. Sometimes, they are no longer able to see the wood for the trees and pursue the prospect of money at all costs. And at no time has this been more apparent than during the expenses scandal.

PART FIVE:

Expenses forever

The scandal that never left

Looking at him now, you'd never guess that Denis MacShane used to be an MP. We meet in a drab cafe opposite Victoria Station – his request – and I nearly double-take when he trudges in. Satchel in one hand, bike helmet in the other, he sports a grubby pair of corduroy trousers, a cheap blue fleece and the most crumpled T-shirt that I think I've ever seen. I'm not much of a smart dresser myself, but MacShane is *so* scruffy that I wonder, for a moment, whether he's deliberately trying to portray himself as an outsider to the Westminster establishment. But no. He looks completely knackered by life. Sad, deep-set eyes stare blankly, jaded by everything they have seen.

Once upon a time, this now tragic, dishevelled man was a prized politician: a privy councillor and Tony Blair's minister of state for Europe. His glittering career had taken him from Oxford to the BBC, and then to Westminster. But in 2013, aged sixty-five, he found himself sitting in a cell in Belmarsh Prison after being found guilty of expenses fraud.

MacShane had faked nineteen receipts, which were charged to the taxpayer. In total, the bills amounted to some £12,900. When he finally landed up in court, the MP was accused of 'deliberate, oft repeated and prolonged dishonesty over a period of years.'[1]

As he begins to tell me his story, MacShane slumps into his chair and groans. 'I mean, what can I say? I have to start by fully acknowledging that I made a terrible mistake and what I did was undoubtedly wrong.' His honesty is admirable, but he immediately goes on the defensive: 'I made no personal profit, it wasn't done deliberately to gain money,' he claims, slurping coffee from a paper cup.

His arrest followed the expenses scandal in 2009, after Westminster authorities alerted Scotland Yard. They soon discovered MacShane's fake receipts, which covered 'research and translation' bills. Although the court accepted he had incurred genuine expenses, the judge said the MP 'chose instead to recoup by dishonest false accounting'. When he was found guilty, MacShane muttered '*quelle surprise*' under his breath as he was led away from the dock.[2] He became one of only seven politicians to be jailed in the wake of the expenses scandal that shook Parliament in 2009.

These days, he styles himself as the expenses scandal's ultimate victim – a careless buffoon, not a monster. 'The original twit,' his Twitter profile says. '*Adieu a la politique*', (goodbye to politics).[3]

He's still on the defensive. 'That was an entirely politically-driven, or media-driven prosecution,' he tells me. 'There were people in the Commons who were absolutely determined to make an example of me.'

MacShane's argument is this: what he did was bad, but he was singled out and used as a scapegoat. Dozens of other MPs were equally bad, but got away scott-free. 'There were many people who themselves had made serious profits from the expenses scheme,' he says. 'I think finding someone to be a scapegoat for the broader fiddling was very convenient.'

It's surprisingly easy to sympathise with him on this – but not for the reasons he would probably like. MacShane *was* a scapegoat, but that doesn't mean he shouldn't have gone to jail. Rather, many believe that more politicians should have been locked up alongside him. While he was rightly recognised as a criminal, others got off with nothing more than a slap on the wrist and were allowed to continue their high-flying careers.

It's worth remembering the sheer scale of abuse exposed in the expenses scandal. Parliament was truly mired in corruption. It touched all the main parties; everyone from lowly backbenchers right up to the prime minister had been cashing in. In the end, more than half of the MPs in the House of Commons were ordered to pay back expenses claims totalling more than £1.1m.

In another world, these disgraced politicians would have been booted out without hesitation. Yet most of them are still shamelessly plugging away in Westminster, hoping that their contemptible claims are slowly forgotten about. One former Tory MP I talk to even describes the scandal as 'unpleasant history' – the implication being that it is no longer relevant.

Far from being pushed out of power, most of those involved have been forgiven and allowed to carry on in top jobs. Just take a look at some of the main figures implicated in the scandal:

- George Osborne 'flipped' his home (switching round the address given for 'main residence' on official forms, which makes it possible to avoid tax charges).[4] He also charged taxpayers for a horse's paddock.[5] He became chancellor of the exchequer in 2010, in charge of the whole country's money.
- John Bercow also flipped his home to a £540,000 London property and claimed maximum allowances.[6] But that didn't stop him being speaker of the House of Commons.
- Tory MP Douglas Hogg claimed £2,200 to clean out the moat on his country estate.[7] A few years later he was appointed to the House of Lords, where he's entitled to claim even more expenses.
- Labour's Jacqui Smith, who was home secretary at the time, pocketed at least £116,000 by claiming expenses for a second home while living with her sister.[8] She has since been handed a series of lucrative jobs, including the head of an NHS Trust.
- Ed Balls claimed £1,610 for cleaners without ever submitting a receipt.[9] He went on to become shadow chancellor, under Ed Miliband.

The list goes on and on and on. It's as if the expenses scandal never happened. So why was it only MacShane and a small handful of others who really felt the repercussions of the scandal? Even if only seven MPs broke the law, dozens more disgraced themselves.

'My case was sent to the police by people, some of whom I think had a vendetta against me,' he claims. 'The House of Commons uniquely said: "we don't give a fuck about the police or the CPS [Crown Prosecution Service]. We will get Denis".'

It may be true that MacShane was used as a scapegoat to offload blame for the abuses of hundreds of MPs, but it's nevertheless hard to get over his incredulity. He seems to be in denial about what he did. Certainly, he doesn't sound like a man plagued with guilt. At one point he even exclaims: 'I produced receipts for everything!'

'Yes Denis,' I want to scream, 'but you faked the receipts! Remember? That's why they locked you up!'

★   ★   ★

MacShane isn't the only one who has struggled to take responsibility – it was a running theme of the scandal. The problem was that abuse wasn't just caused by a few rogue MPs; it was woven into Westminster's culture. Gang mentality justified the wrongdoing and expenses fraud became completely normal.

'You'd see seminars in the tea room [after the General Elections] in 2001 and 2005, where MPs would teach the incomers how to fiddle and max up,' MacShane says. 'You'd sit down and people would tell you their fiddles.' He recalls a fellow Labour MP who boasted that he'd managed to get an entire year's worth of expenses claims paid to him in a lump sum at the start of the year. He shopped around for the best savings account he could find and reaped the rewards.

Another MP has similar memories: 'We go into the tea room and people are talking about how they made money on this, or how they've got some deal going . . . They thought it was a legitimate perk of the job that they could do a little fiddle on the side and get more money in.'

This was institutionalised, systematic corruption. Though many politicians didn't technically break the law, that was largely because the rules themselves were so shoddy. Most of them knew they could get away with murder. Even those who didn't fiddle their expenses were still guilty of a conspiracy of silence: an *omertà* that kept the whole sorry business behind closed doors for years.

When the scandal eventually exploded out into the open, MPs turned to blame anyone and anything but themselves. Apologies were deliberately crafted to avoid taking any personal responsibility. 'I'm sorry for the *anger caused by* my expenses claims,' they would say. Rather than simply: 'I'm sorry for making the claims in the first place.'

The blame game was adopted by politicians of every party, clinging together to defend each other. But there really was no defence. Either they knew what they were doing was wrong, but did it regardless. Or they were so inept or lacking in a moral compass that they didn't think there was anything wrong with it.

Many of the most pitiful excuses were forced out on editions of *Question Time*. MPs stuck two fingers up at enraged audiences and tried to duck responsibility. These clips now haunt the annals of YouTube, endlessly re-living the depths to which politicians fell.

In front of an audience in Newcastle, Eric Pickles tried defending the fact he had claimed expenses for a second home in London, despite his main house being just twenty-nine miles away in Essex.[10] His excuse? 'The House of Commons works on clockwork,' he said, explaining that commuting to work might make him late. 'You have to be there precisely,' he said.

'Like a job, in other words?' asked David Dimbleby.

'Yes,' Pickles replied. 'Exactly like a job.'[11]

On the same programme, former home secretary Charles Clarke palmed blame on to unnamed rogue MPs. But he didn't point fingers at any specific people. 'There is not an ethos of cheating, dishonesty and dishonour in the House. There is not. There are individuals who have done bad things.'[12]

Another edition of *Question Time*, in Grimsby, saw minister Margaret Beckett pulling out the classic move: blame the system. 'This is a system that's grown up over many years,' she said. 'It has many flaws and it has to be changed. And that is, if you recall, something the prime minister proposed quite some considerable time ago.'[13]

One bloke in the audience got the chance to quiz Labour's Jacqui Smith, during an edition in Wales. 'If you realised you made a mistake, why didn't you realise at the time you were doing it wrong?' he said.

Smith nodded, stony faced, trying to look sympathetic. 'One of the reasons was because I received advice that I was doing it right,' she replied. 'But, you know, somebody else has made a different judgement. I accept that.'

'Surely we all know [when] we're doing things wrong?' the man pointed out.

'Well, if you seek advice and you're told you're doing it right, it's reasonable to follow that advice . . .'

'But still inside of you, you still know it's wrong. The thing is, you still used the system knowing it that. You can't deny that, surely?'

'Well I didn't believe that what I was doing was wrong at the time.'

Reeling in disbelief, the guy in the audience just gave up. 'Well, you're very naïve then,' he muttered.[14]

Actually, Jacqui Smith had the best excuse of all – the political equivalent of claiming her dog had eaten her homework. 'I know there's an appearance thing here,' she said, during an interview on *The Andrew Marr Show*. 'I'm claiming less money this year than I was last year. But I also understand that people want that to *look as if it's fair*.'[15]

Yes, the fact that MPs were fiddling their expenses wasn't the bad bit, apparently. The bad bit, Smith reckoned, was the *appearance* that they'd done anything bad.

This one quote sums up Westminster's whole response to the expenses scandal. Rather than genuine reform, they launched a PR campaign. They wanted it to 'look as if it's fair'. So they just went through the motions. MacShane and six others were jailed, giving the appearance that all the worst offenders had been dealt with properly. Then, a new watchdog was set up and extra transparency was brought in. Hey presto, everything is totally reformed and wonderful. Nothing more to see here.

It's true that most of the changes have been for the best. But no effort has ever been made to tackle the real underlying problem that caused the scandal in the first place.

The old system did not *force* people to fiddle their expenses. Individuals chose to do so themselves.[16] Ultimately, the main cause of the scandal was not an out-of-date system, lack of transparency, misguided rules or anything else. It was just greed, pure and simple. A deep-set culture of entitlement, privilege and corruption. And that can still be found in Westminster to this day.

As Denis MacShane finishes his coffee, I ask him if he feels resentful about going to prison, given that other MPs may have dodged the bullet. 'I don't give a toss,' he grunts. 'Every time you look at yourself on Twitter there's usually some little turd who says "urgh, who's that convict MacShane? He's a convicted expense fiddler".' But he adds: 'It's part of life's rich tapestry. I mean, I'm completely philosophical.'

I'm not so sure. He seems pretty bitter, so far as I can tell. He's lost most of his Westminster friends and certainly has little sympathy left for any other politicians caught out in controversies. He talks about his former colleague Lord Sewel as 'that silly Labour lord who was caught sniffing coke off the tits of some tart'. And on Jack Straw he offers: 'I hope he gets his seat in the House of Lords. I couldn't give a fuck, at the end of the day.'

Nice guy.

IPSA ('I'm Paid Sod All')

In the aftermath of the scandal, politicians were forced to make out that they'd learned their lesson. They said they would draw a line under expenses and promised a complete reform. Three key things needed changing: transparency, the rules and the culture. Years later, however, and the radical sweeping reforms still don't seem to have materialised.

There's no doubt that the expenses system is a million times better than it was. Nowadays, a new watchdog called the Independent Parliamentary Standards Authority (IPSA) has control over MPs' pay and expenses. 'Our rules are a clean break from the old system of allowances,' it claimed when it was set up in 2009. 'The new rules are fair (to MPs and the public purse), workable and transparent. We subject all expense claims to rigorous verification and auditing.'

As well as scrapping many of the things politicians can claim for, IPSA also set about publishing all expenses data on its website. Now, anyone can check how much their MP gets, and what they're spending it on – petrol costs, hotels, rent, and so on.

It's also true that the most extreme type of abuses have been almost completely wiped out. MPs are no longer claiming money for birdhouses, or to have their moats cleaned out. That's mainly because of IPSA's new rules, but partly it's thanks to the fear of being caught out by the press, which still engulfs Westminster.

However, despite what MPs may claim, these largely superficial changes do not mean the expenses problem is fixed. In fact, some aspects have even got worse.

During the first five years of Cameron's premiership, claims by MPs rose by 43%. Total business costs and expenses went from £79m in 2010/11, to £113m in 2014/15. And that was on top of their regular salaries.[17]

Parliament's spendthrifts started claiming more and more on things like air travel and rent. Flight expenses went up by 50%, to more than £1m a year. And expenses for renting second homes rose from £6.2m before, to £9.3m in 2014/15.[18]

As for the great transparency push? It wasn't quite as revolutionary as MPs like to make out. In fact, the data that IPSA now publishes with great pride online would not, in itself, be enough to expose the worst abuses of the 2009 scandal. Many of those were only uncovered because the *Telegraph* got hold of the original, uncensored files, which contained every last detail in them.

The trick of 'home flipping', for instance, was only revealed because journalists could see the addresses that MPs had registered. Similarly, the files contained the full names of every company that politicians had paid money to. This meant journalists were able to find out about cases such as when Gordon Brown paid his brother's company £6,577 to clean his London flat.[19]

A senior spin doctor in Westminster at the time of the expenses scandal tells me: 'What no one had expected was that the *Telegraph* was going to get leaked [the files] . . . The *Telegraph* [had the files] un-redacted, which meant you could see addresses, which meant you could then do some proper digging.'

Yet crucial details like these are not included in IPSA's prized new database. Instead, we're just told basic information, like the date and cost of each claim. It's a good start, but it still hides scores of potential scandals.

There is one way around this: the original documents can sometimes be accessed by making a request under the Freedom of Information Act and waiting four weeks for IPSA to respond. But even then, the documents are often still censored and will arrive in your inbox marked with black ink, covering up various details that could have proved crucial to exposing more fiddling.

In December 2012, an account using the handle @IPSA_watch began posting on Twitter. 'Exposing the lunacy which is the Independent Parliamentary Standards Authority,' it said. 'I tweet to show IPSA as punitive, pointless & wasteful.'[20]

With a Portcullis logo and a handful of high-profile journalists following, it almost looked like something official. Its aim was very clear: to bring down the new expenses system. The account is run anonymously, but whoever is behind it has a particular interest and knowledge about Stewart Jackson MP, who had a legal dispute with IPSA over the repayment of expenses claims.[21]

'Surely #IPSA need to be held to account over arbitrary treatment of Stewart Jackson?' one tweet read. Another said: 'Think all those who attacked @SJacksonMP & accused him of profiteering on 2nd home need to say "sorry".'

Intrigued about the identity of the Twitter account, I emailed Jackson, requesting an interview about IPSA. 'I cannot contribute anything which is conceivably printable,' came the response.

But if Stewart Jackson hates the new expenses watchdog, he's in good company among his fellow MPs. Everyone in Parliament will tell you the same thing: IPSA is probably the most loathed organisation in Westminster. However, many MPs are scared of being too vocal in their opposition. IPSA represents the new system, so they worry that publicly criticising it could look like they want a return to the old fraud and fiddling. Instead, they wage a silent war against it. 'They know that MPs hate them,' one backbencher says about IPSA. 'They're rubbish.'

There are some valid criticisms. The watchdog's CEO, Marcial Boo, is himself paid far more than most MPs. In fact, his annual pay cheque of between £120,000 and 125,000 is not that far off what the prime minister earns. Other senior executives are also on lofty salaries: the director of policy and communications earns up to £95,000 and the finance director is on up to £110,000.[22] It's easy to understand how galling it might be for MPs to have their finances ruthlessly controlled by these overpaid managers. When IPSA's chair, Sir Ian Kennedy was appointed, MPs booed and hissed in the Commons chamber.[23]

A top political adviser, who I meet in the House of Commons, doesn't hold back with his criticism of IPSA. 'The system is shit,' he says. 'The phone lines are only open from ten to three each day, and you're like "well just do a full day's fucking work".'

Other insiders complain about errors that the watchdog has made, failures to process payments and being too strict with the rules. 'They get very touchy about things called taxis,' a Tory MP tells me. 'MPs aren't allowed taxis cos it's emotive.

'IPSA aren't interested in what's fair – they're only interested in the rules. MPs call it "I'm Paid Sod All".'

The MP adds: 'They're very, very expensive. We should get rid of IPSA and just have allowances . . . it would save the taxpayer a fortune of money.'

IPSA certainly shouldn't be allowed an easy ride. But rather than criticising its most serious flaws, like the continued lack of transparency over expenses claims, MPs spend their time moaning about efficiency and the day-to-day issues which get on their nerves. That's not to say these things shouldn't be dealt with, but many politicians have got their priorities wrong. After all, the expenses scandal did not cause a public outcry because the system was 'inefficient'. Rather, it was the sheer audacity of the claims and corruption that shocked people.

In fact, IPSA's records suggest the organisation isn't actually all that bad. For every £1 it hands over to MPs and their staff, the watchdog spends around 5p processing the payment. Furthermore, 99.9% of salary payments are accurate and – when the office *is* open – phone calls are answered in an average of 19 seconds. On top of all that, each year it publishes 206,000 expenses claims online, processes 235,000 public consultation responses and answers 173 freedom of information requests.[24]

Even if you still think that's inefficient, it's a darn sight better than many other systems. Compare IPSA to the government's fitness-to-work scheme, say. Over three years, the Department for Work and Pensions paid private companies £1.6bn to conduct controversial health checks on people claiming disability benefits. Their errors were devastating. One report said that one in five people who appealed against their assessment results had their complaints upheld.[25] In 2015, the *Guardian* even claimed that almost ninety people died every month after being declared 'fit for work' by official assessments.[26] But after all the pain, it turned out the health assessments were *not even economically efficient*. The National Audit Office found the system was actually spending more taxpayers' money in assessing people, than it was saving by removing their benefits.[27]

So even if IPSA *is* inefficient and nightmarish to work with, the problem is dwarfed in comparison to other issues that MPs could spend their time complaining about.

IPSA, meanwhile, is well aware that it is under a disproportionate amount of fire from politicians. One member of the watchdog, Ken Olisa, wrote angrily to the Commons Speaker, John Bercow, before quitting in 2013:

> The fundamental changes introduced by IPSA were always going to engender opposition and scrutiny. But, the scale of the reaction from within Westminster has been astonishing – especially given that our job was to clean up a mess not of our making.
>
> The time, money and effort exerted by Parliament and Parliamentary bodies poring over an organisation with an operational budget equal to the taxpayers' subsidy for the Commons bars and restaurants has been entirely disproportionate . . .
>
> It is a shame that so many of those who should have most welcomed a system that is fair, workable and transparent should have invested so much energy in undermining our work.[28]

So why do MPs have this unhealthy obsession with attacking IPSA? You can't help feeling there's some bitterness involved. As one top parliamentary aide tells me: 'They feel very hard done by, by the perception of the expenses scandal.'

Although some MPs are happy with the new system, a great many resent the restrictions over what they can claim. They resent the amount of scrutiny they are placed under. They resent that IPSA won't bend the rules or do favours. And they resent the fact that it won't trust MPs on their word, and always demands evidence for every claim.

One day, while I was doing research in the British Library, a former government adviser popped in to meet me. We trudged down to the cafe and he launched into a rant about Westminster's attitude towards IPSA. Before he quit, he'd become steadily more exasperated hearing MPs whinging about petty grievances, which he reckoned were born out of a sense of entitlement. But he warned that their complaints will only become more vocal over time, as they get more confident in talking about expenses again.

'The only pressure that there's going to be in Parliament for this cycle is MPs moaning about it, saying "oh they insisted I submit receipts! Why don't they trust my word? And it took them a month to pay!"

'Everybody these days is expected to provide a receipt for their expenses! That's just the way the world works these days. We don't do expenses on trust because people lie.'

He added: 'If you're used to signing your expenses off, saying "I'm a Member of Parliament, on my word these things are true", and they say "oh we now don't trust you any more", it's going to be irritating. And I just think "welcome to the real world!" '

Another source has this to say about MPs' attitude to the new watchdog: 'All the complaints just seemed administrative. I haven't got a huge amount of sympathy for MPs when it comes to things like that . . . Frankly it's just admin and delay and process problems. I don't know what the real issue is beyond that.'

An anonymous survey of MPs that IPSA conducted in 2014 revealed some remarkable attitudes from a Parliament that's meant to have moved on from the expenses scandal. One MP called for a return to 'paper-based claims', saying: 'I work 60/70 hours a week and resent being used as your unpaid data entry clerk.'[29] Another called for transparency to be curbed so that she could travel first class without the press finding out. 'It's very difficult to work in standard class,' she complained. 'But if you go 1st . . . IPSA still publishes it as 1st class travel and the papers love "greedy MP" stories . . . It really annoys me.'

One MP even seemed to look back nostalgically at the good old days of fraud and fiddling when he told IPSA: 'Your annual cost is hugely greater than the cost of wrongful over-claiming by MPs in the past.'

Others demanded that IPSA started 'treating my staff with greater respect' and stopped 'dabbling in things which are none of their statutory business'. When asked how the watchdog could improve, one MP suggested: 'Treat MPs with even the slightest amount of respect?' Another moaned that he was 'unable to recover' his bills for entertaining people.[30]

A similar attitude can be found in the House of Lords, where expenses have been shaken up but are still regulated in-house. One peer complained: 'Having one's veracity and honesty constantly distrusted and questioned as a matter of course is extremely unpleasant.'[31]

A more poetic inflection of this sentiment can be found in Paul Flynn's book *How to be an MP*:

> Mortified by guilt and shame the Commons gripped IPSA in an embrace of revulsion. There is no other solution. A malign beast invaded and occupied MPs' territory. It has little sight or hearing and communicates in incomprehensible jargon and hieroglyphics . . . They re-invented a discredited but efficient wheel and came up with a square one with spokes.

An adequate response to all this is simple: stop whinging and get on with it.

The Westminster disconnect

All this moaning about IPSA represents a deeper, more fundamental issue in Westminster. MPs may not have forgotten about the expenses scandal, but they consider it well and truly behind them. It's ancient history, as far as they're concerned, and the problems have now been totally cleared up.

They're still scared of negative publicity that occasionally snares one of their rank, but they've come to believe this is *despite* their actions, not *because* of them. They believe the public and media will always hate them and there's nothing they can do. Few of them stop to consider that – just maybe – expenses are not quite as reformed as they think they are.

'I don't think enough's actually been written or understood about the expenses scandal,' one insider tells me. 'It was a big scandal in the Westminster village for six months, but then Westminster kind of moved on. They got bored of it and moved on to the next thing. I don't think the public did.

'Everyone forgot about MPs' expenses because it was boring – apart from the public who are still seething about it. For a lot of them it confirmed their worst fears.'

Another senior policy wonk agrees: 'There's a big disconnect.

People absolutely hate this place, and I don't think people here really get that because most MPs have no life. The only people they meet outside are people in a political context.

'They sort of think "yeah that was ages ago, we sorted it, and actually IPSA's terrible and they're really annoying and they are really crap and the real problem is that we're not paid enough and IPSA's too restrictive, blah blah blah". And they don't understand that it's still a massive, massive issue for the public.

'There's a sense of "oh well we've got IPSA now so it's done". And actually I don't think there was ever the full root and branch change here that there should have been.'

Even the SNP – who have often railed against Westminster traditions – seem to think the new system is pretty good. 'It's pretty well screwed down, to be honest,' one of their MPs tells me. 'There's lots of things you can't claim for, but that is fine. It's as it should be. It's not quite a sledgehammer to crack a nut, but they have come down, I think, pretty firmly.'

The extent to which Westminster has tried to forget about the expenses scandal is reflected in a recent report by the Committee on Standards in Public Life. 'For five years now IPSA has provided *complete* transparency regarding the expenses of Members of Parliament,' it says defiantly. 'The expenses scandal is now over.'

It also dismisses the idea that transparency can improve trust in the system, claiming: 'Perception of low and declining standards is not necessarily matched by the facts . . . To some degree, such public moods are uncontrollable.'[32]

There's another hidden ingredient to Parliament's disconnect with the public over expenses: bitterness. Many politicians are still annoyed about the way they were treated during the scandal. Parliament is still entangled in a web of personal accusations and grudges.

Some are angry that authorities allowed – and even encouraged – excessive expenses claims. Speaking anonymously, one MP tells me that even as a prospective parliamentary candidate he was dragged in by the chief whip and pressurised to make claims – even if he didn't need the money.

I was told in no uncertain terms: . . . 'You might think you want to have a cheap headline by saying I'm not going to claim all these expenses or allowances. You will not do this. Your colleagues need that money, it's part of their pay – we haven't had a pay rise in years. You will claim. And if you don't need any, you will find something to claim.' . . .

Within six months, it was all out and then they hung everybody out to dry who was only doing what they'd been told to do . . . But nobody in the party has ever wanted to admit that.

Others have painful memories of being attacked by the public over expenses. 'I couldn't bloody walk down the street, never mind go in the club for a pint,' one MP says. 'I think they would have cut my throat.'

So the idea that they should now be subjected to yet more scrutiny over expenses does not sit well with many. They're happier to draw a line under the whole thing, move on and forget about it.

However, if you thought the expenses scandal was over, think again. The rules may have changed, but the claiming culture lives on.

17

Penny pinchers

Let's be honest, £15 isn't a lot. Not in the grand scheme of things. The overall bill for MPs' expenses is nearly £113m per year. So a few quid is hardly going to break the bank. The problem is, if we judge their claims by value alone, we overlook the underlying cultural problems that led to the scandal in the first place. It's not so much *what* they claim that we should be looking out for; it's what they feel *entitled* to claim. What does that £15 *represent*?

MPs say they're on heightened alert and have learned their lessons. They should now know that sticking to the rules isn't necessarily enough: they also need to show personal judgement and responsibility. Yet despite everything that's happened – the scandal, the apologies, the promises – the old attitudes persist.

This is not about the money; it's about the principle. We don't want our representatives to be on the make.

What's in a chicken curry?

Late in the evening on 27 October 2014, Labour MP Ronnie Campbell walked into the Kennington Tandoori, a small London restaurant just south of the river. Its proximity to Westminster has helped it build a good reputation among MPs and the restaurant staff say that politicians dine there regularly.

On this particular occasion, Ronnie Campbell sat down at a table on his own and ordered a chicken tikka curry, with an onion bhajee on the side. He's an old-school backbencher and lives just around the corner from here, in a flat paid for by taxpayers. He's got his own cooker there, and all his bills are covered by expenses.

But Ronnie had had a long day, and he didn't fancy cooking. So, he paid £15.90 for the curry, ate up and went home. But he kept hold of the restaurant bill. Later, the scrap of paper was photocopied and sent to IPSA. He claimed the money back on expenses.[1]

'I always used to go and nip along to the Indians,' Ronnie tells me, in his thick Geordie accent. 'We were allowed fifteen pounds a meal, if Parliament sat after half past seven.'

'I would do a deal with the Indians round the corner,' he says, explaining that the restaurant would do him a meal for £15. 'I'd get a little bit of chicken tikka, a little bit samosas. And that was me – that was my supper.'

We're sitting next to each other on a shabby sofa in a crèche, somewhere in the maze of Parliament. It was the only quiet place we could find to talk – Ronnie explains that people still get angry when they hear politicians talking about expenses. Our interview is not anonymous or off-the-record (indeed, my dictaphone is right in front of him), yet he is alarmingly candid about his expenses, shedding light on Parliament's claim culture.

In the wake of the expenses row, MPs vowed to scrap food subsidies. After all, they don't need to eat any extra just because they're politicians. So there's no good reason why taxpayers should foot their restaurant bills, unless they're away from home without access to a kitchen. But the £15 food allowance was kept on for years and was only dropped at the election, in May 2015. Until then, dozens of MPs carried on bagging free dinners from London restaurants after 7:30 p.m., despite having houses nearby. One source aptly describes the food allowance as 'nuts'.

Rumour has it that some establishments even learned to adjust their prices to entice more politicians in. Fifteen pounds often became the standard rate for a meal, no matter how cheap or expensive it really was.[2]

'If I knew it was after half past seven, I knew I could get a meal for fifteen quid,' Ronnie explains. 'I've seen me get paid fifteen quid for a meal and it were two minutes after half past seven. And I've seen me getting a one refused because it was a minute before half past seven.'

'I still go in,' he says of the Kennington Tandoori. 'I was in last night . . . I still have a little bit of supper.'

Despite everything that the expenses scandal taught MPs about responsibility, Ronnie's notion of fairness still appears to be entirely dictated by whatever the rules say. 'That's fair because it's claimable,' he explains. 'We could claim it.' He felt entitled to his curry and, technically, he probably was. Rules is rules. But shouldn't we expect higher standards from our politicians, even if they are 'within the rules'? Even if claiming curries on expenses was understandable before the scandal, nowadays it's just baffling.

'If I was an MP, I'd be worried about the perception,' I tell him.

'I think some MPs never bothered claiming,' Ronnie says. 'And I says "well as long as it's legit. As long as it's right and you're never going to get wrong for it".'

'And you think that's right?' I ask.

'Well if it was legit and that's what they were paying, that's fine. That's legit . . . Good God, if it wasn't legit, you wouldn't have get paid!'

This money didn't even make a difference to him financially – he just claimed it because he could. 'To me it was neither here or there, fifteen quid,' he admits. 'I mean I used it once/twice a week if I was lucky.' 'Lucky' is the key word here; it was a perk, not a necessity.

He goes on: 'The public would say "no, give them nowt, they can pay for it from their own wages". And I accept that,' he says. 'But at the minute, we're lucky enough to get it paid. I'm not going to argue with them.'

There is a funny inconsistency in his argument: although he reckons he was justified to claim for his chicken curry, he also says IPSA made the right decision when it finally scrapped food allowances in 2015. 'In a little way I'm pleased that it has [been cut], because it was more of an irritant than anything else,' he says. So if he didn't want to claim for food, why did he bother?

As we talk, I worry that Ronnie's views on expenses are still widespread in Westminster. He accepts that reforms were needed and even supports IPSA. But he doesn't seem to have grasped the core reason behind public outrage over expenses. People weren't angry so much because of the lax regulations – we were angry because we got a rare glimpse of MPs' personal ethical standards. Whatever the official rules say, we have our own sense of right and wrong. And we can tell when MPs are taking the piss.

Ronnie neatly sums up the situation, as MPs see it: 'People do think they're entitled to certain things, which they cannae get, because they know that other Members of Parliament throughout Europe gets them. Unfortunately for us, we were caught on a disk,' he says, referring to the leaked expenses files.

This is a man who has not moved on from the past. His eyes still light up when he talks about the free stuff he got on expenses. He genuinely doesn't seem to understand why the public might not be cool with it.

By now Ronnie is really getting into the swing of chatting about his expenses. He seems almost nostalgic about the things he used to get. So I ask him whether he claimed anything particularly fancy under the old system. 'I've got something nice because I had the money to do it,' he tells me. 'I had me allocation and when I wanted a three-piece suite I said "well, I've got at least three or four thousand pounds here I can get a nice three seater . . . and a double seater." Which I did.'[3]

He adds: 'I've still got me bed, I've still got me three-piece suite . . . I've moved a couple of times, but I've still got the original furniture.'

Like many MPs, he moved out of his own London flat when the rules changed and started renting a place instead. The new rules banned claims for mortgage interest payments, but they could still get rent covered on expenses. So, with renting now more cost-effective than mortgages, politicians quickly sold off their old taxpayer-subsidised houses and pocketed the profits.

Ronnie admits he made 'about thirty thousand profit' when he sold his house. He now lives just down the road in another flat, courtesy of the taxpayer. He explains: 'I've had to sell it. I've made a little profit – and that's mine, not yours. And I'm charging you, now, one thousand two hundred quid [for rent].'[4] His main regret about this appears to be that he didn't manage to make even *more* profit.

'I had a cleaner. Now I've got to clean the flat me-bloody-self!' he complains. 'I've got to go round with a hoover and a duster and clean the bath, the toilet! Ay my God! . . . [My wife] comes down, I always get it in the neck – cos, like all men, I just mop it up! It's a typical man's flat!'[5]

What makes Ronnie's ranting all the more cringe-worthy is that he partly blames the public for the flaws in the new system. The changes brought in after 2009 were a result of 'the knee-jerk reaction of the people', he says. The reforms were rushed though, allowing MPs like him to cash in on the profit from their subsidised houses. 'If they had of stopped and thought for a little bit,' he says.

'I wonder whether the public have really ever moved on,' I ask.

'Well *my* public did, cos they elected us again and again and again. So I was alright at the end of the day . . .

'I *think* they've moved on,' he adds. 'There isn't any more scandals.'

The expenses furore was the biggest upset in Westminster for years, yet even that has not made politicians stop and think about what they're claiming. They still don't get it. MPs from across the political spectrum are still filing petty claims that they don't need, which (rightly or wrongly) can leave a bad impression with the public.

One Labour MP tells me the temptation to claim is just too great. 'If I say to you "every month you can claim X hundred pounds for food," are you looking me in the eye and telling me that you would say "no, I think that is inappropriate, I'm not"?' she says.

As if to prove the point, I received an email with an interesting document attached. A scanned copy of a receipt which had been filed with IPSA. I copied down the address that was written on it and jumped on the Tube.

A short walk from Westminster Station, I met Zach, who works behind the till at Yum Yum, a Chinese takeaway with a zero-star hygiene rating.[6] Zach is used to serving up food for politicians. 'We do Foreign Office delivery,' he says. 'They're always ordering big orders. Individually they come in here as well.' But he doesn't think highly of them: 'I don't like politicians, man. But this is our job,' he says.

According to the document I'd been sent, one of those individuals was Simon Danczuk – the prominent Labour MP who was suspended by the party in January 2016 over sordid allegations about his private life. Like Ronnie Campbell, he also rents a home in London which is subsidised on expenses.[7]

Yet, despite being near his own cooker at home, he turned to the Yum Yum takeaway for his dinner, at just before 10 p.m. one December night in 2014. For £15.40, he got a chicken curry, hot-and-sour soup and ribs. He kept hold of the receipt and charged the taxpayer.[8]

Benefit scroungers?

Wealthy people claiming tiny amounts that they don't need might look petty at the best of times. But at a time when the government is targeting so-called 'benefit scroungers', it seems incredible. The MP John Mann has said: 'The rule in Parliament seems to be the richer you are, the more you don't just watch the pennies but claim the pennies.'[9] But while some of these small bills do, clearly, represent a money-grabbing culture, the issue is far more nuanced than many let on. The media can be too quick to jump to conclusions about politicians.

Most of us would agree that MPs shouldn't have to fund their offices out of their own money. They shouldn't have to pay for all the stationery themselves. But the way IPSA's expenses system works means that every individual cost is registered as a separate claim. The result is that small claims can end up looking miserly – even if they're not.

Take David Cameron, for instance. Records from IPSA show that he claimed back 7p on expenses for a bulldog clip.[10] Likewise, Francis Maude claimed 5p for a pencil sharpener while he was the government's paymaster general. Several others put in claims for 2p pencil sharpeners.[11]

The media reaction to this type of story has been predictable: MPs are 'squeezing every last penny out of the taxpayer', according to the *Mail*.[12] But it seems unfair to label this as miserly scrounging. They are in a different category altogether from the likes of Ronnie Campbell's curry.

Campbell *deliberately* chose to exploit a perk and cash in on a free meal. But it's hard to imagine the prime minister filing a 7p claim just so he could claw back the coppers. Healthy cynicism is one thing, but the debate over expenses can easily spill out into spin and name-calling. After all, the chances are that Cameron and Maude don't even look at these expenses claims themselves – they would have been sent off by their staff.

One Tory MP tells me: 'Stationery is annoying because you buy a packet of paper clips and it all just goes through automatically. And then you discover you've claimed for 35p. And that's so irritating because that is so easily a little news story about mean MPs. You probably could find I've claimed for some of those very small things.'

With so many expenses claims to process, it's easy to imagine how things might slip through the net occasionally. However, if politicians are serious about making a good impression, they should be more careful.

Take the Labour stalwart Paul Flynn, for instance, who has campaigned hard against sleaze and corruption for years. Within the context of Parliament, he's undoubtedly one of the good guys in this story. And when I meet him in his Westminster office, he rattles on about lobbying (which 'we've done bugger all about') and criticises MPs' sense of entitlement. But he openly admits getting confused by IPSA's new expenses scheme.

'It was hugely complicated,' he says. 'When it started out I never really understood the system. I'd be going through it and there's all these various categories – I mean dozens and dozens of categories – of things that you never use.'

Flynn is quite adamant that he doesn't claim for anything small or petty. The six or seven hundred Christmas cards he sends each year are paid for out of his own pocket. 'You have to buy them, you have to put the stamps on,' he says. 'You can't put that down as an expense. But people have.'

'You don't think there's an excuse for that?' I ask.

'. . . No, it's never a legitimate expense.' He explains that he gets his assistant to do all his expenses for him, saying: 'It's something you shouldn't do, but I trust her absolutely.'

As the interview progresses, Flynn begins to panic. Midway through, he calls his assistant in to check that she does indeed know the score. 'I've just thought about this,' he says to her. 'We haven't had an in-depth discussion about this . . . We're just talking about people claiming for poppies and things. But I mean, you're well aware of this – that we don't claim for things like that – aren't you?'

The assistant reassures him and he turns back to me. 'It's a relief we've got staff who do it for us. But you're responsible anyway,' he adds. 'I'm just worrying now, thinking now if we understand we don't put in for tiny amounts.'

Actually, Flynn did make one rather embarrassing expenses claim, which has so far gone unnoticed. In August 2013, his close friend and colleague Ron Jones died after giving fifty years of service as a councillor in Newport, south Wales. The two had first met in 1972, when Flynn joined the same council.

At his funeral in a local Roman Catholic church, more than six hundred people turned up to pay their respects. Paul Flynn drove the short four-mile journey to the funeral, from his constituency office and gave the eulogy. 'He was a unique politician unlike others,' he told the congregation. 'Rest in peace, comrade.'[13]

So close was their friendship that Flynn also dedicated a blog post to Jones on his website, calling him a 'loyal and dedicated comrade' and a 'generous friend'.[14]

What makes the situation awkward, however, is that after making his heartfelt eulogy, Flynn claimed £1.80 on expenses for the petrol he'd used to drive to the funeral.[15] The claim form clearly states: 'Cllr Ron Jones Funeral'.

Flynn tells me it was 'a mistake by a member of staff of which I had no knowledge or consent'. And you'd have to be a real cynic not to believe him.[16] He points out, also, that this gives a 'misleading impression', because he actually under-claims for lots of other items.[17]

But the fact remains: if Parliament wants to win back public trust over expenses, claims like this need to be prevented. Every MP says they're being extra vigilant after the scandal and only claim what they really need to. Yet drill down into the details and you'll find, time after time, that they continue to make claims that appear (on the face of it, at least) to be 'penny-pinching'. If they're so keen to prove they've learned from the scandal, why aren't these embarrassing claims rooted out?

Flynn is not the only politician who has claimed expenses to drive to a funeral. Graeme Morrice, who lost his seat in 2015, put in claims covering petrol expenses to attend four separate funerals in 2013 alone. He made the claims despite each one being under £5. The lowest was just £2.25: a five-mile journey to the funeral of one of his own constituents. Morrice also billed taxpayers 90p when he visited a local foodbank, and another 90p to drive two miles down the road to a curry night with local business leaders. Then, come Remembrance Sunday, he filed a £1.70 expenses claim after driving to a nearby memorial service.[18]

One politician, John Cruddas, even tried to claim back £30 on a bunch of white flowers he'd bought for a funeral. The flowers were sent along to the service in Essex with a message attached: 'With deepest sympathy, John Cruddas MP,' it said.[19] However, when IPSA saw the documents, his expenses claim was rejected.

Others are buying cheap drinks and snacks for their hard-working interns and volunteers, and then billing the taxpayer. John Denham filed a 45p claim for a volunteer's bottle of water. And Margot James asked for 85p cashback for some lightly salted popcorn.[20] Meanwhile, the Tory MP Geoffrey Cox sent IPSA a receipt for a 45p bottle of milk that someone had bought from the Co-op.[21] A few months later, Cox was ranked as the second-highest earner outside the Commons, raking in more than £820,000 a year from moonlighting, on top of his MP's salary.[22]

Silly claims like these are still occasionally exposed in the press, but politicians don't seem to change their ways. Recently, the *Sun* branded an MP 'dead cheap' for claiming petrol costs to drive to constituents' funerals.[23] And in 2015, the *Metro* newspaper reported how another MP, Rob Wilson, claimed 9p for a 0.2-mile drive to a meeting that was on the same street as his own house. 'You might have thought that MPs would have learned not to make ridiculous expenses claims,' said the paper. 'But no.'[24]

Incredibly, Wilson defended his 9p claim, saying that 'over a year the mileage does add up'. He said: 'I can see how small claims might look odd but it is important that all MPs do the job properly and stay connected with local people . . . I have never claimed a single penny in accommodation expenses despite late Commons sittings. However, as I do commute most days it does mean I incur parking and mileage expenses instead.'[25]

Yes, the boundary between what's acceptable and what's not isn't always clear. But the solution is simple: if in doubt, leave it out. If MPs are serious about winning back public trust, how about buying your own funeral flowers and going easy on the curry? Claiming expenses isn't compulsory. You don't need to claim it just because you can.

The reason petty claims still persist cannot be put down to mistakes and bureaucracy alone. There is a sense of entitlement that seeks to justify billing taxpayers for anything and everything, no matter how ridiculous.

Poppy poppycock

When they're talking anonymously, political insiders will happily defend expenses claims for small items.

Perhaps the most politically embarrassing small expense that politicians have claimed repeatedly is for poppies and wreaths. During the expenses scandal, Boris Johnson and ex-shadow chancellor Ed Balls were both exposed for claiming money to cover Remembrance Sunday wreaths.[26] More recently, in 2015, Labour MP Sarah Champion was also caught claiming £17 for a poppy wreath.[27]

When they're named and shamed in the press, these politicians cower, grovel and apologise. They blame it on admin errors and quickly pay the money back. But here's what some Westminster insiders really think about poppies:

> I spent a bloody fortune over the last couple of years on poppies . . . You'll get a kicking if you're not wearing a poppy – like in the press or wherever. So you always have to make sure you're wearing one. But then you change your suit the next day and you forget. You're getting on the tube in and you think 'oh for fuck's sake, I've left the poppy on the other suit'. So you've got to go and buy another one.
>
> It's not very much money, but over the course of bloody November, or whatever . . . it's not tons but, ask anyone . . . It's only a few quid but it's going to add up.
>
> Senior special adviser

When the council leader puts it down, he doesn't pay for it. When the commanding officer of the air force cadets puts it down, he doesn't pay for it. When the British Legion guy puts it down, he doesn't pay for it personally. But it is expected that MPs will. Also, there's a fair number of funerals you go to as an MP and on the whole a wreath is appreciated . . . A lot of MPs are very, very short of money, but there's no point moaning about it.[28]

Ex minister

People always moan about MPs claiming for poppies, right? And you go 'oh my god, how disgusting'. But remember, they have to buy ten of these bloody things, and they cost about £6 a pop for these big wreaths . . . So [sometimes] they can't actually afford it, unless they're millionaires. But even if they are millionaires, why should they?

The poppy wreaths thing is interesting because, one sense is, at a gut level you go of course you don't [claim expenses for it]. It's a sign of respect. On the other side of it, you're asking people to pay a massive chunk of their salary on something . . . A lot of MPs just feel slightly put upon that they earn less than they probably should, that they're never allowed to take a pay rise, and then they're expected to pay for all these things. A lot of them just go 'sod it, I'm claiming for this stuff as an expense'.

Former special adviser in Downing Street

Big spenders

I can't tell you where I'm going: MPs say it would be a breach of privacy. I'm not supposed to have the address either. But, with a bit of detective work, it was easy to figure it out.

Following my map, I arrive at a glitzy hotel, not far from the Houses of Parliament. I don't have a booking, but I fancy a nosey around. You see, according to some new documents I've been given, this hotel is where dozens of MPs choose to spend the night. Their bills are claimed on expenses and charged to the taxpayer.

I walk in through the main entrance and sneak down one of the side corridors. At the end is a lobby with eight lifts. I get in one and go up to the top floor.

Here, the views are spectacular: Big Ben and the River Thames sparkle in the early evening lights. Around me, a labyrinth of silent corridors are illuminated in low-level lighting giving a futuristic feel. Eventually, I find my way down to one of the restaurants, where I sit and read a magazine while smartly dressed waiters serve cocktails to the tables around me. Just buying a drink and a sandwich here can set you back £67. I decide to give it a miss.

This is by no means the most luxurious hotel in the world, but it's certainly pretty plush. Guests get free access to a swimming pool, sauna, steam room and gym. There's also a 'paradise' spa where you can get full beauty treatments.

But for lots of politicians, this place has become their second home. Under the new expenses system, MPs can claim up to £150 for every night they stay here.

With many other expenses curbed by IPSA's new rules, hotels are one of the few things remaining that MPs can really go to town on. In one year alone, they claimed more than £700,000. The vast majority of this bill was for places in London, rather than overseas travel.[1] And the hotel chain I was in is probably the most popular of them all, having made at least £127,000 out of our trusted politicians over the course of a single year.[2]

There is one MP in particular who has really maxed up his bills at this hotel: the Conservatives' Andrew Bridgen. When his wife left him a few years ago, Bridgen ditched his Westminster flat and adopted this very hotel as his new pad. One year, he stayed here for 45% of the time – a total of 165 nights.[3] Inevitably, Bridgen racked up a huge bill, amounting to nearly £25,000. Then, he claimed it back on expenses.[4]

This is the same Andrew Bridgen who proudly told me: 'I used to earn a million pounds a year.' Yet here he was charging taxpayers for his hotels. His bills have gone down somewhat lately, but he still frequents the same place.

After the expenses scandal, it's hard for politicians to justify any claims that might look lavish. But when I ask Bridgen if it's acceptable for MPs to claim £150 a night for hotels, I hit a nerve.

'I mean, what do you want?' he snaps. 'We could get some cardboard boxes and kip out on the bridge at Waterloo Station. That would be handy, although we might look a bit of a mess when we arrive to work the next morning. Might not be presentable. Where do you want us to go?'

'Is it a nice hotel?' he laughs. 'No, it's bloody awful. I'd rather be at home.'

Bridgen sees nothing distasteful about the fact that he – and many of his colleagues – charge taxpayers for his second life in a hotel. He reckons it's 'cheaper than having a flat', and adds: 'I stay at the [hotel] because it's a quick walk. When we finish late at night – just walk home.'

Yet, for many people, no amount of economic rationale will justify MPs funding fancy hotel stays off expenses. Again, it's not the money; it's the principle. Indeed, when the expenses scandal hit in 2009, the most controversial claims were not always the most expensive ones. Rather, public anger derived from the fact that politicians appeared so greedy.

But this kind of practice continues. A close look at IPSA's files reveals that MPs claimed more than £156,000 on hotels in the first two months after the 2015 General Election. They included a string of high-class establishments.

Among them were two Tory MPs – Mike Wood and Andrew Turner – who enjoyed nights at London hotels owned by the Ritz-Carlton chain, together claiming more than £500 on expenses.[5] The Ritz-Carlton group owns three places in London, all of which describe themselves as 'luxury' hotels: the Bulgari, the London Edition hotel and the Ritz hotel itself.[6] 'Live London's charm at the capital's most iconic hotel, The Ritz,' says the website. 'Nestled between the attractive neighbourhoods of Mayfair and St James, the five-star luxury hotel is synonymous with prestige.'[7]

In another case, the disgraced former Labour minister Eric Joyce racked up a £426 bill for two nights in a hotel in Glasgow, before he left Parliament in 2015. It was just forty minutes' drive from his own constituency.[8] The Hotel du Vin describes itself as a 'luxury boutique hotel with that little bit more', adding: 'The most famous of Glasgow's hotels has an enviable reputation for service and style, with forty-nine stunning bedrooms and suites, bistro, bar, cigar shack and whisky room.'[9] Afterwards, Joyce kept hold of his receipt and tried to claim back part of it on expenses. He was rebuffed by IPSA who told him it did not fall under the scheme.[10]

Conservative Chris Skidmore successfully claimed £150 expenses for a stay at the Crowne Plaza in London.[11] And his colleague, Jack Lopresti, claimed £750 for several nights spent at one of the Marriott hotels in London, over the course of three months.[12] On the Labour side, Gordon Brown's former Treasury minister, Liam Byrne, charged taxpayers a total of £1,361 in 2014 after staying in London hotels operated by Hilton.[13]

It's important to see this in context. In 2013, Parliament decided that ordinary families have no right to a spare room at the public expense. They introduced the 'bedroom tax', saying it was a luxury we can't afford. But many of those same MPs see no inconsistency in claiming for all the pointless luxury that comes with one of these hotel rooms.

The imbalance is even apparent within Westminster itself. Plenty of other MPs make do with cheaper hotels. While their colleagues spend £150 a night for a room, they just check into places like the

Travelodge or Premier Inn. Meanwhile, lots of Parliament's back-room workers have a completely different lifestyle altogether.

While Andrew Bridgen is settling down in a comfy hotel, where do his own staff spend the night?

As my interview with Bridgen draws to a close, he suddenly reveals something that adds a whole new level of craziness to his hotel stays: his staff get absolutely nothing.

'I don't have any staff in London,' he says, explaining that his people are all based in Leicestershire. 'They travel down two days a week, stay overnight. They have to fund their own staying over-night, because that's not funded under expenses – even though, because they're not based in London, they're paid less.

'But they come down and work for me two days in London – stay at their own expense down here – and then go back and then work in the constituency the rest of the time.'

How does Bridgen justify this? 'It'll save the country a fortune,' he says. 'I claim a lot less than my allowance for staff because I don't need them, but I do like to have them here two days a week, yeah? So they're peripatetic. They move.

'I'm the only MP who does that,' he says proudly. 'And my staff can't claim expenses.'[14]

'How do they survive?' I ask, horrified.

'Harpreet's a Sikh lady – lovely – and she stays with a relative. And Woody stops in one of these Easy hotels which . . . it's like being in a morgue apparently, they just sort of slide him in.'

The contrast between these two worlds is stark. A millionaire MP staying in a £150-a-night hotel, paid on expenses, while his personal staff have to crash the night in spare rooms and budget digs paid out of their own meagre wages. It's quite literally a case of one rule for them, another rule for everyone else.

I ask Bridgen: 'Do they mind that they can't claim for that, when you and other MPs can claim lots of expenses?'

'It seems wrong to me, when that's the way I choose to run my office,' he admits. Yet he is the only MP who subjects staff to this type of setup. Doesn't he take any responsibility for this?

'We run it very efficiently: our emails are always out on time,' he says, trying to justify it. 'I believe I've got the most efficient parliamentary office – or one of them anyway. But, I mean, there's no flexibility in the expenses system to say "that's the way I chose to run it, I think I'm saving the taxpayer a lot of money". I've got good staff, they're very loyal. But if they weren't willing to do that, my system wouldn't work.'

When I ask IPSA about Bridgen's situation, it suggests he might be being needlessly harsh on his staff. Whether deliberately or accidentally, he seems to have misunderstood the rules. He is, in fact, allowed to claim hotel expenses on behalf of his staff – but the claims must be signed off by Bridgen himself.[15]

He can blame IPSA all he likes, but it's his own decision to claim £150 a night in a hotel. And it's his own decision to run his office in a way that means his staff lose out financially.

The mindset Bridgen adopts is one that can justify (or at least excuse) some of Parliament's most outlandish expenses claims. The public are going to hate you, the logic goes, so you shouldn't take their outrage too seriously. Just get on with the job and claim up to the max.

Bridgen compares current public attitudes over expenses to historical cases of public discontent, trying to prove the point that people will never be happy. He gives the example of the Great Fire of 1834, which burned down most of Parliament: 'When the building was getting going, and the flames were licking up, crowds appeared on the south bank of the Thames cheering and shouting "lock the doors",' Bridgen says. His conclusion? 'Perhaps it's not as bad as it used to be.'

Generation rent

Most MPs don't live their lives out of hotels. But that doesn't mean their lifestyles aren't still fuelled by taxpayer cash.

Rents in London are notoriously expensive and buying a flat of your own is out of the question for most young people. In summer 2015, the average monthly rent in the capital hit £1,500. But MPs need to live somewhere convenient for work and we shouldn't expect it to come cheap. Still, if they already have a main home in the constituency, maybe a bog-standard one-bedroom flat would be sufficient for weekdays. But no. Dozens treat the average as the bare minimum.

Using the Freedom of Information Act, I unearthed copies of some of the housing contracts that politicians have signed. At the top of the pile of big spenders are MPs like Simon Danczuk, who has claimed £2,142 per month for rent. In a letter to IPSA, he said this was 'within my budget'. But it wasn't him who was paying – it was the taxpayer.[16] His rent claims come on top of any other accommodation expenses he might choose to claim, like electricity, council tax and a TV licence.

Another MP, Ian Paisley Jr., used to claim £2,592 a month on rent, which you might think was enough. But in September 2015, he signed a new contract, worth £2,925 a month.[17]

Government minister George Freeman has been charging taxpayers £2,817 for a room in Bloomsbury. Meanwhile, his colleague in the Home Office, Karen Bradley, moved into a shared property in Little Venice, a picturesque part of west London. She claimed the £2,167 monthly rent on expenses.[18]

One new Labour MP, Marie Rimmer, managed to fix up her accommodation before she was even elected. Documents suggest she was given the keys to her Westminster flat a month before the 2015 General Election. Her set-up meant she wouldn't miss a day of expenses. Indeed, one of Rimmer's rent claims is dated for the very next day after the election.

Even extortionate allowances are not enough for some politicians. One Tory minister quit his job in 2014, complaining that expenses did 'not allow me to rent a flat that could accommodate my family'. He said: 'It doesn't stretch anywhere near the cost of renting a flat in Westminster.'[19] Living in a cheaper part of town and getting the bus to work was obviously not considered as an option.

If MPs' rent claims aren't excessive enough, it turns out that some of them are cashing in twice. Many own properties in London, but rent another place out on expenses, regardless. This allows them to operate a double-rent system: Flat One is where the MP lives, with rent covered by expenses; Flat Two is the place they actually own, where they act as a landlord and rent it out to other people.

Research done in 2015 by *Channel 4 News* found that at least forty-six MPs had this kind of system in place – a move which one Labour backbencher described to me as 'a new fiddle'. Channel 4 reported:

> Our investigation found many of the MPs bought their London properties with the help of the taxpayer when the previous expenses system allowed them to claim back mortgage payments.
>
> But when those claims were banned following the expenses scandal they switched to letting out their properties, in some cases for up to £3,000 a month. They then started claiming expenses for rent and hotels in the capital.[20]

Among those identified in the report was Chris Bryant, the shadow leader of the House of Commons. He had already bought a penthouse in London back in 2005 and claimed around £1,000 a month in mortgage claims under the old system.

But after the expenses scandal he started renting the property out. It's since been advertised by estate agents as having a private lift and a porter, with rent at about £3,000 a month. Meanwhile, Bryant moved into a new flat and claimed his own rent on expenses, charging taxpayers more than £35,000 over two years.[21]

In an article about the 'new fiddle', the *Guardian* noted: 'Although the practice does not break any rules, it fuels concerns that politicians are still able to profit from Commons allowances.'[22]

'Downright frivolous'

Gloriana is an opera by Benjamin Britten. Originally written to celebrate the coronation of Queen Elizabeth II, it's now considered one of the composer's finest operatic works. So when a performance of it was put on in the Royal Opera House recently, the speaker of the House of Lords, Baroness D'Souza, decided to go along. She was accompanied by the chairman of the Federation Council of Russia.

It was only later, when the Press Association made enquiries under the Freedom of Information Act, that it was revealed the baroness had charged taxpayers £230 for her night at the opera.[23] A chauffeur-driven Mercedes took D'Souza to the event in Covent Garden, just one mile from the Houses of Parliament. The driver then sat outside for four hours waiting for the concert to finish, before taxiing her back to Parliament again. The bills were paid on expenses. If she'd caught the Tube, it would have cost £4.60.[24]

As you'd expect, when the story broke, there was much seething and fuming in the press. The Taxpayers' Alliance, a right-wing pressure group, labelled it 'downright frivolous' and the *Sun* said it was 'shocking'.[25] But extravagant and frivolous expenses claims like this should not be much of a surprise.

Because there has never been a root-and-branch change of Parliament's culture after the expenses scandal, the system is still open to abuse. Politicians like D'Souza, who want to exploit the perks, are still relatively free to do so.

The night at the opera was just one of a catalogue of D'Souza's controversial expenses receipts that the Press Association had got hold of. Others included a £627 chauffeur bill to drive to the enthronement of Archbishop Justin Welby in 2013. She attended with John Bercow, the speaker of the House of Commons, but the pair took separate cars for the same trip. Bercow claimed an additional £525 for the journey.[26]

Ridiculous claims are even filed by top government figures. Among the many receipts I uncovered was one from the health secretary, Jeremy Hunt. In 2014, he used his expenses to buy expensive designer glasses for his staff.

Official work guidelines say that employers should *contribute* to the cost of specs, if staff need them to use a computer. But the health secretary filed claims on behalf of his staff covering the entire cost. Documents show that one of his staff visited Chandlers Opticians in Surrey and bought a £275 pair of glasses, which Hunt then billed to taxpayers. The glasses were eleven times the price of Specsavers' cheapest pair. The opticians' practice is run by a bloke called Stephen, who has a 'flair for fashion', according to the website. So rest assured that Hunt's assistant is now looking incredibly stylish![27] A second opticians' bill for another staff member was also filed on Hunt's expenses. This time, it covered a £25 eye test and a £180 pair of glasses.

It seems Hunt was fully aware that the expenses claim was being made. He told me: 'In advance of submitting the claim, my office checked it specifically with IPSA to ensure that everything was being done in the proper way – and we would contest any allegation to the contrary.'[28]

It may have been within the rules, but the health secretary ducked my question: was it *appropriate*?[29] Of course, Hunt was only following in the footsteps of his predecessor at the Department for Health, Andrew Lansley, who claimed £229 for prescription glasses and eye test costs for an adviser in 2013.[30]

Expenses claims like this leave some insiders less than impressed. 'When you employ staff in a business, you don't pay for their fucking glasses,' one ex-MP says. 'Literally unbelievable!'

So what's the best way to police an expenses system? The dilemma may be familiar to any business manager: set up a system that relies on trust and some people will be untrustworthy (most of them, in this case); but go the other way and impose strict rules and they will play those rules. Tell them they can claim up to a maximum, and that maximum soon becomes a target to be aimed at. There is no technical fix. So does that mean we should just get used to it?

Even the most cynical of us would probably agree that our democratic representatives should be held to a higher standard. This is not a business – it's Parliament. Surely we can expect them to stick to the rules *and* exercise some degree of personal judgement as well? Is that really too much to ask?

Money for old robe

'Are there still lavish expenses in the House of Lords?' I asked a Conservative peer.

'There aren't any,' came the reply. 'You can't make outlandish expenses claims because it's a limited sum of money.' So that's that sorted, then.

The scariest thing about the House of Lords expenses system is that it looks fine. At first and second glance, it really does look completely reformed. There's certainly been a dramatic shake-up. Most peers can now only claim expenses for three core categories:

- An allowance given to them for each day they turn up in Parliament
- Travel to get to Westminster
- Basic expenses for certain overseas travel

It seems reasonable. But the devil is in the detail.

Taxpayers fork out £18m a year for the attendance allowance alone.[1] It currently stands at a generous £300 a day, which is about four times the London Living Wage.[2] But it gets better: the allowance isn't taxed, because it's not technically regarded as a 'salary'. Even when you factor in peers who opt out of the allowance, it still works out as an average cost of £260 per peer, *per day*.[3]

Meanwhile, the travel expenses look completely dull and unremarkable when they're published in a huge spreadsheet online – as you can probably imagine. Everything about it screams 'no scandal here'. It's only when you get your hands on the original receipts that things start to liven up a bit. And – using the Freedom of Information Act again – we can do just that.

*   *   *

When an urgent debate is called in Westminster during recess, expenses go through the roof. If a politician wants to speak, or even just watch the debate, they can claim thousands of pounds to get there. It doesn't matter whether they're travelling from Croydon or Kraków. The rules state: 'Should the House be recalled during a Parliamentary recess, Members may recover the costs necessarily incurred in attending a sitting of the House, including the cost of travel from overseas.'[4]

So when Parliament was recalled in September 2014, for an urgent debate on tackling ISIS in Iraq, the Lib Dem peer Brian Paddick had no qualms about flying over from New York to attend.

Paddick is a former senior officer at Scotland Yard and once ran for London Mayor. Now getting on for sixty, he is the Lib Dem spokesman for home affairs in the House of Lords.[5] Paddick clearly thinks he has an important contribution to make in politics, which is why he felt justified to travel 3,500 miles for a single parliamentary debate. You be the judge of whether it was worth it.

Information about his trip had been deeply buried from the public and only became apparent after a long trawl through expenses data. After spotting that he'd claimed for a flight, I then tracked down copies of his original travel documents.

The file reveals in meticulous detail how Paddick flew back from his US trip in style – an overnight flight from New York's JFK Airport at 7 p.m. the night before the debate. Paddick flew with British Airways and booked himself into the so-called 'Club World' cabin, seat 06B.

Club World is BA's long-haul business-class service. It 'combines premium levels of comfort and service with the freedom and flexibility to make every journey unique and unforgettable'.[6] A ticket will get you everything you could ask for: a seat that converts into a completely flat bed, access to 'private lounges and luxurious spa treatments', food and drink options, and priority boarding. BA also chucks in a quilted blanket, a memory-foam headrest and a 'luxury amenity kit with Elemis skincare products'. When you land at Heathrow, your ticket will also get you access to 'a luxury facial treatment or relaxing massage'.[7]

Paddick landed in London just after 7 a.m., on the day of the debate and made his way over to the House of Lords. Whether he had time to fit in a quick massage beforehand, I don't know. But by 11:40, Parliament had begun proceedings for the day.

Paddick was among a rabble of fifty-eight peers who requested to speak about ISIS. 'The debate for us to contribute to, is how we keep the British people safe from the threat posed by ISIL [aka ISIS],' their Lordships were told. 'In particular, what role our Armed Forces should play in the international coalition to dismantle and ultimately destroy what President Obama has rightly called "this network of death".'[8]

It wasn't until mid-afternoon that Paddick finally got his time in the spotlight. It must have been a big moment for him. After all, this is what his entire trip from New York had been about. But when he finally stood up, the best that can be said about his speech is that it was short – 446 words, in fact.

'The term "Islamic terrorism" is a contradiction in terms,' he told his colleagues, making a simple point that had already been widely aired. 'It gives a wholly false impression of Islam.'[9]

Then he turned to the prospect of military action, which he helpfully pointed out was 'a very serious issue with very serious consequences'.

Finally, he closed by offering these supreme words of wisdom: 'In my *professional experience as a police officer*, the overwhelming majority of Muslims in this country are law-abiding and peace-loving.'[10] (As if you need 'professional experience' as a copper in order to reach this hopefully obvious conclusion!)

And that was that.

He packed up and went back to New York for the rest of his trip. His return flight on British Airways left from Heathrow that evening. He paid for the Club World cabin again. Seat 15F.

The following month, Brian Paddick filled out a form. He was claiming back expenses for all the money that he'd spent on the flights.

And the total bill? £8,897.84.

The House of Lords authorities approved his claim and he cashed the money, courtesy of the taxpayer.[11]

You're welcome, Brian.

After I got hold of his travel documents, I contacted Paddick to ask whether he thought his claim had been appropriate. Did he want to explain himself? His response was short and to-the-point. 'No comment,' he said. And with that, he deleted me on Twitter.[12]

Here's another example of outright extravagance in the House of Lords.

In 2009, Lord Taylor of Blackburn became the first peer to be suspended from Parliament since the seventeenth century, alongside his Labour colleague, Lord Truscott. The pair were caught in an undercover sting – reportedly prepared to change legislation in exchange for money. Both men escaped criminal investigation because the police said it was too difficult to obtain evidence.[13] However, a House of Lords inquiry later found there was 'comprehensive' evidence against Taylor and said his defence was 'implausible'.[14] He was kicked out of Parliament for six months.

But then he came back. No questions asked. And now he's found a different way to cash in from the House of Lords.

From his home in Blackburn, the drive to Westminster takes at least four hours. But that hasn't deterred this disgraced peer from showing his face. In the space of just two months – in the quieter summer period between June and July 2014 – Taylor turned up for an impressive thirty-five days in the House of Lords.

Each day he was there, Taylor pocketed the maximum £300 allowance. That would have been more than enough to cover hotels and food. But instead, he took the money and repeatedly drove back and forth from his home. Meanwhile, he filed separate claims for his petrol expenses.

In two months, Lord Taylor made eighteen trips between London and Blackburn, which he said was a 248-mile drive. For each trip, he claimed £111.60 travel expenses, on top of his daily allowance. Over the period he managed to rack up a £12,508 bill, which was charged to taxpayers. The claims were approved, for the privilege of having him in Parliament. Authorities clearly thought this was money well spent.

So what was this old rogue doing in Westminster that was so important? Erm . . . not much. According to official records, Lord Taylor didn't make any speeches or interventions throughout the two months.[15] And during this entire time, he only got around to voting once, on a new law about knives in schools.[16]

Back in 2009 he was given a free pass, when police decided not to launch a corruption investigation against him. Now, the House of Lords has welcomed him back with open arms, giving him another free pass to cash in thousands of pounds on expenses. Any justification for paying this guy's extortionate bills will be lost on most people.

Silent Lords

Peers don't have to do anything for their money. It's not quite the same as an actual job. They don't have to make a speech; they don't have to vote. They could spend most of the day in the tea room, if they fancy. All they have to do is turn up and walk to the chamber for their attendance to be noted. That – and that alone – entitles them to £300 a day, plus travel expenses. The rules state:

> A member is counted as having attended if they have been present on a given date at a sitting in the House of Lords chamber, at a Grand Committee or Select Committee sitting or if they have been recorded as voting in a division in the main chamber.[17]

'You just have to show your face to qualify for money,' one peer explains. 'It's possible for people to be here for a very short time, not do any work, and get the same amount of money as people who do.'

As you'd expect, this system is incredibly easy to abuse. And it regularly is. In 2013, the *Daily Mirror* managed to expose a lord in a 'clocking in' scandal. Lord Hanningfield had already been in trouble over expenses, having served a nine-month prison sentence in 2011 for fiddling his books and falsely claiming more than £13,000.[18] After being released, however, he was allowed back to the Lords where he started claiming again.

A secret video shot by the *Mirror* shows how the burly septuagenarian nips in and out of Parliament with just enough time to be registered, allowing him to then claim the £300 attendance allowance.

Here's the paper's account of what its journalists saw:

He appeared smart and professional, looking like he was ready to take on a day's work, possibly joining in an important debate in the main chamber. But after strolling through the House and getting his attendance recorded by the Journal Office, he was off again – leaving via the same entrance at 3.01 p.m.

Our video proves Hanningfield was inside just 24 minutes and five seconds to qualify for his £300 fee.[19]

In September 2015, it was announced that Hanningfield would be charged over the 'clocking in' allegations, which he denied.[20] He defended himself, saying: 'I've actually spent my whole life serving the taxpayer, and I am now trying to get back again.'[21]

However, at the eleventh hour before his trial, Parliament intervened and effectivley forced prosecutors to drop the case. House of Lords lawyers insisted that courts cannot rule on what activities constitute 'parliamentary work'. The judge explained: 'Parliament was saying it is a matter for us parliament to make that determination, not for the criminal court.'[22]

Not surprisingly, the *Mirror* accused the House of Lords of a stitch-up.[23] 'Parliament makes the laws by which the rest of us live,' it said, 'lawmakers must be punished if they are found to have broken them.'

Hanningfield may have been alone in having faced the prospect of court, but he's certainly not the only peer accused of milking the system. To get a sense of the scale of the problem, I started weaving together three different sets of data, which are all publicly available online. First, I took a copy of peers' expenses claims, using all the claims made in the 2014/15 parliamentary year.[24] These figures were then cross-referenced with two more sources: comprehensive voting data and a list of peers who didn't speak in the main Lords' chamber at all that year.[25]

Mix these together, and the result: Silent Lords.

The Silent Lord is a mysterious creature. They wield considerable political power and influence, but choose instead to ensure a steady trickle of money is flowing into their bank accounts. These are the unknowns of Parliament. Some of them are rarely ever sighted. If you're lucky, you might spot one entertaining pals in the tea room, or skulking off to the expenses office. They are the ancient reprobates who haunt Westminster like a bad dream. Even the most old-fashioned and unsavoury peers will tell you: they've got no time for the Silent Lords.

According to the data, there were forty-three peers who claimed expenses despite never speaking. These included the likes of Lord Taylor of Blackburn, who claimed £43,000 that year.[26]

Labour colleagues Lord Kirkhill and Baroness Smith of Gilmorehill put in £41,000 and £36,000 of claims respectively, without joining in any debates.[27] And Baroness Eccles of Moulton, from the Conservative Party, claimed £33,000.[28]

Together, this group of forty-three politicians claimed more than £621,600 in one year alone, without uttering a single word.[29]

Then, there are another thirty-four peers who may have spoken a few times, but didn't vote on any legislation. Among them is James Dalrymple, who goes by the name 'The Earl of Stair'. He turned up for just seventeen days of the year but claimed almost £14,000 on expenses, including more than £6,000 on air travel.[30] That's an average cost to the taxpayer of £798 per day. Throughout the time, he didn't vote on anything in the main chamber. And, for nineteen of those twenty days he remained silent. He only rose once, to make a short speech in the Scottish referendum debate.[31]

The gang of thirty-four non-voters filed expenses claims that added up to more than £130,000.[32]

There's a final group. These are the *completely* silent ones – peers who have neither spoken *nor* voted, but have still claimed expenses. There are eight peers who fell into this category, not including government office holders. I should point out, though, that a couple of them may have had a decent excuse (e.g. the man who died).

Here's what they claimed in 2014/15:

1. Lord Steyn (cross bench)   £11,250
2. Lord Lisvane (cross bench)*   £5,785
3. Lord Macfarlane of Bearsden (Conservative)   £5,320
4. Viscount Allenby of Megiddo (cross bench)†   £2,915
5. Duke of Somerset (cross bench)   £1,650
6. Lord Kerslake (cross bench)*   £900
7. Bishop of Leeds (bishops)*   £821
8. Lord Feldman (Conservative)‡   £150

* *Introduced to the Lords during the year*
† *Died during the year*
‡ *Not to be mistaken with Lord Feldman of Elstree*

Together these Silent Lords claimed £28,791 in one year. Parliamentary documents have no record of them contributing to any debates in the main chamber, or voting on anything. Yet their expenses were handed to them unquestioned.

Two of these peers have been named over the controversy before. The *Sun* ran a story about Steyn and Macfarlane in late 2015.[33] But details of their actual expenses, along with the other Silent Lords, have remained unreported.

One reason for this is that the Electoral Reform Society – which has been at the forefront of raising this issue – deliberately chooses not to publish the peers' names in its reports. One of its researchers tells me that the organisation's ethos is not one that likes 'pointing fingers at particular individuals – that's not our style'. She adds: 'For us it's a structural argument; for other people it can be quite personal.'

However, their expenses are well worth highlighting because they are just so ridiculous.

Lord Johan Steyn is a former law lord who now, in his eighties, is semi-retired. He lives in Fulham, just fifteen minutes' drive from Parliament, where he has a modest house on a quiet street. Steyn has not spoken in a Lords debate since June 2009 and last voted in 2013.[34] But he hasn't stopped claiming expenses. In 2014/15 he made the quick journey to Parliament a total of eighty-six times, pocketing £11,250 in expenses along the way.

Steyn's counterpart in silence, Lord Macfarlane, has a more extravagant expenses file. Based in Glasgow, the Conservative peer has charged taxpayers to regularly fly down to London. EasyJet and Ryanair both do the route for about £45 return, but Macfarlane prefers to fly with British Airways. According to the travel documents, he charges taxpayers up to £362 for a return flight.[35] And when he gets there, he doesn't speak or vote. There's also no record of him taking part in any committees in the Lords during the year 2014/15. Quite what he does in London is a mystery, but he cashes in regardless.

PART SIX:

Damage assessment

20

Confirmation

When you've been investigating something for ages, you begin to doubt yourself.

What if I'd got it all wrong? What if financial interests aren't a big problem in Westminster after all? Maybe I was being too puritanical about this whole thing.

It's at times like this when you want Parliament to turn around to you and say 'yes, this really is a problem'. And, luckily, that's exactly what happened.

It was early 2016 and, looking for confirmation about my concerns over financial interests, I began writing an anonymous survey. Over the next few days, I sent it out to every one of Parliament's 650 MPs. There were questions about salaries, expenses, lobbying and second jobs. I wanted to know what politicians really thought, without fear of being named and shamed.

Ironically, a lot of MPs refuse to do surveys unless they're paid. Big market research firms like Ipsos MORI and ComRes are prepared to pay for political insights – and it's a popular way among politicians to make a bit of pocket money. The Register of Interests mentions surveys no fewer than 405 times.[1] Conservative MP Peter Bone, for instance, has listed payments for completing sixteen surveys, earning anywhere between £10 and £200 a pop. In total, he's declared £1,350 from doing them.[2]

There was no money on offer for my survey. I also realised that certain MPs were more likely to respond than others: senior ministers may have less time, while those with more extreme opinions (at both ends of the spectrum) were likely to be more interested in the subject. Nonetheless, the final response rate was still pretty decent, at ten per cent.[3] Although the survey would not give a completely watertight analysis of attitudes, the sample was large enough to paint a picture.

As the responses trickled in, I stayed glued to my computer, reading each new comment with childish delight. Here, at last, were politicians' true, honest feelings about their earnings.

The very first MP to reply disagreed with the policy of every main political party over salaries. Behind the veil of anonymity, they said politicians weren't paid enough.

'Politicians aren't greedy, but the media unfairly distorts the truth,' they said.[4] This MP wanted to scrap IPSA. What's more, they said that MPs with 'significant outside interests' should be applauded.

This was just the start.

Overall, just eight MPs thought they were paid too much. Most thought their current wages were about right. But over a quarter of them wanted a further pay rise.

Compare this with national opinion polls and the Westminster disconnect becomes apparent. Research by YouGov in 2013 showed that two thirds of the public wanted MPs to be paid less.[5] Since then, Parliament has handed out a series of pay rises, with wages going up by almost £9,000. But for more than a quarter of MPs, it seems that still isn't enough.

'MPs should be paid salaries that reflect the status of the role,' one demanded. 'The concept of a reasonable wage for the work we do is not understood,' said another.

Asked if there was a sense of entitlement in Westminster, some MPs agreed but tried to defend it. 'If you work eighty hours a week, are on call twenty-four hours a day and have no private life you will feel you are due some form of entitlement,' said one.[6]

Another added: 'Being an MP is not a normal job. It must have high status.'

But Parliament is clearly divided. Plenty of politicians are critical of Westminster's image. 'It's a club,' one MP admitted. Another said: 'The culture of Parliament (particularly the huge amount of corporate lobbying) contributes to a sense of "If I'm being lobbied by people paid much more than MPs then I deserve more." '

Others suggested how this sense of entitlement may have come about. 'Some MPs can get caught up in the Westminster bubble,' said one. Another reckoned: 'Many who have that attitude [entitlement] do so before they become MPs.'

Do you think MPs are paid a fair salary?

26%

- No – we're not paid enough
- No – we're paid too much
- Yes – it's about right

61%

13%

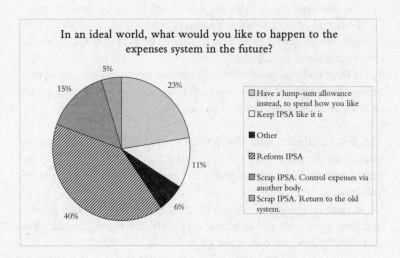

In an ideal world, what would you like to happen to the expenses system in the future?

5%

15%

23%

- Have a lump-sum allowance instead, to spend how you like
- Keep IPSA like it is
- Other
- Reform IPSA
- Scrap IPSA. Control expenses via another body.
- Scrap IPSA. Return to the old system.

11%

40%

6%

The biggest divide was over expenses. Judging by the survey, there is no clear consensus among MPs about what they want. But what it confirmed for sure is that they really hate the current system. In fact, only seven of the MPs who responded wanted to keep IPSA like it is.[7] The most popular suggestion was to reform it (40%) – but almost one in five MPs wanted to scrap the watchdog altogether.

Incredibly, three MPs even felt nostalgic about the days of fiddling and corruption and called for a return to the previous expenses system. Even the almighty expenses scandal was not enough to put them off. (Perhaps it is telling that two of these three also complained that their salaries weren't high enough.)

There weren't many kind words for the new expenses watchdog. 'Funny that IPSA and the processes in place now – despite cutting MPs' income and "expenses" – is costing the taxpayer c.£1.5m [per year] more than the old system cost,' said one MP. 'So who wins – taxpayer is still being ripped off . . . Well done *Daily Telegraph*.'

'IPSA is imperfect and feels, like MPs, that they have to perform to the demands of the *Telegraph* and the Twitter-sphere,' another said. 'But no one sensible thinks there is any realistic chance of the system changing at the moment so we just need to knuckle down and get on with our lives.'

A third complained that 'the current system stops MPs doing their jobs effectively and makes it feel that we are just administrators and having to continually justify what we do.'

So far, so predictable. This was roughly what I'd expected: a handful on either side who vigorously attack and defend financial interests. But there was one question that caught me by surprise.

It read: 'Have you ever been worried that an MP is biased because of their own financial interests?' I gave them three options: 'Yes, regularly', 'Yes, but only once or twice', or 'Never'.

In person, most politicians I spoke to about this seemed fairly relaxed, apart from the small minority who actively campaign on the issue. So I imagined there can't be much concern about the influence of private business. But speaking anonymously, MPs' admissions squeaked out. The survey revealed the worrying scale of Parliament's conflicts of interest:

More than *three quarters* of my sample MPs have worried that their colleagues are biased because of their personal financial interests. What's worse is that this is clearly not just a problem surrounding one or two rogue politicians: 33% of these MPs say that it happens frequently.

The implications of this are terrifying. It's not just the public who worry that Parliament is corrupt. Most of our politicians think it too. They think that financial influence may be twisting politics before their very eyes.

'MPs should not vote on issues where they have a financial interest (as per councillors in local government), including landlord MPs voting on housing issues,' said one respondent. A second agreed, saying: 'The rules for councillors and interests are far stricter and should be applied to MPs.'

'Very concerned about vested interests, who are winning government contracts,' said another. One lone voice pointed out: 'The Register of Interests is not precise or detailed enough!'

Weirdly, however, MPs' overwhelming concern about conflicts of interest does not seem to translate into a desire to actually solve the

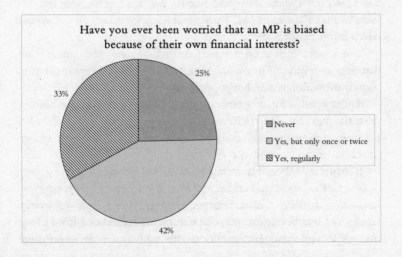

Have you ever been worried that an MP is biased because of their own financial interests?

25%

33%

42%

- Never
- Yes, but only once or twice
- Yes, regularly

problem. Many were strongly defensive of second jobs. 'An MP should be more highly regarded for having them.'

Far from trying to curb outside interests, some people want more. 'All MPs should have outside interests otherwise they become just professional politicians,' one of them wrote. Another added: 'MPs with outside interests (I am one such) have much to bring to Parliament and public policy and it is childish and silly to portray us as MPs who don't concentrate or give value for money.'

Blame everyone else

Looking at the survey responses, the overriding impression I got was this: these people must really hate me. More than anything, the survey paints a picture of a Parliament that begrudges journalists for digging dirt on their financial interests.

'What right has anybody to know what your full detailed financial interests are?' one MP ranted. 'The media are always looking for an easy story,' said another. 'Lazy journalism.'

'There are some "corrupt" journalists and media outlets who get *journalism* a bad name.'

The message was that politicians aren't the bad guys; the press are the bad guys. I thought it would be good to scrutinise Parliament in this book, but apparently people like me are just 'ruining democratic institutions'. Politicians only have a bad reputation because of 'media witch hunts', they said.

Resentment runs even deeper than this. It's not just a matter of blaming journalists. They also blame *you*, the public. People are just stupid and will never be happy, they say.

'There is still a lot of ignorance about MPs' work and pay but it's what the public want to believe. They love to hate us,' said one. 'The public mood on this issue is ugly . . . and will not change for a long time.'

'It seems an MP will be criticised whatever they do.'

One MP even suggested he was planning to stand down because his private earnings caused 'jealousy' among other people: 'There is far too much hypocritical and puritanical self-aggrandising from a few noisy MPs and commentators about those MPs who maintain their outside interests . . . I would prefer it if my private earnings were private but I abide by the rules of the House and declare them. It causes jealousy and resentment. But if you don't like it, you can leave. I intend to and rejoin the real world!'

The inability to take responsibility seemed to be a feature of this survey – just like it was in the expenses scandal. Time and time again, MPs palmed the blame off on others.

In one question, I asked them: 'The media often portrays politicians as "greedy". Why do you think this is?' One in ten MPs responded, saying: 'The public are just cynical.' And almost 30% said: 'Politicians aren't greedy, but the media unfairly distorts the truth.'

Out of all the MPs who responded, only three admitted: 'Greed and corruption *is* still a huge problem in Parliament.'[8]

What's more, most MPs refuse to accept any more transparency. Only a tiny handful said the system was not open enough. But almost a quarter of MPs thought there was *too much* transparency, and not enough privacy. And that's even despite one in five MPs admitting to making mistakes on their *own* declaration of interests.

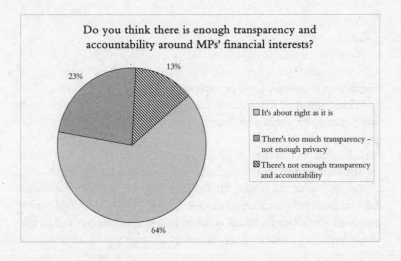

Do you think there is enough transparency and accountability around MPs' financial interests?

13%

23%

64%

- It's about right as it is
- There's too much transparency – not enough privacy
- There's not enough transparency and accountability

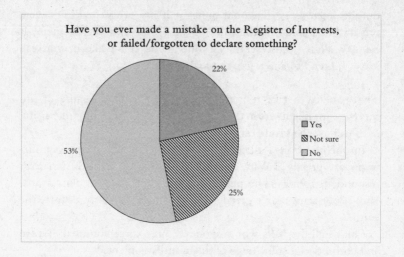

The survey paints a sorry picture of Parliament. It seems politicians know that financial interests could cause serious problems, but they aren't prepared to take action to improve things. They do not accept the need for more transparency, nor do they support scrutiny by the press.

MPs know that they're sitting on a scandal, but they don't want to poke it in case it turns around to bite them.

Breeding cynicism

Politicians might think we're cynical. And maybe we are. But we're not *born* cynical, it has to come from somewhere. It brews, as – year after year – we feel increasingly betrayed and disappointed by the representatives we elect.

I decided to travel to south Wales, where I grew up, and found myself back in my old comprehensive school. I wanted to know what first-time voters felt about MPs. Were they already 'cynical' about what makes the wheels of government turn? Or did the whole thing just seem irrelevant to them? What impact was all this having outside the Westminster bubble?

I stood in front of an A-level History class, who sat staring at me with blank, bored faces. The media constantly tells us that young people aren't interested in politics and – for a moment – it seemed to be true. This class was where I first learned about the nineteenth-century Chartist movement, which was defined by an ambitious desire to make politics fairer. But has that sentiment now been lost?

Before I told the students about my investigation, I got them to quickly write down the first word that came to mind when thinking about Britain's current MPs.[9] Overwhelmingly, the words were negative. And (unprompted) many had connotations with money and greed. When I asked if anyone had written a neutral word, one student put his hand up. 'Err . . . I've written "snakes",' he said. The class burst into laughter. 'Some snakes aren't nasty!'

Here's the full list of their words:

- Arrogant
- Clever
- Competitive
- Competitive
- Competitive
- Competitive
- Disconnected
- Elite (Oxford educated)
- Elitist
- Entertaining
- Extreme
- Greedy
- Greedy
- Male
- Manipulative
- Manipulative
- Manipulative
- Out-of-touch
- Pretentious
- Privileged
- Self-interested
- Self-preservation
- Smart
- Snakes
- Unorganised
- Unorganised
- Unrealistic
- Unreliable
- Varied

Then I asked them to write an explanation for their word.

'They are privileged people who have come from an upper class lifestyle and struggle to relate to the ordinary people,' wrote Callum, a seventeen-year-old at the back of the class. Another student, Siân, said politicians are 'motivated by self-interest rather than the good of the country'. And Madeline – who wrote down 'self-interested' as her word – explained: 'Many work for outside companies, and I believe many use their position in Parliament for their personal benefit.'

We ended up talking about politics for nearly an hour. They told me how they were pissed off with 'privileged, upper-class' MPs. They talked about politicians being corrupt. And about how politics *should be* in a perfect world.

A theme was emerging. These guys weren't *cynical*. They didn't lack political ideals: they still had hope, principles and visions. They just felt that MPs weren't living up to their expectations. They saw them as a gang of self-serving toffs. Of course, this was just one class-room out of thousands across the country. But if these views are prevalent among other first-time voters their age, it wasn't good news for politics, because their disillusionment was underscored with anger.

Don't mistake this for the seemingly timeless phenomenon of teenage rebellion, either. That kind of concept is often used as an excuse to ignore young people. Actually, teenage disillusionment with politics is a relatively modern trait and its growth (perhaps not coincidentally) has correlated with increased exposure of political scandals over the decades.

In 1967 – a time famous for teenage rebellion – a survey revealed how conservative most young people really were. Far from snubbing the entire system of government, they actually admired and respected political leaders. Teenagers ranked the prime minister, Harold Wilson, as their fourth most popular 'personality'. He was beaten by 'Mother' and 'the Queen'. And when asked what one law they would most like to change, 68% of teenagers said they wanted to bring back the death penalty.[10]

The point is, if politicians moan that 'the public mood on this issue is ugly,' then they fail to appreciate that they are partly to blame.

In this A-level class, a lot of their frustration derived from the perception that politicians are self-interested. As the students started to debate, it became obvious that this undermined their entire faith in the political system. One student explained: 'They're supposed to be representing us, but actually we feel like they're representing big business.'

It's hardly surprising that they think MPs are 'greedy'. For them, the biggest political scandal in recent times happened when they were eleven, just as they were starting to become more aware of politics.

Though Westminster may be keen to forget about it, it's still fresh in the minds of these students. And whereas my generation was politicised by the Iraq War, these students have been *de*-politicised by the expenses scandal. They have grown up in an era with plenty of sleaze, but very few positive principles to put in its place.

'It seems like it's in the past, but everyone knows that there's still problems with it. It's just that nobody talks about it any more,' said Luke, who is the most political in the group. 'People act as if it's been dealt with but, at the end of the day, people still claim expenses and it's still a problem.'

Absolutely no one in the class thought that MPs should be allowed to have paid second jobs. If they want outside experience, they should do it for free, they said. One student added: 'If the Conservative government is so happy to force university graduates into unpaid internships, surely they should force MPs into the same thing?' The others agreed and several students broke out into applause.

Here's the thing that politicians often fail to appreciate: this stuff really matters. When the public smells dodgy dealing, it's no good dismissing it as silly Westminster gossip. It has a deep, underlying impact on people's trust in politics. True, it may not directly influence the outcome of elections, because all the main parties are implicated. But it certainly makes people disillusioned. The longer this goes on, the harder it will be for political parties to win back the kind of widespread support they all dream of.

If the nineteenth-century Chartists walked into Parliament tomorrow, they would be met by the same smug attempt to portray them as cynical or ignorant. If the system is going to be cleaned up, the first step must be for Westminster to accept responsibility. So politicians, take note: young people are disillusioned, they are angry – but don't call them cynical.

21

What's next?

Red smoke rose into the air opposite Big Ben as protesters yelled out their angry chants. A small group of young men had broken away from the main demonstration and started scuffling with the police. From somewhere in the crowd, an empty beer can hurtled through the air and clipped one of the officers on the cheek. A slow streak of blood trickled down her face and on to her uniform.

For a moment, the fury over MPs' financial affairs had boiled over. It was two days after David Cameron admitted that he'd once owned shares in a tax haven following the Panama Papers leak and protesters had hit the streets to demand his resignation. They held banners with slogans like 'Time to go, chum', and 'We will shout till Cameron's out'. But for all their shouting, Cameron showed no sign of moving just yet. A few days earlier, the Icelandic prime minister had quit over a similar issue, after huge protests in Reykjavík. But there was going to be no repeat of that here. Financial controversy was not to be his downfall.

Cameron had learned from Parliament's grand history of financial sleaze: nothing will change. Nothing substantial. If he quit, it would just be a symbolic gesture. But would the rules be tightened? Would attitudes shift? The depressing truth is that Westminster slides from scandal to scandal without ever reforming its ways. Those involved simply do not get it. They don't understand why their private finances could possibly make people so angry. And when a fresh scandal comes along, all they want to do is sweep it under the carpet and move on.

Everyone in Westminster will tell you the same thing – there's no 'appetite' to do anything substantive about any of these issues – secret investments, salaries, moonlighting, conflicts of interest, lobbying, entitlement. Political leaders don't want to wade into this stuff too far. It will upset their own MPs and embarrass their parties. If this were only a problem in one party, they would quickly be rounded on by everyone else and forced to clean up their act. But all sides are guilty, so a strict *omertà* prevails. The way Westminster hurriedly moved on after the scandal over Cameron's offshore investment was testament to that.

I arrive in Westminster for one final time, hoping to get an insider's perspective on why MPs never learn from their mistakes. It's late April 2016 and the early evening light shimmers playfully over the Victorian Gothic architecture. Parliament Square is peaceful now. A sole campaigner lies snoozing on the grass, holding a placard between his legs, while tourists mill around taking photographs. The remnants of past protests seem neatly hidden under a glaze of sunshine. It's all too easy to forget that, a couple of weeks ago, this place was the centre of national outrage over the prime minister's financial interests.

In the midst of the scandal, Labour's John Mann was the first MP to call on Cameron to quit. 'He has no choice but to resign,' he Tweeted. 'If it's good enough for tiny Iceland it's good enough for the UK. Cameron must go.'[1] But now that the initial headlines have passed, I want to know if Mann still holds out hope of cleaning up politics?

As we talk in his Westminster office, he explains why he thinks Cameron should have stepped down straight after the Panama Papers came out. 'Morally and ethically, there was no question: he was duty bound to declare [his shareholdings], and he didn't. And that's dishonest,' Mann says. 'He should resign . . . The sanction in this country isn't high enough.'

And there could be a surprisingly simple solution to improve transparency. 'It should be a criminal offence for an MP not to declare things,' Mann suggests. 'That would concentrate the mind. If that was criminal law, David Cameron would have declared [his offshore investment].

'Transparency is what's needed. If an MP wants to get involved in an arms dealing company, it's up to them, as long as the public's able to see that. The public can make a judgement about whether that's a good or a bad thing. I trust the general public. The public needs to have the information available.'

Suggestions for how to deal with sleaze are not common in Parliament. Instead, pessimism dominates. When I ask a former government adviser what hope there is of improving things, he replies: 'I think no hope. No hope at all.' He explains: 'The Tories have got the hint that, provided they don't change anything, they'll be alright. I don't see any further clean-up of the way that MPs behave. The only thing that I can see is the opposite.'

Another source agrees: 'No one cares . . . At the end of the day, is this going to affect how people vote? If it's not something in a political party that's actually making a difference in an election, why would you bother?'

And so the sleaze continues. 'They've got away with it before, so they're happy to get away with it again,' John Mann says. 'Obviously, some have got their comeuppance in the expenses scandal and are no longer here, but self-interest is a powerful motivator.'

'Do you think there are some MPs who just don't get it?' I ask.

He stops to think. 'No. I think they *choose* not to get it,' he says. 'People create their own justifications. Some of them are wilder than others, in terms of the leaps that are required . . . People are rational on these things. They know what's right and what's wrong. They know what's borderline – and there are very few things that are borderline.'

Just another failed revolution

Every now and then, there's a glint of hope. One of those occasions came in spring 2015: it looked like there was a chance to reform MPs' finances. The then Labour leader, Ed Miliband, called for a ban on paid directorships and consultancies. 'We've got to settle this issue of second jobs once and for all,' he said, 'so we remove any suspicion that MPs are working not for their constituents' interests, but someone else's interests.'[2]

Labour's Angela Eagle, who was shadow leader of the House of Commons, moved the proposals, saying: 'The time has come to make a decisive break with the status quo on Members' remunerated interests. I believe the current situation has become untenable.'

The public deserve to be safe in the knowledge that every Member of Parliament works and acts in the interests of their local constituents, and not in the interests of anyone paying them . . . We have to take radical action to ensure that we bring ourselves back in line with the levels of conduct that our constituents expect of all of us . . .

Being a Member of Parliament is an extremely demanding and tough job, and it is done with integrity and dedication by the vast majority of colleagues in all parties. Unfortunately, however, the perception is growing that some MPs are in it only for what they can get, rather than for what they can give, and that is not an impression that we can allow to fester any longer.[3]

Another Labour MP chipped in, saying: 'We should really accept that this is about money. It is about Members – primarily Government Members – who want to be paid extra . . . The public are not prepared to put up with this any longer.'

But the proposals didn't stand a chance. For a start, they weren't watertight enough and it was easy for critics to pick holes. More importantly, however, was the sheer scale of Parliament's outside earnings, which meant that a big section of the Commons had vested interests in keeping the rules exactly as they were.

Several well-paid Tories mocked the idea of reform and boasted about how many outside jobs they had. One grandee, Sir Tony Baldry, joked: 'It will take me five minutes to read out my entry in the Register of Members' Financial Interests.'[4]

Meanwhile, other MPs who joined the debate were not entirely clear about what interests they had. For instance, Alan Duncan spoke without mentioning what his interests were and later clarified: 'The reason I did not declare an interest is that I have not got any.' In fact, although he had no directorships or consultancies, the Register of Interests at the time did indicate that he earned a 'substantial income' by renting out a property in London.[5]

Because of the shoddy transparency, it was hard for those arguing in favour of reform to point to any specific wrongdoing among MPs. 'That's how I got a bit stuck in the debate,' one of the key Labour politicians involved tells me. 'I had to start off by acknowledging that I have no evidence of any individual being individually corrupt.

'I thought "I'm damned if I'm going to be part of an institution that's regarded so badly by the wider public". It would be better to make a bit of a stand. People know that there's something wrong, and we've got to clean our act up.' The MP adds that people would be more angry about Parliament's financial impropriety, 'but they don't know quite the extent of it'.

Labour's proposals were swiftly thrown out, with the government claiming they were 'unclear'.[6] They were certainly not as detailed as they could have been. But in rejecting this modest invitation to reform the system, Parliament slammed the door shut on cleaner politics.

New politics

There was one final ray of hope. Campaigners for cleaning up Parliament might have taken solace in the rise of Jeremy Corbyn to the Labour leadership in 2015. Once hailed as Westminster's lowest expenses claimer, he quickly became a figurehead for honest politics.[7]

It's one thing to have good intentions, but it's quite another to translate them into reality. For a start, the issue was clearly far from the top of Corbyn's priority list when he was first elected. He hadn't spoken in Ed Miliband's debate on second jobs and has been fairly quiet on lobbying, transparency and expenses.

It's probably unfair to burden Corbyn with the responsibility of singlehandedly spearheading the changes that are needed – and there's no doubting his principles on the matter. But after his election the question became, if not *him* then *who*? And if not *now*, then *when*?

Shortly after Corbyn's rise to power I asked a top-level Labour insider whether his 'new politics' could cut the sleaze. 'No, I don't think they'll get anywhere near it,' the adviser said bluntly. 'They are so, so overwhelmed by all the stuff they have to do, just the day-to-day bread and butter. Just to respond to each day's press, try and set out your agenda, try and actually set out some space to do what you want to do. It's so far down the list.'

Pushing for tighter regulation of financial interests would create friction throughout Westminster too, the source added. 'You're pissing off all your backbenchers. We're already pissing backbenchers off over nonsense stuff, so do you really want to start bringing up this stuff? And the thing is, we're not going to get anywhere close to it because the Tories aren't going to support us on it.

'Jeremy [Corbyn] could say "we're going to be the cleanest party ever, blah blah blah blah, we're not going to have second jobs". But all those backbenchers who have second jobs will be like "well fuck you, I'm doing it anyway" . . . So what can you do to them really?'

But the biggest reason why the issue will be ignored is simply this: it won't affect the election results. 'Are people going to vote for the cleanest party ever, but they think they're fucking incompetent and can't run the economy?' the senior Labour insider said. 'It doesn't matter, ultimately.'

But when I met him in April 2016, arch Corbyn critic John Mann took a different view. Corbyn *could* clean up politics, he said, but he hasn't yet. 'I haven't seen any practical changes at all,' Mann told me. 'I think it would help him and the Labour Party if there was. But I haven't seen it yet.'

But could the Labour leader actually make a difference? 'Yes, quite easily,' the MP replied. 'The general public would back it. The media, for different reasons, would back it.'

As for Corbyn's image as Parliament's lowest expenses claimer, Mann was critical. 'That's the spin that he's put out and he's allowed to continue,' he said. 'He's not the lowest spending MP and he hasn't been. That's simply not the case. He's created this mystique about it . . . It's not a criticism; it's simply not true.'

Squabbles aside, the question remains: who will step up to the plate and do something about financial interests? Neither Cameron, Corbyn – nor their critics in Westminster – seem to do much except talk.

The fight for democracy

There's little doubt that the private money trails which flow through Westminster are a threat to democracy. We've seen how financial excess and impropriety has plagued politics, and how the public have been left in the dark. It's easy to brush these issues off as individual cases; exceptions to the rule. But so long as the system remains unregulated and uncontrolled, politicians' personal finances will continue to undermine trust in British politics.

Let's not be naïve though, our politicians will never all be saints. No matter what happens, there will always be cheats and crooks among them. There will always be some who put money before morals and those who think that rich people make better MPs than anyone else.

We could change the rules – and we should. Tighter regulations could drag Westminster into the twenty-first century and bring in a new era of open politics. But that alone won't change attitudes. Whatever system we set up, there will always be some rotten apples who don't care what the public think of them.

'The manipulation of greed still seeks to corrupt the power of Parliament,' writes Paul Flynn MP. 'The fumigation of the Palace cannot prevent re-infestation . . . sleaze is ever-present, ravenous to re-infect.'[8]

So that leaves us with the only remaining answer: vigilance.

Quiz your MP; set up a blog; investigate expenses; campaign for transparency. There is no magic button that will suddenly clean everything up – this is an ongoing struggle that will never end. But if we want to live in a fair and open society, we've got to continually fight for it. Sleazy politicians should not come out of this story as the winners.

The press get a bad press, and often it's justified. But over the years, journalists, bloggers and researchers have brilliantly exposed some of the worst abuses – from undercover lobbying stings to the expenses scandal. 'A rumbustious, noisy, sneering press keeps people on the straight and narrow,' one MP tells me. 'Politicians who have real power should be subject to both exposure, disclosure, accountability.'

But the media will never have the capacity to do everything: to expose *every* dodgy MP. And in the spaces between headlines, the scandals don't disappear – they are just hidden.

If everyone reading this book spent the next half-hour researching the personal finances of their own MP, British democracy would be better for it. Politicians will not police themselves – it's up to us. And it's so easy for them to make money and behave badly. One former MP, disillusioned with Parliament's love affair with money, tells me simply: 'If you want to cash in, you could.'

Parliament Ltd

As I came to the end of my investigation, I realised there was something I'd never checked.

While MPs sold off their political credibility to the highest bidder, I wondered if Parliament itself was now just another facility for businesses. Had any private companies actually used the House of Commons as their registered address?

That's when I found out about 'UKIP Parliamentary Resource Unit Limited' – a private vehicle used to control thousands of pounds of funding for Nigel Farage's party.[9] Incorporated as a limited company in July 2015, it was registered at . . . Parliament.[10] The official document, filed at Companies House, spelled it out, bold and clear:

A6	Registered office address ❷						
	Please give the registered office address of your company						
Building name/number	HOUSE OF COMMONS						
Street							
Post town	LONDON						
County/Region							
Postcode	S	W	1	A	0	A	A

I printed out the document and sellotaped it to the wall above my desk. Nothing was sacred any more – not even the halls of democracy. And this was my constant reminder.

Parliament had surrendered itself to money and business. Now, it had become 'Parliament Ltd'.

Afterword

Seven months after this book was first published in 2016, I got an email from Parliament's Select Committee for Standards. They said they were reviewing the MPs' Code of Conduct and asked me to give evidence as part of a panel of witnesses. It all seemed very exciting – until I actually got there.

It's easy to mistake a genuine desire to reform with a routine box-ticking exercise. But this definitely seemed like the latter.

It shouldn't have come as any surprise, though, because – as I already knew – the Standards Committee itself is as controversial as anything. In fact, in the last year alone, three of the six MPs sitting in front of me had themselves been found in breach of the rules. Even the chairman, Sir Kevin Barron.[1]

(Barron's particular case was shrugged off as 'minor' and 'inadvertent' in a report by Kathryn Hudson, the Commissioner for Standards.[2] By happy coincidence, Barron himself had sat on the board that interviewed Hudson when she applied for her job.[3] But when I suggested there was a conflict of interest, because she was appointed by the very MPs she's meant to investigate, Barron jumped in, shaking his head and demanding an explanation.)

The audacity of the committee's position was lost on them. How could these people ever be expected to run an adequate inquiry into all this, when the members were so caught up in it themselves? The result was that most of the hearing was about superficial things, instead of anything substantial. Rather than focusing on important questions, like 'How can the Register of Interests become more transparent?' or 'How can we strengthen the rules against lobbying?', they seemed more keen to just give the Code of Conduct a quick polish.

'Would a shorter, more focused [Code of Conduct] document be regarded as a step forward?' one of the committee members asked – as if MPs only acted badly because they couldn't be bothered to read a long rulebook. Someone else added: 'Would you like to see more social media used?' Others talked about printing the rules on the back of MPs' lanyards, to remind them.

'I agree with a lot of that, but I would add that this is a bit like rearranging the deckchairs on the Titanic,' I replied. 'Sorry to sound like a broken record but I would come back to transparency.'

Sadly, the select committee hearing follows a string of near-pointless review exercises by Parliament's various watchdogs. They tweak and refine stuff occasionally, not always for the best, and certainly never do anything meaningful.

Hudson launched a public consultation in early 2016 but it was buried deep on Parliament's website, riddled with technical questions. It got just nineteen responses, of which only eight were from members of the public. Other submissions came from four MPs, the head of the Civil Service, three official standards commissioners, two parliamentary committees and Transparency International, whose short submission explained: 'We do not currently have the resources to respond in detail.'

All future consultations on the subject seem destined to die in the same way.

Upon writing this book, I reported several MPs to Hudson, asking her to investigate potential conflicts of interest.

But the following month I got a letter telling me that only a couple of them would be placed under official investigation. No time limit was set and no updates were given. The inquiries were kept strictly behind closed doors. What's more, I was formally banned from disclosing the contents of any letters I sent or received from Parliament about it all.

There were some rather odd excuses given for the cases she chose not to investigate. On Royston Smith (the Southampton MP who had worked for a development business) Hudson offered only: 'I do not think the evidence justifies beginning an inquiry.' And on Bob Neill (who worked for lobbying firm Cratus Communications), she reckoned that, as non-executive director, he didn't have any personal involvement with clients. So that was perfectly alright, apparently.

In another case, Hudson managed to get a key fact wrong. My complaint about Nigel Adams explained his financial interests were particularly important because he's a member of the Culture, Media and Sport Committee. But in her response, excusing the MP, she referred instead to the Communities and Local Government Committee (of which he has never been a member).

Meanwhile, Gisela Stuart was investigated, but cleared. Despite standing to be chair of the Public Accounts Committee, which investigates tax avoidance, Stuart had held an undeclared stake in Vestra Wealth, a partnership which helped tax-avoiding non-doms. However, Hudson said no rules were broken because she judged that Vestra did not 'meet the test of relevance'. She said: 'It is a general investment manager with no specific focus on a specialist area.'

You might wonder whether Stuart should have declared the investment anyway, regardless of the Public Accounts Committee election, just because it was worth so much. Indeed, when she finally updated the Register of Interests it was estimated to be £93,000 – well over the £70,000 threshold for declaration. But Hudson yet again said this wasn't a problem because it had only increased in recent months, and the public had no right to know about it beforehand. Estimates of investment values only have to be updated once a year, she explained, and Stuart 'had no cause to re-estimate the value' any earlier than she did.[4]

My complaints had more success in the House of Lords. In July 2016, after weeks of waiting, a report was published into the conduct of Baroness Greenfield (the peer who made a speech about university intellectual property, despite failing to declare a directorship at Tekcapital plc).

The inquiry ruled against her. 'Baroness Greenfield has accepted that she breached the Code of Conduct by not registering her directorship of Tekcapital within one month of acquiring it, and by not declaring the interest during the debate,' the report explained. 'She said these were down to a misunderstanding of the rules and an oversight respectively.'[5]

And the punishment for this major oversight? A fine, perhaps? Suspension from Parliament? No. Greenfield simply wrote 'a formal letter of apology' to the chairman of a sub-committee. And that was that.

It will be a long time before Westminster gets into shape – and the arguments over specific details will always continue. But even if MPs keep their second jobs, here are some tentative ideas for a more transparent, less corrupt Parliament:

- Make it a criminal offence for MPs and peers to fail to declare relevant financial interests. (Bodies like the Welsh Assembly have similar laws to this already.)
- Ban parliamentarians from voting on issues where they, or companies they work for, stand to gain from the decision more than the standard population. (Again, laws like this already exist elsewhere.)
- Scrap Parliament's internal watchdogs and hand responsibility to an independent organisation.
- Expand the rules on disclosure to include all financial and property interests, all outside jobs (including unpaid jobs), and all directorships, without exception.
- Publish the Register of Interests in an accessible spreadsheet format, which provides a full breakdown of the details. This should include the unique company number for each business interest and a standardised method of reporting external jobs and income.
- Make MPs disclose the contracts for any outside jobs they have and publish these online.
- Introduce a regular, independent audit of the Register of Interests.
- Rewrite the rulebook if necessary.

Acknowledgements

Huge thanks to all the people who helped make this book possible:
Mum and Dad, for everything. My agent, Andrew Lownie, took a gamble on me, helped me develop the original idea and has been hugely supportive throughout. My editor, Rupert Lancaster, did the same – along with everyone at Hodder, particularly Maddy Price, Vero Norton and the lawyers. The incredibly generous team at DueDil.com (and particularly Norval Scott) saved me months of work by devoting their time and expertise to compiling some of the crucial data used in this book. My friends Jim Norton, Emily Fairbairn, Rebecca Ratcliffe and Simon Murphy were a constant source of advice, wisdom and support throughout. 'Lord' Gordon was a great sport for getting involved, although he is sadly still not a lord. Rhys Cater is the king of spreadsheet formulas. Rhodri and Natalia read drafts and have been extremely supportive. Josie Long has been an inspiration to collaborate with in our shows together, in which some of the ideas for this book were developed. Beth Middleton and Ade Colborne helped organise my meeting with the fantastic history students at Cowbridge Comprehensive School. Caroline Lucas and her staff have also been very helpful, as have my friends Josie Whittle, Andy McGrath, Emily Mears, Mike Regan and Sammy Cowley, among others.

Special thanks to journalists Daniel Kraemer and Rebecca Ratcliffe who worked on some of the data-crunching with me.

I am grateful to everyone I interviewed, including a great many who I am not able to name in order to protect their anonymity. Also to the experts, academics and researchers who gave invaluable insights and guidance, particularly Lord Paul Bew, Jessica Garland, Dr Seth

Thévoz and Prof. Prem Sikka. Thanks also to the dozens of helpful press and FOI officers who I spammed with requests (especially Chris Veck and Matthew Lumby at IPSA). Many other press and FOI officers were, of course, distinctly *unhelpful*.

I am indebted to all the journalists, authors and researchers I have cited. This book would not have been possible without the brilliant work of countless other people over many years.

The following books were also especially insightful, and which I recommend: *Honourable Friends?* (Caroline Lucas); *How to be an MP* (Paul Flynn); *The Establishment* (Owen Jones); *A Quiet Word* (Tamasin Cave and Andy Rowell); *The Great Tax Robbery* (Richard Brooks); *As Used On the Famous Nelson Mandela* (Mark Thomas); *The Shadow World* (Andrew Feinstein); *A Century of Spin* (David Miller and William Dinan); *The Best Democracy Money Can Buy* (Greg Palast).

All mistakes are my own and not the fault or responsibility of any of the people mentioned above.

Endnotes

1. In conversation with Mark McGowan: https://www.youtube.com/watch?v=WUtVXD4Tp-M (accessed 18/09/15)
2. *Mark Thomas Comedy Product*, episode 5, series 6: https://www.youtube.com/watch?v=uEoTEsMjUZE

Introduction

1. http://www.theguardian.com/commentisfree/2016/apr/10/the-guardian-view-on-david-cameron-the-warping-ways-of-wealth
2. Antonia Fraser, *Perilous Question: The Drama of the Great Reform Bill 1832* (2013), Chapter 15. Also (re his oratory, politics and insults): David Moss, *Thomas Attwood: The Biography of a Radical* (1990)
3. Hansard: HC Deb, 30 May 1839, vol 47 cc1143
4. http://www.parliament.uk/about/living-heritage/transformingsociety/electionsvoting/chartists/case-study/the-right-to-vote/the-chartists-and-birmingham/1839-petition/
5. http://www.historyofparliamentonline.org/volume/1820-1832/survey/vi-members
6. Within the context of modern history. Parliament's website notes that some systems of payment did exist in earlier eras: 'From the 13th century shires and boroughs sometimes paid their MPs and met some of the expenses of sending them to Westminster. This practice ceased by the end of the 17th century.'
7. From a speech by Rev. James Rayner Stephens at a demonstration on Kersal Moor, 1838, and reported in the *Northern Star*, 29 Sept 1838. Quoted in, for instance: Howard Martin, *Britain in the 19th Century* (2002), p.160
8. Hansard: HC Deb, 12 July 1839, vol 49, cc236
9. Hansard: HC Deb, 14 Aug 1911, vol 29 cc1625

10. Ibid.

11. Calculated using the Bank of England Inflation Calculator, adjusted to 2015 inflation levels.

12. Hansard: HC Deb, 10 Aug 1911, vol 29 cc1382

13. http://hansard.millbanksystems.com/commons/1911/aug/14/class-ii-payment-of-members#S5CV0029P0_19110814_HOC_379

14. Hansard: HC Deb, 10 Aug 1911, vol 29 cc1383. My emphasis.

15. Michael Rush, *Parliament Today*, (Manchester University Press, 2005) p.114

16. http://www.publications.parliament.uk/pa/cm201012/cmselect/cmmemex/1484/148404.htm

17. IPSA, *MPs Pay In The 2015 Parliament: Final Report* (July 2015)

18. In nominal value.

19. Calculated using the Bank of England Inflation Calculator, comparing salaries in 1915 and 2015. According to the Inflation Calculator, MPs' salary in 1915 (£400) is equivalent to £37,090.91 in 2015 money. The £400 nominal value is given on Parliament's website at: http://researchbriefings.files.parliament.uk/documents/SN05075/SN05075.pdf NB: the 2015 salary was still in place at the start of 2016, before rising again in April.

20. Real terms values between 1985 and 2015, adjusted to 2015 inflation levels using the Bank of England Inflation Calculator. NB: the salary from 2015 was used, rather than 2016, because (a) at the time of writing in Feb 2016 the £1,000 pay rise has not yet been introduced (due in April 2016); and (b) because the Bank of England's inflation calculator works only for full calendar years, meaning that 2015 is the most recent date available to which it's possible to adjust prices.

21. Rounded to nearest thousand. (£74,962). As of 01/04/16: http://parliamentarystandards.org.uk/NewsAndMedia/Pages/LatestNews2.aspx?ListNews=739f9c00-b7d4-4282-bffd-9ae51fd8d92d&NewsId=96

22. Rounded up from £80,880.96. This is the real terms value in 2002, adjusted to 2015 inflation levels

23. Because Roth looked at both past and present business connections, his findings are not directly comparable to the new data on the current Parliament that is published later in this book, which only includes roles which were current at the time of writing.

24. Andrew Roth, *The Business Backgrounds of M.P.s* (1965)

25. James Callaghan, quoted in: Andrew Roth, *The Business Backgrounds of M.P.s* (1965)

26. http://www.parliament.uk/briefing-papers/SN01528.pdf (NB: occupation statistics only cover MPs from the three main political parties)

Part One: A bit on the side
Chapter 1: Criminal journalist

1. Email to me from Equiniti Ltd (10/06/15)
2. Section 116 (2) of the Companies Act, 2006 states: 'The register and the index of members' names must be open to the inspection.' It goes on to add that fees may be prescribed for this service if the requester is not themselves a 'member', i.e. shareholder. Therefore, charging for this document is perfectly within the law – it is the law itself which is questionable; not companies making use of it.
3. This name has been chosen arbitrarily. There is no suggestion that this individual is necessarily a female.
4. The value of the shareholding is not known and it could therefore have not been within the registrable threshold. Therefore, there is no suggestion that parliamentary rules were necessarily breached.
5. BAE Systems plc, Annual Report, 2004 and 2006.
6. BAE Systems plc, Annual Report, 2004
7. Companies Act 1985, 1985 c. 6, Part XI, Chapter II, Section 356: http://www.legislation.gov.uk/ukpga/1985/6/section/356/enacted
8. There is no suggestion that G4S would have restricted transparency if I had been a campaigner, merely that they wanted to research and find out more about my background and purpose of my research.
9. Recorded phone call with G4S press office
10. Email from Peter David, G4S (30/09/15)
11. Email from Peter David, G4S (01/10/15)
12. Statement emailed from BIS (02/03/16)
13. A Companies House spokeswoman said: 'A traded public company or a company that has shares admitted for trading to a recognised investment exchange or regulated market only need to disclose details of those shareholders who hold at least 5% of any class of shares as at the made-up-date of their Annual Return. If they are also subject to the Vote Holder and Issuer Notification Rules (DTR5) then they wouldn't have to disclose any details on their Annual Return.' (03/03/16). NB: 5% of a FTSE 100 company is enormous, therefore the vast majority of ordinary shareholders are not included. Indeed, when I requested a full version of BAE's shares from Companies House, it only named two stakeholders.

14. See, for instance: http://www.linklaters.com/Insights/Publication 1005Newsletter/UK-Corporate-Update-5-March-2015/Pages/ comply-request-non-member-inspect-registers.aspx

15. Companies Act 2006: Section 116, (1) (a)

16. http://www.theguardian.com/business/2015/mar/27/sports-direct-takes-rangers-fan-to-court-over-effort-to-access-shareholder-register

17. To be clear, John Hunter acknowledged both sides of the argument and said it was a tricky issue. He said: 'There are quite difficult issues in terms of personal security.'

Chapter 2: The great transparency myth

1. £10m figure refers to difference in turnover (£32.7m and £22.9m): Osborne & Little Group Limited and Osborne & Little Ltd – accounts ending March 2011 and Annual Return 2012 for both companies (these were the most recent documents at the time). There is no suggestion that Osborne profited from his investment during the time that his public declaration was inaccurate. Indeed, no dividends were paid by Osborne & Little Group Limited for this year.

2. http://www.publications.parliament.uk/pa/cm/cmregmem/121022/ 121022.pdf

3. Register of Interests for Lords and Commons, as at Aug 2015.

4. http://www.parliament.uk/mps-lords-and-offices/standards-and-financial-interests/house-of-lords-commissioner-for-standards-/code-of-conduct-for-the-house-of-lords/guide-to-the-code-of-conduct/ #jump-link-4

5. On the Register of Interests, Grieve says that his shareholdings are 'held jointly with my wife, and were controlled by a blind management trust whilst I was a member of the government'.

6. http://www.independent.co.uk/news/business/news/shell-and-vw-top-list-of-ngos-most-hated-brands-in-the-uk-a6818946.html

7. The company's full name is Royal Dutch Shell plc

8. http://www.theguardian.com/business/2012/jul/03/glaxosmithkline-fined-bribing-doctors-pharmaceuticals ; http://www.bbc.co.uk/news /business-26970873

9. http://www.publications.parliament.uk/pa/cm201415/cmselect/ cmstandards/772/772.pdf

10. Exempt under FOI s.34(1) (an absolute exemption). As outlined in responses to FOI requests I sent to the House of Commons (2015). NB:

some emails might be published as part of Parliamentary reports, e.g. by the Commissioner herself, but these would of course be Parliament's choice of what to disclose and what not to. It is also possible that some communication from the Commissioner's office that does not concern Members' activities may potentially be subject to FOI.

11. Parliamentary Commissioner for Standards, *Annual Report 2014–15*, http://www.parliament.uk/documents/pcfs/Annual-Report-2014-15.pdf. NB: Time taken for inquiries based on averages for 2013/14 and 2014/15 (55% over 3 months).

12. http://www.telegraph.co.uk/news/politics/11874776/When-I-read-Kathryn-Hudsons-report-into-Jack-Straw-and-Malcolm-Rifkind-I-laughed-out-loud.html

13. The exact complaint was that he had not declared it within the 28-day deadline.

14. http://www.parliament.uk/documents/pcfs/rectifications/Dr-Vince-Cable-MP.pdf

15. http://www.parliament.uk/documents/pcfs/rectifications/Dr-Vince-Cable-MP.pdf

16. http://www.theguardian.com/politics/2015/jan/09/vince-cable-apologises-not-declaring-donation-polling

17. http://www.telegraph.co.uk/news/politics/12190163/Commons-watchdog-chair-Sir-Kevin-Barron-steps-aside-from-committee-over-rules-breach.html NB: Barron said the money from the pharmaceutical firm had all been paid to charity. He said that this meant he had not broken any rules, but he referred himself to the Commissioner anyway, in light of the allegations.

18. http://www.telegraph.co.uk/news/uknews/12188113/MPs-must-no-longer-police-themselves.html

19. http://www.theguardian.com/politics/2015/dec/23/parliamentary-standards-kathryn-hudson-yeo-straw-rifkind

Chapter 3: Stinking rich

1. http://politicalscrapbook.net/2015/03/grant-shapps-plane-and-car-boasts-stinking-filthy-rich-online-michael-green/ and http://www.theguardian.com/politics/2015/mar/15/grant-shapps-admits-he-had-second-job-as-millioniare-web-marketer-while-mp

2. http://politicalscrapbook.net/2012/09/grant-shapps-wrote-stinking-rich-guide-boasted-of-two-aircraft-michael-green/

3. http://politicalscrapbook.net/2015/03/grant-shapps-plane-and-car-boasts-stinking-filthy-rich-online-michael-green/

4. http://www.theguardian.com/politics/2015/mar/15/grant-shapps-admits-he-had-second-job-as-millioniare-web-marketer-while-mp

5. http://www.theguardian.com/politics/2012/sep/21/grant-shapps-posed-web-guru

6. http://www.theguardian.com/politics/2012/sep/02/grant-shapps-google-howtocorp-adsense

7. http://www.theguardian.com/politics/2015/mar/15/grant-shapps-admits-he-had-second-job-as-millioniare-web-marketer-while-mp

8. http://www.theguardian.com/politics/2015/mar/16/revealed-grant-shapps-threat-to-sue-constituent-over-michael-green-post

9. http://www.telegraph.co.uk/news/investigations/11428075/The-MPs-who-topped-up-their-salaries-with-1600-an-hour-second-jobs.html (Dates were just over a year: 01/01/14 to 06/01/15).

10. http://politicalscrapbook.net/2012/02/david-cameron-binge-drinking-urbium-tiger-tiger/

11. http://www.theguardian.com/politics/2005/aug/25/conservatives.uk

12. Unless specified otherwise, analysis of the Register of Interests throughout this book is based on the records as they stood in Aug 2015 for the House of Commons, and 23/08/15 for the House of Lords. These were the most recently published versions when I started my analysis. Earnings are only declared in the Commons Register, not the Lords. However, declarations are not published uniformly between different MPs, making watertight analysis impossible. For instance, one MP might declare gross income, while another declares net. Some declare payments dating back years; others only list payments received in the last 12 months. And so on. The whole thing's a mess. I have therefore tried to clean the data as far as reasonably possible. That has meant things like expanding out certain regular incomes into annual figures. For instance, Ian Blackford MP says he is 'paid £1,000 a month' for one job, so, for the sake of this analysis I have recorded that as an equivalent annual income, i.e. £12,000. Similarly, Boris Johnson has only listed two instalments of his salary as London Mayor, both of different amounts and without stating the annual salary. Therefore, the annual salary figure published by the Mayor's Office (£47,970) has been used in place of the Register's figures. This method seems, to me, to be making the best of a bad dataset, but I equally appreciate it is not an exact science and other people could probably analyse the same document and get a range of different results for the total income. This

is, therefore, meant as a rough guide only. It's also worth pointing out again that the Register obviously changes and updates all the time and there is no suggestion that any of the employment details mentioned are still ongoing now.

13. Figures rounded to nearest 100. The total number of individual entries on the Register of Interests, not a reflection of the number of jobs etc. It is included here to give a picture of the size of the document, rather than a reflection of earnings, etc. It does not include entries which said 'Nil' or 'No registrable interests'. Peers on leaves of absence were also not included.

14. This is an approximation, which is necessary because of the format of the Register of Interests. Earnings are not recorded in a uniform way, so it is not always possible to record exact figures. For instance, some MPs say they earn X amount per month, while others will list each individual payment as it comes in. The figure included here is conservative because wages have only been calculated as an annual salary when it is obvious that payments are regular and consistent.

15. Based on the 303 MPs who have declared outside income; not representative of the whole of the Commons. Calculation uses the basic £74,000 MP salary that was introduced in 2015 and does not include any ministerial or other parliamentary salaries. This is only a rough working, given the flaws with the data (see previous notes). The figure has been rounded to the nearest 10p.

16. Register of Interests as at Aug 2015 ('from June 2015 I receive £22,916.66 a month for writing articles for the Telegraph Media Group Ltd . . . Hours: 10 hrs a month').

17. Income and salaries mentioned in this list are based on what is declared in the Register of Interests as at Aug 2015. The total figure given for each MP represents the amount of earnings declared on the Register over a 12-month period. However, there is no suggestion that these figures represent an annual income, or are reflective of any work contracts – the Register does not specify exactly when these amounts were earned, only when they were declared. Therefore it is perfectly possible that some of this money was earned outside of the 12-month period. The 12-month period may vary slightly between MPs, but is generally the period immediately before publication of this version of the Register of Interests (Aug 2015). NB1: With Boris Johnson, his Mayoral salary has been included based on an annual figure from the Mayor's Office (see previous note). NB2: With Nicholas Soames, some of his declarations are given as X amount per month/quarter. Where

this is the case, the figures have been expanded out to an annual figure. NB3: All salary figures in this list are rounded to the nearest thousand.

18. The basic pay for MPs in 2014 was £64,060. This calculation is based purely on this standard pay rate and earnings declared in the Register of Interests as at Aug 2015. NB: I have included the word 'potentially' because although all these earnings were registered in 2014, they may not necessarily have all been earned in that year.

19. http://www.telegraph.co.uk/news/politics/conservative/11940456/ Tory-MP-Geoffrey-Cox-resigns-from-sleaze-watchdog-after-failing-to-declare-hundreds-of-thousands-of-pounds.html NB1: At the time of writing (04/01/16), details of this failure to declare earnings are not entirely clear because very little has yet been published by the Parliamentary Commissioner. The *Telegraph* notes: 'According to the latest register of members' financial interests, Mr Cox received £325,000 on June 15 and 16 this year for 500 hours of work carried out between June 2014 and March 2015. Under Commons rules external income needs to be registered within 28 days, but the sum was not declared to the authorities until September 30. A number of other payments also appear to have been registered late.' Therefore, it appears that not all of this amount was earned in 2014. NB2: Cox did not respond to a request for comment.

20. http://news.bbc.co.uk/1/hi/england/london/8148899.stm; Register of Interests (as at Aug 2015) says: 'Until further notice, from June 2015 I receive £22,916.66 a month for writing articles for the Telegraph Media Group Ltd'. NB: Johnson did not respond to a request for comment.

21. Garnier pointed out: 'I don't have a salary as a barrister but fees for each item of work, but you may think that's a distinction without a difference save that I am self-employed and can therefore choose my own hours and place of work and can therefore be far more flexible than an employee in an office.'

22. Hourly rate is rounded up to the nearest £10. Percentage is rounded up to nearest whole number and is based on MP salary as at the date of this version of the Register of Interests (Aug 2015), which was £74,000. NB: Phillips did not respond to a request for comment.

23. http://www.mirror.co.uk/news/uk-news/tory-toff-nicholas-soames-who-3119800; Register of Interests, as at Aug 2015. ('Senior Advisor on Strategic Issues to Intrepid Capital Partners . . . Until further notice, I receive an annual payment of £19,988 for an expected commitment of 30 hours.'). NB: Soames did not respond to a request for comment.

24. Companies House, *Statistical release: Incorporated companies in the United Kingdom – November 2015*

25. Rounded to nearest hundred.

26. National stat: rounded to nearest whole number (17.79), based on Companies House statistics from Nov 2015 cited previously, and using UK population figure of 64.6m. Westminster stat: rounded to nearest whole number – 1.67 companies per politician, based on Parliament size of 1,476 and 2,465 companies.

27. One company for every 0.6 parliamentarians. Based on Parliament size of 1,476 (826 peers and 650 MPs).

28. Not all corporate information was available for every company (for various reasons including firms that were newly incorporated or late filing accounts). The statistics that follow are likely to be *incredibly* conservative.

29. Full-time workforce is 22.98m according to ONS (Oct–Dec 2015): http://www.ons.gov.uk/employmentandlabourmarket/peopleinwork /employmentandemployeetypes/bulletins/uklabourmarket/ february2016

30. https://www.sheffield.gov.uk/your-city-council/sheffield-profile/ population-and-health.html; https://www.bristol.gov.uk/statistics-census-information/the-population-of-bristol; http://www.aberdeencity.gov.uk/ nmsruntime/saveasdialog.asp?lID=65068&sID=3365

31. The London stat of 49% is based on a sample of 1,817 companies where the addresses were clear in the data. Stats for Scotland and NI are based on the standard prefixes attached to company numbers that identify companies registered in those countries. Therefore the percentage for these is based on the entire selection of 2,456 companies since company numbers for each one was known.

32. Net assets.

33. Rounded to nearest whole numbers. As already mentioned, this is not an exact science and the figures are meant as approximations only. NB1: there is no suggestion that all of the directorships should have been declared under parliamentary rules. Non-declaration can often be perfectly legitimate within the rules. NB2: I am grateful to the journalist Rebecca Ratcliffe, who helped me cross-reference the DueDil data with the Register of Interests, and who is credited in the acknowledgements page.

34. As at 31/10/15 ; https://issuu.com/embassykazakhstan/docs/second_ kazakhstan-u.s._convention_b. In an email, Lord Watford explained: 'Thank you for your note and opportunity to respond to your query

about the non-declaration of my interest in Strategic Matters LLP. Albeit the latter was, indeed, one of the sponsors of the December 2014 Kazakh-US Convention, it, in fact, only subsequently started to trade recently earlier this year as I and my business partner, Alan Spence, were pre-occupied with a series of other projects. This being the case, my interest will shortly be registered in the Register of Interests where all my business interests have always been duly declared in a timely manner.'

35. As at 26/10/15.

36. Mark Field said: 'All clients of M.C.Field Consulting Limited are listed in my register of interests, which declares in full the time spent and money earned from my non-parliamentary activities.'

Chapter 4: Honest graft?

1. Lords Hansard: 19 Nov 2015, Column 365 http://www.publications. parliament.uk/pa/ld201516/ldhansrd/text/151119-0003. htm#15111946000199

2. According to http://www.commsworld.com/corporate/board-of-directors NB: This biography says he left investment banking in 2002.

3. Register of Interests, as at 14/12/15.

4. The website says: 'Our solutions include Fibre Ethernet, VPLS, EFM, EoFTTC and Broadband.' http://www.commsworld.com/ (accessed 09/03/16) ; http://www.commsworld.com/news/scottish-businesses-urged-to-use-grant-for-faster-broadband (accessed 31/12/15)

5. For instance: http://www.publications.parliament.uk/pa/cm201516/ cmhansrd/cm150624/halltext/150624h0002.htm. Following the initial publication of this book, the Parliamentary Commissioner for Standards agreed to launch an inquiry into Blackford for failing to declare his interests while speaking in a debate. The inquiry ruled that he was 'in breach of the rules'. However, the Commissioner added: 'I do not believe Mr Blackford was activley trying to conceal his financial interests,' saying it was a 'genuine mistake'.

6. http://www.publications.parliament.uk/pa/cm201516/cmhansrd/ cm150624/halltext/150624h0002.htm

7. Lord Marland: http://www.publications.parliament.uk/pa/ld201314/ ldhansrd/text/130516-0002.htm#13051661000853

8. Lords Hansard: 9 April 2014, Column 1337–40

9. Tekcapital Topco plc, 'Appointment of Director' document (date of appointment: 17/02/14. Received by Companies House: 21/02/14).

Greenfield is a non-executive director, according to the firm's annual accounts ending Nov 2014.

10. http://tekcapital.com/ (accessed 30/11/15)

11. As at 31/10/15. NB: 'Tekcapital Ltd' is named in Greenfield's 'Biography' page on Parliament's website, but is not listed in the Register of Interests.

12. Following the initial publication of this book in May 2016, the House of Lords Commissioner for Standards agreed to launch an inquiry into Baroness Greenfield over this case. The report concluded there had been a breach of the rules and said she had wirtten a formal letter of apology to the chairman of the Sub-Committee on Lords' Conduct. The Commissioner said: 'Although I accept that Baroness Greenfield's late registration of the interest was due to a misunderstanding of the rules (she thought interests need to be registered only if they exceed £1,000 in value per month), all members of the House of Lords are expected to understand the requirements of the Code of Conduct. The general threshold below which financial interests do not normally need to be registered is £500 per year. That is a lot less than £1,000 per month, which is a considerable amount. The requirement to register all directorships is equally clear. Even if there was doubt about the Code's requirements the Registrar of Lords' Interests was available to advise. I regret that Baroness Greenfield's understanding of this aspect of the Code was so faulty. That said, I repeat that I accept that her mistake was genuine, as is her apology.'

13. https://uk.linkedin.com/in/clifford-gross-715b9029 (accessed 30/11/15) and http://finance.yahoo.com/news/q-interview-ceo-tekcapital-open-130000404.html

14. Screenshot from Clifford M. Gross, Joseph P. Allen, *Technology Transfer for Entrepreneurs: A Guide to Commercializing Federal Laboratory Innovations* (2003) p.105. The book cites the following source for the diagram: 'Gross, Reischl and Abercrombie 2000'.

15. Tekcapital plc (previously Tekcapital Topco plc), annual accounts ending Nov 2014 (the most recent annual accounts to be filed with Companies House at time of writing). Re share options, it says of Greenfield: '75,000 shares at 25p per share'.

16. http://dev.tekcapital.com/about/background-values/ (accessed 30/11/15)

17. http://tekcapital.com/services/ (accessed 30/11/15)

18. Full comment from Baroness Greenfield (received 15/04/16): 'I am very grateful to Mr Williams for bringing this issue to my attention. I now learn

that I should indeed have included the directorship of Tekcapital plc in the Declaration of Interests and am very sorry for the misunderstanding on my part. I was originally under the impression that I needed only to declare income over £1,000.00 per month: since the stipend I receive from Tekcapital is below this amount, I did not include it in my monthly statement. I am now aware that I was in error and should have declared any directorships irrespective of income: I've immediately corrected this mistake. Please note that as far as I'm aware my entry of the Declaration of Interests now complies with all requirements. You might also like to note that I claim no daily attendance allowance nor any other expenses.'

19. http://www.independent.co.uk/news/uk/politics/tory-mp-royston-smith-is-least-active-among-parliaments-new-members-a6886761.html

20. http://www.publications.parliament.uk/pa/cm201516/cmhansrd/cm150713/debtext/150713-0002.htm#15071328000058

21. http://www.publications.parliament.uk/pa/cm201516/cmhansrd/cm150713/debtext/150713-0002.htm#15071328000058

22. http://www.dailyecho.co.uk/news/13376306.REVEALED__Take_a_glimpse_at_Southampton_s_new___36m_hotel/

23. Ibid.

24. Ibid.

25. Register of Interests, as at 26/10/15. NB: it is registered on Companies House as Vigilo Ltd. His Register of Interests explains: 'Vigilo Ltd trading as RMJ Public Relations.' ; https://www.linkedin.com/company/rmjpr?trk=ppro_cprof (as at 12/12/15)

26. He only lists his shareholdings in the company. Separately, he also declares a list of consultancy work, although it is not clear from the Register whether this work was done via the company.

27. https://uk.pinterest.com/johnnicolson/7-fournier-street-spitalfields/ (accessed 07/02/16)

28. http://www.heraldscotland.com/news/13807613.John_Nicolson__an_SNP_MP_with_a_good_eye_for_property/?ref=mc&lp=3 NB: There is absolutely no suggestion that Nicolson's work in Parliament has been influenced in any way by his personal financial interests, or that he has done anything inappropriate.

29. http://www.theguardian.com/housing-network/2016/jan/14/mp-landlords-number-risen-quarter-last-parliament-housing-bill

30. http://www.publications.parliament.uk/pa/cm201516/cmcode/1076/107604.htm NB: they also have to declare it if they receive more than a certain amount of rental income from the property.

31. Figures (and the breakdown that follows) are based on the Commons' Register of Interests, as at Aug 2015. 'Forestries' includes woodland. 'Farms' includes entries described as 'farmland'.

32. http://www.parliament.uk/mps-lords-and-offices/standards-and-financial-interests/house-of-lords-commissioner-for-standards-/code-of-conduct-for-the-house-of-lords/guide-to-the-code-of-conduct/#jump-link-3 Another difference is that peers are required to declare property where rental income is more than £5k, rather than £10k in the Commons.

33. Figures (and the breakdown that follows) are based on the Lords' Register of Interests, as at 23/08/15. Some declarations include multiple properties, e.g. they might simply refer to 'houses'. Where it is clear there are multiple properties, but the number is not given, I have taken the most conservative approach and listed it as 2 properties. NB: 'Houses, mansions, flats and cottages' includes entries which are simply declared as 'residential'. Also, 'farms' includes farmland. 'Forestries' includes woodlands.

34. http://www.independent.co.uk/news/uk/politics/tories-vote-down-law-requiring-landlords-make-their-homes-fit-for-human-habitation-a6809691.html

35. http://www.independent.co.uk/news/uk/politics/landlord-tory-mp-philip-davies-law-requiring-homes-be-fit-for-human-habitation-unnecessary-a6696931.html

36. http://www.independent.co.uk/news/people/philip-davies-bills-the-tory-mp-has-attempted-to-filibuster-a6743121.html NB: There is absolutely no suggestion that Davies' work in Parliament has been influenced in any way by his personal financial interests, or that he has done anything inappropriate.

37. http://www.parliament.uk/business/committees/committees-a-z/commons-select/culture-media-and-sport-committee/inquiries/parliament-2015/establishing-world-class-connectivity-throughout-the-uk-15-16/

38. http://www.parliament.uk/business/committees/committees-a-z/commons-select/culture-media-and-sport-committee/news-parliament-2015/terms-of-reference-connectivity-15-16/ Writing in Feb 2016.

39. As at 08/02/16.

40. http://www.parliament.uk/documents/commons-committees/culture-media-and-sport/Formal_minutes_2015-16.pdf

41. http://www.ngcnetworks.co.uk/about-us.html (accessed 01/12/15)

42. http://www.parliament.uk/documents/commons-committees/culture-media-and-sport/Formal_minutes_2015-16.pdf

43. http://www.publications.parliament.uk/pa/cm/cmregmem/150608/adams_nigel.htm and http://www.publications.parliament.uk/pa/cm/cmregmem/150713/adams_nigel.htm NB: it is possible that the value or proportion of his shareholding became lower than the registrable threshold. There is no suggestion that he broke any parliamentary rules or acted improperly.

44. http://data.parliament.uk/writtenevidence/committeeevidence.svc/evidencedocument/culture-media-and-sport-committee/establishing-worldclass-connectivity-throughout-the-uk/oral/25468.html

45. http://www.parliament.uk/documents/commons-committees/culture-media-and-sport/Formal_minutes_2015-16.pdf 'Nigel Adams declared a non-pecuniary interest as his wife was a director and shareholder of two telecommunications companies.'

46. Director since 2006, according to Companies House. Shares have been rounded up to one decimal point. See NGC Networks Limited, Annual Return (15/11/15)

47. http://www.selbyandainsty.com/meet-nigel/ (accessed 01/12/15)

48. http://www.publications.parliament.uk/pa/ld201212/ldhansrd/text/120229-0002.htm#12022976000053

49. Public Whip, as at 15/12/15 – http://www.publicwhip.org.uk/mp.php?mpn=Wolfson_of_Sunningdale&mpc=Lords&house=lords&display=allvotes#divisions

50. http://www.theguardian.com/commentisfree/2013/mar/30/health-act-means-death-of-nhs

51. http://www.unitetheunion.org/uploaded/documents/unite%20politics%20briefing%20-%20privatised%20nhs11-15356.pdf

52. https://www.google.co.uk/url?sa=t&rct=j&q=&esrc=s&source=web&cd=1&cad=rja&uact=8&ved=0ahUKEwjn6efFyN7JAhVGthQKHRmaAOMQFgggMAA&url=http%3A%2F%2Fwww.healthlogistics.co.uk%2Fwp-content%2Fuploads%2F2015%2F11%2FHealthlogistics-Services-for-Suppliers_-1015.pdf&usg=AFQjCNGsSKqmxqJYEULqNWYWuld1lPvNRQ&sig2=cVN4PSgKI5P_WMx0DD5i8g (PDF file download)

53. http://www.healthlogistics.co.uk/nhs-suppliers/ (accessed 15/12/15)

54. http://www.healthlogistics.co.uk/services/ (accessed 15/12/15)

55. Healthlogistics.co.uk Limited, annual accounts ending March 2015. NB1: £1.8m refers to total shareholder funds. NB2: Lord Wolfson is one of a number of people on the board of directors. The latest Annual Return (Jan 2015) does not list him as one of the shareholders. There is no suggestion that he has ever personally profited from the company.

56. As at 09/03/16.
57. http://www.patients-association.org.uk/organiser/lord-wolfson-of-sunningdale/ (accessed 15/12/15)
58. £580,850 as at 15/12/15, according to the Electoral Commission.
59. https://groupdf.com/en/ and https://groupdf.com/en/our-business/gas-distribution/ (accessed16/01/16)
60. http://www.publications.parliament.uk/pa/ld201415/ldhansrd/text/150324-0001.htm#15032472000376
61. ICE Futures Europe: accounts ending Dec 2014, and 'Appointment of Director' document (23/09/15) as filed with Companies House.
62. https://www.theice.com/publicdocs/Linking_Oil_Price_Moves_Events.pdf (accessed 09/12/15)
63. https://www.theice.com/publicdocs/Linking_Oil_Price_Moves_Events.pdf
64. https://www.theice.com/publicdocs/Global_Crude_Products_Outlook.pdf
65. To be clear, his initial appointment was approved by a parliamentary advisory committee and this was published on Parliament's website. But it was not listed in the Register of Interests or mentioned in the speech itself. It appeared on the Register of Interests a few days after the speech.
66. http://www.publications.parliament.uk/pa/ld201516/ldhansrd/text/151202-0001.htm#15120253000409
67. Email from Jeremy Lefroy (24/12/15)
68. Between 1989 and 2000: http://www.jeremylefroy.org.uk/about-jeremy
69. http://ifcext.ifc.org/ifcext/spiwebsite1.nsf/ProjectDisplay/SPI_DP24994 (accessed 28/11/15)
70. http://www.publications.parliament.uk/pa/cm201011/cmhansrd/cm101026/debtext/101026-0001.htm#10102622000422 (NB: the word 'honourable' has been unabbreviated from the original Hansard text for clarity)
71. http://www.publications.parliament.uk/pa/cm201314/cmhansrd/cm140313/debtext/140313-0002.htm
72. http://www.publications.parliament.uk/pa/cm201516/cmhansrd/cm151027/halltext/151027h0001.htm NB: There is no suggestion that Advanced Bio Extracts has ever sought or benefitted from government money, or that Lefroy has ever used Parliament as a means to further his business interests in any way. Rather, the point being made is about transparency.

73. Advanced Bio-Extracts Limited, 'Termination of a Director' document (received 25/12/15; date of termination 24/12/15)

Chapter 5: Time to spare

1. Quoted by Angela Eagle MP (Lab) in Hansard: 25 Feb 2015, Column 388 and subsequently reported across the media. The Hansard is at: http://www.publications.parliament.uk/pa/cm201415/cmhansrd/cm150225/debtext/150225-0003.htm

2. http://www.parliament.uk/get-involved/contact-your-mp/

3. Register of Interests (as at 08/02/16). Yes, his book publisher is the same as mine. And, yes, my advance payment was absolute peanuts compared to his. Where's the justice in that, eh?!

4. http://www.publications.parliament.uk/pa/cm201415/cmselect/cmstandards/383/383.pdf

5. Hours declared in Register of Interests, as at 08/02/16.

6. Register of Interests (at Aug 2015). Mayor of London is declared as 'full time', this is assumed to be 365 days a year, minus 28 days statutory holiday entitlement: 337. This is added to columnist job, which is '10 hrs a month' (so, 120 hours a year). If we assume a working day is 8 hours, this works out as 15 days a year. Combined total is therefore 352 days.

7. Register of Interests (at Aug 2015). Total hours declared for work in 2014 = 680. If a working day is assumed to be 8 hours, this is equal to 85 days. Work was for 'Messrs. Travers, Thorp, Alberga, Attorneys', 'Messrs. Janes, solicitors', and 'Messrs. Khakhar and Co. Solicitors'. This figure does *not* include one of the items declared, which was 450 hours 'for legal services provided between 1 September 2013 and 30 January 2014' as this time period overlaps the 12 months being used for this calculation.

8. Register of Interests (at Aug 2015). The date of the hours worked is not always specified and, since work contracts overlap, it is impossible to work out an accurate figure for a 12-month period. This is therefore based on the 14 months between April 2014 and May 2015. However, I have excluded one item which falls in this period, but which started before it ('legal services provided. Solicitors: Reed Smith LLP . . . Hours: approximately 125 hours between 13 September 2013 and 12 October 2014'). It is clearly impossible to tell from this how many hours were worked within the 14-month period we are concerned

with. NB: Some of his declarations are listed in days, while others are listed in hours. For this calculation, the hours were added up and divided by 8 (usual hours for a working day), to arrive at the number of days. This was then added to items where it was already given in numbers of days.

9. Register of Interests (at Aug 2015). 'Between 10 hrs and 35 hrs a month' as chairman of County Finance Group Ltd. Since the time given is in a bracket, the halfway point between the two figures has been used as an average (22.5 hours a month). Multiplied across 12 months = 270 hours. Plus, London Assembly Member, 'between 10 hrs and 25 hrs a month'. Also taking the halfway figure, the calculation is therefore 17.5 x 12 = 210 hours. Combined total is 270 + 210 = 480 hours. If a working day is assumed to be 8 hours, this is equal to 60 days.

10. Register of Interests (at Aug 2015). Work for Apex Fund Services Holdings is 'expected to be 8 hrs a week'. Weeks per year is assumed to be 52, minus 6 weeks annual statutory holiday entitlement (so, 46). Therefore, hours per year is 8 x 46 = 386. Work as non-exec director of Philip T. English International Financial Services Ltd is 'expected to be about 60 hrs a year'. And work as non-exec director of Allpay Limited is 'four meetings a year; expected hours 5.5 hours each meeting'. Therefore 22 hours per year. Total hours per year is therefore 386 + 60 + 22 = 468. If an average working day is assumed to be 8 hours, then this is therefore equal to 58.5 days. Rounded to nearest whole number = 59.

11. Register of Interests (at Aug 2015). '10 hrs per week' as director of Morden Estates Company Limited. Weeks per year is assumed to be 52, minus 6 weeks annual statutory holiday entitlement (so, 46). Therefore the equivalent hours per year is 460. If an average working day is assumed to be 8 hours, then this is therefore equal to 57.5 days. Rounded to nearest whole number = 58.

12. https://www.youtube.com/watch?v=_ZNeXma48mE

13. http://www.theguardian.com/politics/2015/apr/25/david-cameron-blames-brain-fade-for-getting-his-football-team-wrong ; http://www.bbc.co.uk/programmes/p0093vk1/segments

14. http://www.publications.parliament.uk/pa/cm201415/cmhansrd/cm150225/debtext/150225-0003.htm

15. http://www.dailymail.co.uk/news/article-3279224/Tory-MP-quits-Commons-sleaze-watchdog-missing-dealdine-declare-350-000-earnings-barrister.html

16. Register of Interests (at Aug 2015). 'Received £40,000 . . . Hours: 30 hrs. (Registered 15/10/14).'

17. There is no suggestion that any of the MPs named do not work an appropriate number of hours as an MP, merely that they are spending considerable amounts of time doing other lucrative work, which could be spent doing MP work.

18. https://www.barstandardsboard.org.uk/regulatory-requirements/for-barristers/continuing-professional-development/frequently-asked-questions-about-cpd/ ('All practising barristers who have completed the first three years of practice are required to undertake the Established Practitioners Programme. Established Practitioners are required to complete a minimum of 12 CPD hours each calendar year'. A working day is assumed to be 8 hours, so this is therefore 1.5 days.) The Bar Standards board told me: 'If a barrister wishes to take a number of years off work, they do not have to renew their practising certificate, however, they become what is known as an 'unregistered barrister'. This means they cannot describe themselves as a barrister in connection with the provision of legal services, until they re-gain a practising certificate, which they can apply for at any time, as long as they are still eligible.'

19. Poll on website: http://www.telegraph.co.uk/news/politics/conservative/11940456/Tory-MP-Geoffrey-Cox-resigns-from-sleaze-watchdog-after-failing-to-declare-hundreds-of-thousands-of-pounds.html (Total of 2,468 votes cast as at 04/01/16)

20. https://yougov.co.uk/news/2015/02/25/voters-support-ban-second-jobs-mps/

Part Two: The enemy within
Chapter 6: Banks

1. There is no suggestion that any of these jobs or shareholdings are still active. Nor is there any suggestion that any of these peers were acting on behalf of any financial institutions or external third parties during the banking reform debates, or at any other time. Rather, this list is meant to illustrate the lack of diversity in professional background among peers who joined the debate.

2. http://www.parliament.uk/biographies/lords/lord-flight/4211 (His Metro Bank position is non-executive).

3. http://www.businessinsider.com/a-22-year-career-at-goldman-sachs-didnt-prepare-this-former-banker-for-running-the-london-olympics-2012-6?IR=T

4. newday.co.uk and http://www.parliament.uk/biographies/lords/lord-eatwell/2802

5. http://www.parliament.uk/biographies/lords/lord-lawson-of-blaby/1039

6. http://www.parliament.uk/biographies/lords/lord-mcfall-of-alcluith/4148 ; Companies House documents. NB: he was not a director at the time this legislation was first introduced, but joined the board within the period it was being debated and while he spoke on it. This was fully declared and there is no suggestion he did anything inappropriate.

7. http://www.parliament.uk/biographies/lords/lord-brennan/2550

8. Prudential plc, annual report, 2013; Frontier Economics Ltd, accounts ending April 2014. NB: Both directorships are non-executive. The former is also as an independent directorship.

9. CAABU Management Limited, annual accounts ending Sept 2000. There is no suggestion that he, the company or the trust were involved in any tax avoidance activities.

10. http://www.parliament.uk/biographies/lords/baroness-cohen-of-pimlico/2535

11. http://www.bbc.co.uk/religion/0/19847046

12. http://www.parliament.uk/biographies/lords/baroness-noakes/2554

13. http://www.parliament.uk/biographies/lords/viscount-trenchard/1829

14. http://www.lloydsbankinggroup.com/our-group/directors/. NB: the position at Lloyds is non-executive.

15. http://www.scotsman.com/news/profile-lord-forsyth-1-1371203

16. Jupiter Dividend & Growth Trust plc, annual accounts ending Dec 2013; Lords Register of Interests. NB: the three companies are called 'AREF Holdings (Bermuda) Ltd', 'IREF Australian Holdings (Bermuda) Ltd' and 'IREF Global Holdings (Bermuda) Ltd', so they would appear to be Bermudan companies, but it has not been possible to verify this. There is no suggestion that he or the companies have engaged with tax avoidance activities or drawn any inappropriate benefits from their apparent link to Bermuda.

17. http://www.gpbullhound.com/people/lord-clive-hollick/

18. http://www.publications.parliament.uk/pa/ld/ldreg/ldregold/reg22.htm

19. http://www.elaracapital.com/our-firm/board-of-directors and various Companies House documents filed for Ax Markets Limited

20. The Bill was drawn up in the Commons, but the Lords get to 'design'

in the sense that they can propose amendments and dispute sections they don't like.

21. http://www.ft.com/cms/s/0/e926e9e2-aef1-11e5-993b-c425a3d2b65a.html#axzz3xLQlfc3n

22. *Private Eye*, No.1409 (8–21 Jan 2016), p.3

23. Prof. Prem Sikka, *Banking in the public interest: Progressive reform of the financial sector* (Centre for Labour and Social Studies, Feb 2014): http://classonline.org.uk/docs/2014_Banking_in_the_public_interest_-_Prem_Sikka.pdf

24. Sikka is referring to the overall situation and the relationship between Parliament and the City as a whole, rather than the list of specific peers' names mentioned earlier. Although this was discussed in the interview, he did not see the list himself at the time and is in no way implying anything about the people included on the list. Additionally, there is no suggestion from the author that any of the individuals named on the list have done anything wrong or are corrupt in any way. Rather, it is the overriding institutional setup and relationship of Parliament and the City as a whole which it's suggested is corrupt – something that cannot be pinpointed down to any individual.

25. Worked in finance in 1971: http://www.bloomberg.com/research/stocks/private/person.asp?personId=10287358&privcapId=138416

26. http://www.parliament.uk/biographies/lords/lord-flight/4211   and http://news.bbc.co.uk/1/hi/uk_politics/4384577.stm

27. http://www.theguardian.com/politics/2010/nov/25/howard-flight-rebuked-no-10-poor-people-breeding

28. There is no suggestion that Lord Flight, Tax Incentivised Savings Association, or anyone else involved acted dishonourably, illegally, or in breach of parliamentary rules, nor that they stood to benefit financially or commercially from Lord Flight's activity. Rather, this is included to demonstrate the influence that Flight has in shaping legislation, and his willingness to listen to concerns and issues arising from his business interests in an honest fashion.

29. http://www.theguardian.com/business/2013/nov/26/government-defeat-banking-reform-bill

30. http://www.totalpolitics.com/print/322527/lord-strathclyde-and39when-people-look-at-me-they-see-poshand39.thtml

31. http://www.publications.parliament.uk/pa/ld201314/ldhansrd/text/131216-0002.htm#1312173000146

32. Flight corrected me on his job title, saying 'I'm a regulator in Guernsey, yes.'

33. http://www.bbc.co.uk/news/world-europe-guernsey-33181401

Subsequent reports suggest Guernsey may have since been dropped from the blacklist. See: http://www.international-adviser.com/news/1024244/guernsey-dropped-eu-tax-blacklist

34. https://www.thebureauinvestigates.com/2012/07/10/house-of-bankers-16-of-lords-are-paid-by-city-firms/

35. https://www.thebureauinvestigates.com/2012/07/10/house-of-bankers-16-of-lords-are-paid-by-city-firms/

36. Register of Interests (as at 14/12/15), and the latest accounts for Europe Arab Bank PLC (ending Dec 2014). He is an independent non-executive director.

37. Europe Arab Bank PLC, annual accounts ending Dec 2014. Net profit is before tax.

38. Arab Bank Group, *Annual Report 2014*: http://www.arabbank.com/uploads/File/AnnualReport2014EN.pdf

39. http://www.nytimes.com/2014/09/23/nyregion/arab-bank-found-guilty-of-supporting-terrorist.html

40. http://www.nytimes.com/2014/09/23/nyregion/arab-bank-found-guilty-of-supporting-terrorist.html

41. http://www.nytimes.com/2014/09/23/nyregion/arab-bank-found-guilty-of-supporting-terrorist.html NB: a year later, the Arab Bank reportedly reached a settlement with the plaintiffs shortly before the damages trial began.

42. http://www.nytimes.com/2015/08/15/nyregion/arab-bank-reaches-settlement-in-suit-accusing-it-of-financing-terrorism.html?_r=0

43. Email from Sir Edward Leigh MP (11/03/16). Leigh said: 'I am an independent non-executive director of Europe Arab Bank plc (EAB), which is a UK incorporated bank regulated by the Prudential Regulation Authority and the Financial Conduct Authority and adheres to the highest standards of conduct and corporate governance. I should just make clear that I hold no position with EAB's parent, Arab Bank plc (which is one of the Middle East's largest banking groups) and cannot and do not speak on its behalf . . . The following are matters of public record in relation to the lawsuits:

'1. The lawsuits did not allege that Arab Bank engaged in acts of terrorism, but claimed that it provided banking services to individuals or organisations that it allegedly knew to be affiliated with terrorist groups. Arab Bank denied any wrongdoing throughout; it maintained that it provided lawful and legitimate banking services, including the processing of automated, electronic fund transfer instructions in conformity with governing compliance rules. The

Bank consistently stated that it did not knowingly or intentionally do business with terrorists, but rather adopted measures to combat terrorist financing.

'2. During the course of the lawsuit the US Solicitor General filed an "amicus curiae" (ie "friend of the court") brief supportive of Arab Bank in which it stated that the US Government views Arab Bank as a "constructive partner" in combating terrorism financing.

'3. As announced last year, the parties agreed to settle the litigation without any admission of any wrongdoing on the part of Arab Bank. The terms of the settlement agreement are confidential.

'. . . Not only do I consider my position as a non-executive director at EAB to be entirely appropriate for an MP, but it is an association which I am proud to maintain.'

44. There is no suggestion that the Arab Bank, or any of its subsidiaries, have engaged in tax avoidance activities or used tax havens for any inappropriate purposes.

45. Email from Sir Edward Leigh MP (11/03/16). He said: 'EAB is UK tax resident and pays corporation tax as well as other UK taxes in the ordinary way. UK corporation tax is not charged on revenue (as you seem to suggest) but on profits. EAB's profits before tax for 2014 were €8.9m. As the notes to the audited financial statements in EAB's most recent published annual report (for 2014) make clear, EAB has substantial unused tax losses (estimated at €350m for 2014) which were appropriately offset against profits in accordance with the rules.'

46. http://countyfinancegroup.co.uk/ (accessed 08/01/16)

47. http://www.philiptenglish.com/about.aspx (accessed 08/01/16); and Philip T. English International Financial Services Limited, annual accounts ending March 2015. The £1.5m figure refers to turnover.

48. http://www.pembrokevct.com/

49. Somerset Capital Managent LLP, annual accounts ending March 2015). The £19m figure refers to turnover. Re Rees-Mogg's salary, see Register of Interests (as at Aug 2015). The payments he has registered vary slightly, but are all over £9,000.

50. Emails between me and Jacob Rees-Mogg's Diary Secretary (Dec 2015). The financial figures are from the parent company, of which he is also a director: The American Trading Company (Holdings) Limited, annual accounts (ending March 2015). There is no suggestion that his claim about the company not needing to be declared is inaccurate.

Chapter 7: Tax

1. There is no suggestion that Stuart broke any rules by not declaring Vestra Wealth in the Register of Interests. Rather, this shows that the current rules may not be substantial.

2. Vestra Wealth LLP, Companies House filing: 'Appointment of member of a Limited Liability Partnership (LLP)' document (date of appointment: 30/07/12; received for filing in electronic format: 30/04/13)

3. http://www.theguardian.com/politics/2015/feb/13/miliband-determined-tax-avoidance

4. http://www.theguardian.com/politics/2015/apr/07/ed-miliband-non-dom-tax-status-labour

5. http://www.vestrawealth.com/media/literature2/Vestra_Wealth_Brochure.pdf (accessed 09/03/16)

6. http://www.vestrawealth.com/; http://www.vestrawealth.com/media/literature/Key_Facts_Intermediaries.pdf (both accessed 09/03/16)

7. http://www.vestrawealth.com/media/news/Vestra_Wealth_Brochure.pdf (accessed 09/03/16)

8. http://www.vestrawealth.com/media/literature/Key_Facts_Intermediaries.pdf (accessed 09/03/16)

9. http://www.vestrawealth.com/people/danielfresnais/ (accessed 09/03/16)

10. http://www.wealthadviser.co/2014/02/04/196753/tax-take-non-coms-jumps-record-high (accessed 09/03/16). NB: according to this website, this report was published in 2014.

11. 'Financial Statements, Vestra Wealth LLP', accounts for year ending 30/04/14 (as filed with Companies House)

12. Lord McFall of Alcluith (Lab), Hansard: House of Lords, 9 July 2014, Column 210

13. http://www.wealthadviser.co/2014/02/04/196753/tax-take-non-coms-jumps-record-high

14. http://www.londonlovesbusiness.com/business-news/super-wealthy-are-on-tipping-point-of-leaving-london/3457.article

15. http://www.parliament.uk/business/committees/committees-a-z/commons-select/public-accounts-committee/chair-nominations1/

16. There is no suggestion that either Gisela Stuart, or Vestra Wealth, or anyone associated with it has acted illegally or improperly, or that Stuart has avoided paying any tax.

17. http://www.publications.parliament.uk/pa/cm/cmregmem/160222/stuart_gisela.htm

18. £70,000 is the threshold for registration. Her declaration implies that the investment reached this level on the day of the interview. NB: the £43.50 figure is return on investment, whereas the £70,000 figure is overall value of investment. There is no suggestion that either figure is wrong or that her official declarations are misleading. Following the initial publication of this book in May 2016, the Commissioner for Standards launched an inquiry into this case but ruled that Gisela Stuart had not breached the Code of Conduct, neither for late registration of her interests in Vestra Wealth LLP, nor for failure to declare it (i.e. whilst running to be chair of the Public Accounts Committee). I have discussed this in more detail in the Afterword.

19. It had been an emerging political issue for some time, most notably after the emergence of UK Uncut in 2010 and the protests against alleged tax avoidance by Vodafone. *The Times*'s revelations, however, led to unprecedented coverage and interventions from senior politicians.

20. http://www.theguardian.com/politics/2012/jun/20/jimmy-carr-tax-david-cameron

21. http://www.theguardian.com/politics/2015/feb/13/miliband-determined-tax-avoidance ; http://www.theguardian.com/politics/2011/aug/27/george-osborne-warns-tax-cheats; https://www.gov.uk/government/speeches/deputy-prime-ministers-speech-on-tax-and-fairness NB: Osborne's comment was about illegal tax evasion, rather than legal (if morally questionable) tax avoidance.

22. http://www.taxresearch.org.uk/Documents/PCSTaxGap2014Full.pdf

23. The total bill for MPs' expenses in 2014/15 was £112,653,000 (net), according to IPSA.

24. http://www.taxresearch.org.uk/Documents/PCSTaxGap2014Full.pdf

25. http://www.bbc.co.uk/news/business-31248913. There is no suggestion that all of the people involved had avoided tax or acted in an illegal way. It is likely to have varied greatly between cases.

26. For example: https://www.tuc.org.uk/sites/default/files/GAAR.pdf

27. http://blogs.channel4.com/factcheck/howmanynondompeers/444

28. http://www.bbc.co.uk/news/10535852 ; http://www.theguardian.com/politics/2010/mar/01/lord-ashcroft-reveals-non-dom

29. Michael Ashcroft, preface to: Michael Ashcroft and Isabel Oakeshott, *Call Me Dave: The unauthorised biography of David Cameron* (Biteback, 2015)

30. Hansard, House of Lords, 19 Oct 2010, Column WA168; and 27 Oct 2010, Column WA304. See: http://www.publications.parliament.uk/pa/ld201011/ldhansrd/text/101019w0001.htm#10101929000529 and http://www.publications.parliament.uk/pa/ld201011/ldhansrd/text/101027w0001.htm#10102745000314 My emphasis.

31. Hansard, House of Lords, 19 Dec 2012, Column WA327. http://www.publications.parliament.uk/pa/ld201213/ldhansrd/text/121219w0001.htm#12121958000387

32. No suggestion that he actually worked on the island – just that this is where the company is based.

33. Razzall's Register of Interests says: 'Ardel Holdings Ltd (Guernsey) (formerly Concordia Holdings Ltd (Guernsey)) (holding company) (interest ceased 22 May 2015)' (as at 28/08/15). He was on the board of directors, alongside others, and there is no suggestion that he owned the company. There is no available information about his remuneration. Also see: http://www.careyolsen.com/experience/carey-olsen-advises-ardel-holdings-on-the-sale-of-ardel-trust-to-equiom/

34. http://www.telegraph.co.uk/news/politics/2435740/Party-loving-peer-Lord-Razzall.html

35. Hansard: House of Lords, 9 July 2014, Column 210

36. Ardel brochures: 'Qualifying Non-UK Pension Schemes (QNUPS)' and 'Offshore Protected Cell Company Bond'. Formerly at: http://www.ardelholdings.com/file/58/ardelqualifyingnonukpension-schemesqnups.pdf and http://www.ardelholdings.com/file/55/ardeloffshoreprotectedcellcompanybond.pdf (Both accessed 20/04/15. Website has since been re-made).

37. Various brochures and literature downloaded from Ardel's website (accessed 20/05/15). The site has since been re-made.

38. http://www.ardelholdings.com/file//13/Ardel%20invite%20Edinburgh.pdf (accessed at 20/05/15) The site has since been re-made and this document does not appear to be online any more.

39. Ardel brochure: 'Hold-Over Trust'. Formerly at: http://www.ardel-holdings.com/file/5/ardelholdovertrust.pdf (accessed 20/04/15. Website has since been re-made). NB: There is absolutely no suggestion that Ardel helped people to break the law or that it was involved in any way with illegal tax evasion. Rather, the point is merely that it helped clients to legitimately and legally navigate tax laws.

40. Ardel newsletter, 'communiqueé', issue 6 (07/12)

41. Razzall could not be reached for comment. However, I first revealed Razzall's link with Ardel in an article for the *Guardian* in 2012, with

Rajeev Syal. At the time, he said: 'As an adviser to the owner of Ardel Holdings for the last 25 years I have always been satisfied that the business does not engage in activities of the type criticised by George Osborne.' See: http://www.theguardian.com/business/2012/sep/20/top-tory-britain-tax-haven-millionaires NB: as already mentioned, Ardel has since been bought up, and there is no suggestion that he has any involvement with this any more.

42. With Rajeev Syal, a lobby journalist for the *Guardian*. http://www.theguardian.com/business/2012/sep/20/tory-treasurer-make-uk-tax-haven ; http://www.theguardian.com/business/2012/sep/20/top-tory-britain-tax-haven-millionaires and http://www.theguardian.com/news/datablog/2012/sep/20/peers-mps-directors-companies-linked-tax-havens

43. Email from Lord Fraser (30/08/12). The spacing between words has been corrected.

44. Full response and quotes given in the spreadsheet at: http://www.theguardian.com/news/datablog/2012/sep/20/peers-mps-directors-companies-linked-tax-havens

45. At the time of the *Guardian* report, Arcadia Group Limited (of which Lord Grabiner was on the board of directors) had a parent company, Taveta Ltd, which was registered in Jersey. Sir Philip Green confirmed this on the phone to the *Guardian* at the time. Lawyers for the company which Lord Fraser had a position at, In2Matrix Services Group (Jersey) Limited, confirmed: 'Our client confirms that Lord Fraser of Carmyllie is a non-executive director of In2Matrix Services Group (Jersey) Limited . . . We can confirm that In2Matrix Services Group (Jersey) Limited is a Jersey registered company.' The full details are available at: http://www.theguardian.com/news/datablog/2012/sep/20/peers-mps-directors-companies-linked-tax-havens. There is no suggestion that any of these details have remained the same since the *Guardian* report.

46. http://www.theguardian.com/news/2016/apr/04/tory-donors-links-to-offshore-firms-revealed-in-leaked-panama-papers ; http://www.theguardian.com/news/2016/apr/04/panama-papers-david-cameron-father-tax-bahamas

47. This comment was not made in relation to Arcadia Group and there is no suggestion that Arcadia Group has any links to the Cayman Islands.

48. I am grateful to the journalist Daniel Kraemer, who worked with me on this analysis, and who is credited in the acknowledgements page.

49. There is no fixed definition of a 'tax haven'. For this analysis, I included

jurisdictions listed as tax havens by Ethical Consumer (as listed at Nov 2015), which is calculated using a more balanced approach than some lists (taking the population size into consideration). Added to this were Liberia, Nauru, Cyprus, Dubai, the Bahamas and Mauritius, which are all frequently regarded as tax havens. E.g.:

- http://www.oecd.org/countries/monaco/listofunco-operativetax-havens.htm (re. Liberia & Nauru);
- 'Report raises heat on tax havens', *Financial Times* (23/11/13) (re. Cyprus & Dubai);
- 'Tax fraud trial begins in France of art-dealer dynasty', *Financial Times* (04/01/16) (re. Bahamas);
- http://www.theguardian.com/business/2013/nov/03/deloittes-tax-savings-investments-in-poor-countries (re. Mauritius).
- For the Ethical Consumer list, see: http://www.ethicalconsumer.org/ethicalcampaigns/taxjusticecampaign/taxhavenlist.aspx.

NB: 'tax havens' vary greatly in terms of what benefits a company can get from them (if any). Some may offer zero tax, but others might simply offer the opportunity to keep certain financial information private, or avoid dual taxation. Therefore, while all of these territories might reasonably be described as 'tax havens', that in no way suggests that any company based there has avoided tax or done anything improper.

50. http://www.standard.co.uk/news/uk/everyone-avoids-tax-says-lord-fink-after-he-was-named-by-ed-miliband-in-commons-row-10041040.html

51. Quotes from spreadsheet at: http://www.theguardian.com/news/data-blog/2012/sep/20/peers-mps-directors-companies-linked-tax-havens

52. Marex Spectron Group Limited, accounts ending Dec 2014 (most recently available on Companies House at time of writing). Subsidiaries in Hong Kong, Gibraltar and Singapore.

53. ISAM Europe LLP, accounts ending March 2015. As registered on Companies House.

54. Figure is for turnover: 'Caparo Group Limited', accounts ending Dec 2014. NB: figure rounded to nearest £10m (actual figure according to accounts: £371.2m)

55. Alan Tovey, 'Failed Caparo had over £160m in liabilities including black hole in its pension scheme', *Daily Telegraph* (12/01/16). NB: this report adds: 'Administrators managed to save the bulk of the jobs within the Caparo companies after selling them, but some of the businesses were unsustainable and about 500 redundancies were made.' Also: http:

//news.sky.com/story/1596124/steel-jobs-saved-as-caparo-business-sold

56. According to the latest accounts filed on Companies House at the time of writing: Caparo Group Limited, accounts ending Dec 2014. Responding, Lord Paul's PA simply quoted the latest balance sheet for Caparo Group Ltd (year ending 31/12/14), under the heading 'Ultimate parent company and controlling parties': 'The Rt Hon The Lord Paul of Marylebone, The Honourable Ms Anjli Paul, The Honourable Ambar Paul, The Honourable Akash Paul and The Honourable Angad Paul, directors of Caparo Group Limited, are jointly and indirectly interested in the whole of the issued share capital of Caparo Group Limited through shareholdings registered in the name of Caparo International Corporation, a company registered in the British Virgin Islands. Caparo International Corporation ultimately holds the issued share capital of Caparo Group Limited on behalf of a series of family trusts.'

57. See Cayman Islands company register: http://www.ciregistry.gov.ky/portal/page/portal/reghome   and   http://www.bloomberg.com/research/stocks/private/snapshot.asp?privcapid=314622976

58. http://www.gov.ky/portal/page/portal/cighome/cayman/theeconomy/taxes

59. As at 16/01/16.

60. Somerset Capital Management Limited, accounts ending March 2015. NB: It is not clear what proportion of the Cayman Island company is owned by the UK company. The accounts simply say it owns '50 (2014: 50) ordinary shares of 1 US $ each in Somerset Capital Management (Cayman) Limited, a company incorporated in the Cayman Islands. The company has made a capital contribution of £50,000 to Somerset Capital Management LLP.' [The LLP is a related partnership that Rees-Mogg is also part of.] Responding, Rees-Mogg said: 'The company has no assets and no income as it is purely there in relation to funds that are sold to US investors who receive no tax advantages from investing in the Cayman Islands. Somerset Capital Management has no offshore earnings in tax havens.'

61. Responding, Philp said: 'BP Balkans Pluto (Cyprus) Ltd is a holding company for property businesses in various Eastern European countries. These subsidiaries pay full tax in the local countries in which they operate (unlike Google, Facebook etc which pay virtually no tax in many counties in which they operate, including the UK). The structure

is not designed for tax avoidance, and in fact does not avoid tax as mentioned. The BP Balkans company, and its subsidiaries, have no connection at all to the UK and so are clearly not relevant to my role as a UK MP. So I am afraid you are barking up the wrong tree.'

62. http://www.publications.parliament.uk/pa/cm200809/cmselect/ cmtreasy/355/355we03.htm NB: Philp's company is declared as BP Balkans Pluto (Cyprus) Ltd. The company registry in Cyprus confirms it is registered there.

63. http://www.independent.co.uk/news/people/nadhim-zahawi-from-a -refugee-on-welfare-to-the-heart-of-no-10-9760085.html

64. SThree plc, accounts ending Nov 2014. This shows £218,223,000 gross profit and £(8,066,000) tax. There is absolutely no suggestion that SThree has avoided tax in any illegal or illegitimate way, or that the use of firms based in tax havens is in any way linked to the amount of tax paid overall.

65. http://www.bbc.co.uk/news/business-18944097

66. Quote is from Vince Cable: http://www.bbc.co.uk/news/business -33628020

Chapter 8: War

1. All quotes and detail re al-Huda: https://www.amnesty.org/download /Documents/MDE3130262015ENGLISH.PDF. NB: some punctuation marks have been slightly altered in the quote from the schoolgirl, for the sake of clarity and emphasis.

2. Ibid.

3. Ibid.

4. http://www.theguardian.com/world/2015/mar/31/yemen-in-crisis- air-strike-leaves-40-civilians-dead-at-camp

5. http://www.theguardian.com/world/2016/jan/27/un-report-into- saudi-led-strikes-in-yemen-raises-questions-over-uk-role

6. There is no suggestion that BAE equipment was used in any of these specific attacks – simply that it is one of the most important arms suppliers to Saudi Arabia (including many aircraft).

7. Based on 2013 revenue, according to BAE Systems plc, 'Annual Report 2014'.

8. BAE Systems, Annual Report 2014: http://investors.baesystems.com/ ~/media/Files/B/Bae-Systems-Investor-Relations-V3/Annual%20 Reports/bae-annual-report-2014.pdf

9. http://www.theguardian.com/world/2016/jan/19/human-rights-groups-condemn-steep-rise-in-uk-arms-sales-to-saudis

10. https://www.amnesty.org/en/latest/news/2016/01/shia-cleric-among-47-executed-by-saudi-arabia-in-a-single-day/

11. Channel 4 News online video: https://www.facebook.com/Channel4News/videos/vb.6622931938/10153467145386939

12. Wafic Said

13. Andrew Feinstein, *The Shadow State: Inside the Global Arms Trade* (Penguin, 2012), p.35. NB: BAE Systems was then called 'British Aerospace'.

14. There is a strong archive of reports and investigations into BAE and the Al Yamamah contract on the *Guardian*'s website, at: http://www.theguardian.com/world/bae

15. Lord Goldsmith, quoted in: Andrew Feinstein, *The Shadow State: Inside the Global Arms Trade* (Penguin, 2012), pp.144–5

16. Andrew Feinstein, *The Shadow State: Inside the Global Arms Trade* (Penguin, 2012), p.143 ; and http://www.thesundaytimes.co.uk/sto/news/uk_news/article65009.ece

17. Lords Register of Interests, as at 22/01/16

18. This is fully declared in the Register of Interests.

19. Does not include any committee work, or other work that he may have done.

20. As at 21/01/16, from the start of the year 2006/07. According to the Hansard website. Does not include written questions or contributions to committees etc, only the main chamber.

21. Hansard, House of Lords, 24 Jan 2007 : Column 1143–5 (http://www.publications.parliament.uk/pa/ld200607/ldhansrd/text/70124-0007.htm#07012497000021)

22. http://www.baesystems.com/product/BAES_163698/successor?_afrLoop=2419463726622000&_afrWindowMode=0&_afrWindowId=null#!%40%40%3F_afrWindowId%3Dnull%26_afrLoop%3D2419463726622000%26_afrWindowMode%3D0%26_adf.ctrl-state%3Dfsq1byzfr_73 (Accessed 09/09/15)

23. http://www.baesystems.com/article/BAES_179694/bae-systems-awarded-257m-for-final-phase-of-successor-submarine-design?_afrLoop=2415921126725000&_afrWindowMode=0&_afrWindowId=null#!%40%40%3F_afrWindowId%3Dnull%26_afrLoop%3D2415921126725000%26_afrWindowMode%3D0%26_adf.ctrl-state%3Dex5j0jp02_134 (Accessed 09/09/15)

24. http://www.thetimes.co.uk/tto/opinion/thunderer/article4685219.ece

25. Full quote here is: 'I think you're rather stretching to make a point on that because, let's face it, nuclear weapons has been one of the biggest public policy issues in this country for the last forty or fifty years. And therefore, the idea that people couldn't comment on as broad a public issue as that, and somehow believe there is commercial advantage in doing so, well that defeats me.'

26. As at 10/10/16.

27. Register of Lords' Interests (as at 23/08/15). First declared in the register published 10/06/13. Salary is based on 2015 Register of Interests, which states, for example: 'Received £10,500. Hours: 20–25 hrs'. The £420 figure is therefore the most conservative estimate as it assumes he did the maximum 25 hours work.

28. Not my comparison. The likening of offsets to bribery is made, among other places, in: *The Financial Times*, 'Q&A: What are offsets?' (09/10/13) http://www.ft.com/cms/s/0/87728d1e-197a-11e3-afc2 -00144feab7de.html

29. The point about secrecy is meant about offsets in general, not specifically about Blenheim. Indeed, its website claims: 'Blenheim Capital has been at the forefront of transparency in offset advisory services since its inception, actively seeking regulation around the world and spending around 35% of its annual budget on outside compliance.' http://www. blenheimcapital.net/regulation (accessed 15/09/15)

30. http://www.economist.com/news/business/21578400-more-govern-ments-are-insisting-weapons-sellers-invest-side-deals-help-them -develop

31. As above, this is a comment about the offset market in general rather than specifically linked to Blenheim. Indeed, according to Blenheim's website, it is registered with numerous regulators including the UK Export Control Organisation and was the first offset provider to be authorised and regulated by the UK Financial Conduct Authority.

32. http://www.ft.com/cms/s/0/87728d1e-197a-11e3-afc2-00144feab7de.html

33. http://www.ft.com/cms/s/0/87728d1e-197a-11e3-afc2-00144feab7de.html

34. https://www.gov.uk/government/uploads/system/uploads/attach-ment_data/file/369353/gerald_20howarth_20approval_20letter_20_website_.pdf NB: This document, from the Advisory Committee on Business Appointments, notes the MOD had no formal contractual relationships with the company, and that Howarth did not have access to any commercially sensitive information about competitors.

35. http://www.telegraph.co.uk/finance/newsbysector/industry/defence/7903707/Blenheim-signed-up-for-5bn-Malaysian-defence-offset-deal.html

36. Ibid.

37. http://www.economist.com/news/business/21578400-more-governments-are-insisting-weapons-sellers-invest-side-deals-help-them-develop

38. http://www.ft.com/cms/s/0/353a6ace-356d-11e5-b05b-b01debd57852.html

39. http://www.dailymail.co.uk/femail/article-229926/The-man-doesn-t-damm.html

40. www.publicwhip.org.uk

41. http://news.bbc.co.uk/1/hi/uk_politics/2736339.stm

42. Register of Interests, as at 11/01/16. It is a non-executive position, according to the Register ; http://www.aegisworld.com/. NB: There is absolutely no suggestion that Soames's work in Parliament is influenced in any way by his personal financial interests. Furthermore, Companies House records say that Soames did not join the board of directors at AEGIS until 2005 (i.e. about 2.5 years after the invasion of Iraq), so there is clearly absolutely no suggestion Soames voted with financial or commercial interests.

43. Ann Hagedorn, *The Invisible Soldiers: How America Outsourced Our Security* (Simon & Schuster, 2014), p.87

44. http://www.aegisworld.com/who-we-are/(accessed23/01/16);'Appointment of director or secretary' form, as filed on Companies House, concerning Soames at Aegis Defence Services Limited.

45. Aegis Defence Services Limited, accounts ending Dec 2014.

46. Hansard for 2014/15 and 2015/16 up until time of writing (23/01/16).

47. http://www.independent.co.uk/news/people/profiles/lord-guthrie-tonys-general-turns-defence-into-an-attack-399865.html

48. 'Colt Defense LLC Colt Finance Corp.', Annual Report Amendment, year ending Dec 2013. Filed on Colt's website on 09/12/14 (the most recent annual report available on the site as at Nov 2015): http://www.colt.com/DesktopModules/Bring2mind/DMX/Download.aspx?EntryId=865&PortalId=0&DownloadMethod=attachment

49. Ibid.

50. Ibid. NB: This is written under a section in the annual report titled 'Risks related to our business', and under the subheading 'Misconduct by employees or agents could harm us and is difficult to detect and

deter'. There is no suggestion that misconduct does occur, or that Colt
is unable to prevent it – merely that it recognises this is a potential risk
of the business.

51. Colt commercial catalogue, 2015
52. http://time.com/24735/here-are-the-5-companies-making-a-killing-
off-wars-around-the-world/
53. Register of Interests, as at 23/01/16 ; http://www.generaldynamics.
uk.com/about-gduk ; General Dynamics United Kingdom Limited
(01911653), accounts ending Dec 2014. Committee membership is
listed at http://www.parliament.uk/biographies/lords/lord-levene-of-
portsoken/2035 (as at 23/01/16)
54. Register of Interests, as at 23/08/15
55. Register of Interests, as at 23/08/15, it says: 'interest ceased 6 January
2016'. NB: there are two 'Lord Patten's. The other one is Lord
(Christopher Francis) Patten of Barnes. The one I'm referring to here is
Lord (John Haggitt Charles) Patten.
56. http://www.theguardian.com/books/2013/feb/03/siegfried-sassoon-
poem-atrocities
57. Register of Interests, as at 23/01/16
58. http://www.raytheon.com/capabilities/precision/index.html
59. Register of Interests, as at 24/01/16.
60. According to Parliament's website, Inge declared this interest in April
2010 and made an amendment to the declaration in 2011. See: http://
explore.data.parliament.uk/?endpoint=lordsregisteredinterests
61. According to: http://bahrainsociety.uk/wp-content/uploads/2015/08
/Brig-Sincock2009.pdf (accessed 14/04/16)
62. According   to: http://www.gulf-daily-news.com/Print.
aspx?storyid=263771 (PDF) (Accessed 14/04/16)
63. FOI response, House of Lords (30/09/15). NB1: There is no
suggestion that Lord Inge broke any rules or acted inappropriately.
Since he does not appear to have been working for Bahrain at the
time he sponsored this even, it was perfectly within the rules.
NB2: 'sponsored' is the word used by the House of Lords to
describe this, however this merely refers to the granting of access
for the room used in Parliament. There is absolutely no suggestion
that Lord Inge paid any money towards the event, nor that he
benefitted in any way, or had any financial involvement with the
event whatsoever.
64. http://blogs.telegraph.co.uk/news/concoughlin/100016467/why-is-
britain-harbouring-bahrain-dissidents/

65. http://www.telegraph.co.uk/news/worldnews/middleeast/bahrain/
    8331765/Bahrain-in-turmoil-as-it-risks-rift-with-US.html

66. http://www.telegraph.co.uk/news/worldnews/middleeast/bahrain/
    11196656/The-family-that-protests-against-Bahrains-brutal-regime.
    html

67. In an email on 15/10/15, Lord Inge's PA said he had 'retired from
    everything about two years ago'. She was informed that this position is
    still listed on the Register of Interests, but as at 24/01/16 it has still not
    been removed.

68. Register of Interests, as at 24/01/16. NB: It is not clear from the
    Register how long Lord Richards acted as an adviser, but there is no
    suggestion this had been a long-term thing. The king and government
    of Jordan were personal clients of a strategic advice firm he chairs,
    Palliser Associates Ltd

69. Keith Perry, 'UK should not intervene in Syria, says former defence
    Chief', *Daily Telegraph* (10/03/14, p.8); Steven Swinford, 'Former
    head of the Armed Forces calls for thousands more troops to fight
    extremists', *Daily Telegraph* (06/10/14, p.8)

70. https://www.hrw.org/world-report/2014/country-chapters/jordan

Chapter 9: Corporate irresponsibility

1. http://www.globallabourrights.org/reports/1203-Chinese-Sweatshop
   -in-Bangladesh.pdf

2. Ibid. NB: The term 'slave wages' was used in press coverage of the report:
   http://www.thesun.co.uk/sol/homepage/news/4192900/Sweatshop-
   horror-exposed.html. The report itself describes the salaries as 'a starva-
   tion wage'.

3. Ibid.

4. Ibid.

5. BHS was sold in 2015.

6. He resigned his position in Dec 2015, according to a Companies House
   document (although, at the time of writing, his position is still listed on
   the Register of Interests).

7. http://www.thetimes.co.uk/tto/news/uk/article3097954.ece ; http://
   www.theguardian.com/commentisfree/2011/aug/12/rupert-
   murdoch-lawyers-watergate-news-corp

8. http://www.telegraph.co.uk/finance/bank-of-england/11361253/
   MPs-raise-suspicions-over-Bank-of-England-forex-report.html

9. http://www.lse.ac.uk/alumni/LSEConnect/LSEMagazine/pdf/summer2007/Advocate.pdf

10. http://www.independent.co.uk/news/business/analysis-and-features/lord-grabiner-no-room-at-the-inns-for-dickensian-values-his-great-expectations-come-to-3m-a-year-19009.html

11. Claire Newell Mauritius and Robert Winnett, 'Revealed: Topshop clothes made with "slave labour",' *The Sunday Times* (12/08/07), p1. NB: according to the report, the promise of higher wages were given by 'self-employed agents', not by Arcadia Group Limited or any employee or representative of the company.

12. http://www.independent.co.uk/news/uk/home-news/retail-giants-shamed-by-uk-sweatshops-2128022.html

13. https://www.arcadiagroup.co.uk/fashionfootprint/our-products/Ethical%20Trading (accessed 19/02/16)

14. http://www.ethicaltrade.org/about-eti/our-members (accessed 19/02/16)

15. Quoted in Ted C. Fishman, *China Inc.: The Relentless Rise of the Next Great Superpower* (Simon & Schuster, 2005)

16. Ibid and http://www.heraldscotland.com/news/12510264.Mone_angered_by__apos_sweatshop_apos__claim_over_Chinese_workers/

17. http://www.independent.co.uk/news/people/lingerie-entrepreneur-michelle-mone-reportedly-to-be-made-tory-peer-in-the-house-of-lords-10432161.html

18. http://www.heraldscotland.com/news/13845618.Michelle_Mone_s_firm_posts_big_losses_on_eve_of_her_Lords_unveiling/?ref=mr&lp=2

19. http://www.theguardian.com/world/2014/feb/06/bangladesh-garment-factories-child-labour-uk ; http://www.itv.com/news/story/2014-02-06/exposure-bangladesh-factory-abuse/

20. He is no longer on the board of directors. According to a document filed with Companies House, by Associated British Foods plc, his appointment ended on 30/11/15.

21. Associated British Foods plc, annual accounts ending Sept 2015

22. http://www.huffingtonpost.com/2013/05/02/bangladesh-death-toll-tops-500_n_3199568.html

23. http://www.theguardian.com/world/2014/mar/16/primark-payout-victims-rana-plaza-bangladesh

24. http://www.primark.com/en/our-ethics/news/press-releases/a-summary-of-primarks-rana-plaza-response ; http://www.primark.com/en/our-ethics/news/rana-plaza

25. The company's Annual Report 2000 is the earliest report that Charles Powell appears to be mentioned in. However, the exact date of his

appointment is not known and it is therefore possible it may have been in 1999, after the publication of that year's report.

26. Barrick Gold Corporation, Annual Report (2000 and 2014): http://www.barrick.com/investors/annual-report/

27. Barrick Annual Review 2006. It adds: 'In Papua New Guinea, remediation work is being completed on the West Wall at Porgera . . . Barrick owns a 75% interest in this joint venture and operates the mine. We expect Porgera to be a solid producer for many years to come.' See: http://www.barrick.com/files/annual-report/Barrick-Annual-Report-2006.pdf. However, the company now says it only owns 47.5% of the mine: 'Barrick (Niugini) Ltd. is the 95% owner of the Porgera Joint Venture and is the manager of the operation. Barrick Gold Corporation and Zijin Mining Group each own 50% of Barrick (Niugini) Ltd. The remaining 5% interest in the Porgera Joint Venture is held by Mineral Resources Enga and is divided between the Enga Provincial government (2.5%) and local landowners (2.5%).' See: http://www.barrick.com/operations/papua-new-guinea/porgera/default.aspx

28. Barrick Annual Review 2006: http://www.barrick.com/files/annual-report/Barrick-Annual-Report-2006.pdf

29. https://www.hrw.org/report/2011/02/01/golds-costly-dividend/human-rights-impacts-papua-new-guineas-porgera-gold-mine

30. The report adds: 'Barrick has committed itself to taking steps designed to address both failings, described in detail in the pages that follow. Human Rights Watch welcomes these moves, but their ultimate value will depend entirely on whether they succeed in preventing abuse and ensuring accountability for abuses that do occur.

'Barrick has also committed to providing Human Rights Watch with copies of its most current environmental reports when they are finalised, along with other documents. In Human Rights Watch's view, the company should have made these public long ago.' NB: There is no suggestion that any of these allegations, issues or concerns are still ongoing today, or that Barrick itself has done anything illegal.

31. https://www.hrw.org/report/2011/02/01/golds-costly-dividend/human-rights-impacts-papua-new-guineas-porgera-gold-mine

32. Barrick Annual Review 2011: http://www.barrick.com/files/annual-report/Barrick-Annual-Report-2011.pdf

33. Email from Lord Powell of Bayswater (11/03/16). He said: 'I assume you understand the difference between a company's board which has a statutory role and the responsibility to deal with these matters provide, and an advisory board which meets once a year to provide strategic

advice to the company but has no role in running it and is not necessarily fully informed in detail of all its affairs. I am on the Barrick Advisory Board and have only a broad knowledge of the matters alleged in the Human Rights Watch 2011 report.

'What I do know is that Barrick condemned in the strongest possible terms the crimes alleged in the Human Rights Watch report, made no attempt to conceal the enormity of what happened, conducted a thorough internal investigation and urged the Papua New Guinea police to do the same. It strengthened security at the mine to avoid any repetition and provided mandatory human rights training to all the mine's employees. The author of the Human Rights Watch report said at the time he thought that Barrick responded with the necessary vigour to the allegations in the report. Since those events Barrick has introduced a comprehensive human rights compliance programme and a remediation framework to compensate the victims, making it one of the first companies in the world to undertake the latter.

'In other words Barrick handled these very serious indeed horrific events in an open, effective and ethical way, reflecting the high ethical standards under which the company operates at its various mines across the world. So I have no misgivings about serving on its Advisory Board and don't believe any other fair- minded person, whether a member of the House of Lords or not, would have reservations either. You cannot turn the clock back but you can make sure that everything possible is done to make sure nothing similar happens again and the victims are adequately compensated.' [all sic]

34. http://www.theguardian.com/environment/2012/nov/20/peter-lilley-oil-company-shares

35. Register of Interests as at 30/11/15. He no longer has this position. The Register of Interests says: 'Until November 2014 (Updated 21 November 2014), non-executive director of Tethys Petroleum Limited.'

36. https://www.hrw.org/world-report/2015/country-chapters/kazakhstan; http://www.theguardian.com/commentisfree/2014/may/21/uk-shouldnt-court-kazakhstan-abusive-corrupt-dictatorship

37. http://www.tethyspetroleum.com/system/financial_reports/downloads/000/000/007/original/AIF-2014-FINAL_v002_r2xv8t.pdf?1434678937

38. http://www.parliament.uk/biographies/commons/peter-lilley/68 (accessed 21/02/16)

39. http://www.theguardian.com/environment/2012/oct/25/green-campaigners-condemn-peter-lilley

40. Caroline Lucas, *Honourable Friends?: Parliament and the fight for change* (Portobello Books, 2015), pp.13-16

41. http://www.theguardian.com/world/2010/jul/23/trafigura-dutch-fine-waste-export; http://www.bbc.co.uk/news/world-africa-10735255 ; http://www.theguardian.com/world/2009/sep/16/trafigura-oil-ivory-coast NB: Following a legal dispute between the BBC and lawyers for Trafigura, the BBC acknowledged: 'Experts in the [compensation] case were not able to establish a link between the waste and serious long-term consequences, including deaths.'

42. Ibid.

43. http://www.theguardian.com/world/2009/sep/16/trafigura-oil-ivory-coast

44. Caroline Lucas, *Honourable Friends?: Parliament and the fight for change* (Portobello Books, 2015), p.13

45. http://www.theguardian.com/politics/2009/sep/17/lord-strathclyde-end-trafigura-links

46. http://www.theguardian.com/politics/2009/sep/17/lord-strathclyde-end-trafigura-links; http://www.theguardian.com/environment/2009/may/16/bbc-newsnight-trafigura-lawyers-libel

47. http://www.theguardian.com/politics/2009/sep/17/lord-strathclyde-end-trafigura-links

48. http://www.bbc.co.uk/news/uk-politics-20932061; http://www.ft.com/cms/s/0/20d123d2-a51b-11e2-8777-00144feabdc0.html#axzz40m4iCLEC

Part Three: Politics for sale
Chapter 10: Lobbying: the insiders

1. Tamasin Cave & Andy Rowell, *A Quiet Word: Lobbying, crony capitalism and broken politics in Britain*, (Vintage, 2015), p.9

2. *The Sunday Times* (21/03/10), pp.1, 7, 8; *The Sunday Times* (28/03/10), p.1; and the parliamentary report into the scandal: http://www.publications.parliament.uk/pa/cm201011/cmselect/cmstnprv/654/65402.htm

3. In an attempt to prevent the person being identified, I do not intend to confirm the gender of this person. I am therefore using the word 'he' simply because most of the MPs caught in the sting were male, but this should not be interpreted, in either way, to try to identify the

interviewee. This also applies to gender-specific words within the quotes used.

4. http://www.acwa.co.uk/our_profile and http://www.acwa.co.uk/stephen_byers (accessed 14/01/16). The hours and salary of this job are not known.

5. ACWA Services Limited, annual accounts (ending Dec 2014)

6. http://www.fticonsulting.com/about/newsroom/press-releases/fti-consulting-strengthens-uk-public-affairs-practice-with-new-appointments (accessed 14/01/16)

7. http://www.publications.parliament.uk/pa/cm201011/cmselect/cmstnprv/654/65408.htm

8. There is no suggestion whatsoever that Hoon has used his parliamentary experience or contacts in any illegal, wrong, or unethical way in his job at AugustaWestland.

9. http://www.ft.com/cms/s/0/01fa9156-80aa-11e0-85a4-00144feabdc0.html#axzz42HV19UZ4

10. http://www.exaronews.com/articles/5178/geoff-hoon-set-to-help-defend-westland-at-bribes-trial-in-italy

11. As at March 2015: http://www.amrc.co.uk/news/bank-of-england-governor-praises-the-amrc%E2%80%99s-role-in-manufacturing%E2%80%99s-recovery/

12. http://www.yorkshirepost.co.uk/business/business-news/is-caborn-the-right-man-for-sheffield-city-region-s-top-job-1-7394046 There is no suggestion that he got the job because of the funding, nor that either he or the company have acted improperly in any way.

13. http://www.amrc.co.uk/news/apprenticeship-inquiry/

14. These comments about near-corruption in no way refer to any of the specific names mentioned above. Rather, this is a more general point about making limp excuses for questionable behaviour.

15. http://www.publications.parliament.uk/pa/cm201516/cmselect/cmstandards/472/472.pdf NB: This comment referred to non-secret information only. There is no suggestion that he was prepared to provide classified or confidential information.

16. Malcolm Rifkind interview on the BBC's 'The Daily Politics' programme, 23/02/15: https://www.youtube.com/watch?v=LqseHWFIeEw

17. *Daily Telegraph*, 23/02/15, p.19

18. *Daily Telegraph*, 23/09/15, p.15

19. http://www.independent.co.uk/news/uk/politics/sir-malcolm-rifkind-helped-hire-head-of-parliamentary-watchdog-that-cleared-him-over-cash-for-access-10508789.html

20. http://www.publications.parliament.uk/pa/cm201516/cmselect/cmstandards/472/472.pdf

21. *Daily Telegraph*, 18/09/15, p.1

22. http://stakeholders.ofcom.org.uk/binaries/enforcement/broadcast-bulletins/obb295/Issue_295.pdf

23. Nudge Factory Ltd, annual return (April, 2016) and Register of Interests (as at 21/03/16). NB: his shareholding in the company is declared in the Register of Interests.

24. Both as at 02/02/16.

25. http://www.nudgefactory.co.uk/our-services/public-affairs/ (as at 02/02/16). NB: The website appears to have been updated since this date. At 08/03/16, this link contains less text, but says Nudge Factory has a 'deep understanding of the Westminster Village' and adds: 'Because we understand the forces acting on decision-makers, we can ensure that your engagement is focused, effective and has a measurable impact on policy-making and regulation.'

26. This quote has been slightly tidied up, for the sake of clarity. The original quote began 'Those are the exactly the sort of things that we do.' (I have removed the first 'the' in the main text.) The remainder of the quote is verbatim.

27. The company was founded before Scully became an MP.

28. There is no suggestion that the Nudge Factory, or any other lobby firms, have broken any rules by not being listed on the official register. The rules are complex and there may be good and legitimate reasons why they are not registered at the time of writing. NB: This is based on the Commons and Lords Registers of Interests, as at Aug 2015, and combined with the DueDil data.

29. Phone call to the Office for the Parliamentary Commissioner for Standards (14/03/16)

30. Agreement between Peter Lilley and the 'Eurasian Council on Foreign Affairs Ltd', as filed at the Parliamentary Archives, signed Dec 2014. The document says: '. . . the Member will provide the following services: Will be a Member of the ECFA Advisory Council, attend one annual meeting of the Council in Central Asia or a European capital, and will offer advice from time to time to the ECFA director'. There is no suggestion that this contract is ongoing, or that it involved any lobbying.

31. Agreement between Sir David Amess and The Caravan Club, as filed at the Parliamentary Archives, dated April 2012. There is no suggestion that this contract is ongoing, or that it involved any lobbying.

32. Register of Interests (as at 07/03/16) ; https://registerofconsultantlobbyists.force.com/CLR_Public_Profile?id=0012400000CA7mZAAT NB: pay rounded to nearest £1. Under Cratus, a list of payments includes: '22 July 2015, received £3,333.32. Hours: 8 hrs.'

33. M J Gleeson Group Limited (the parent company), accounts ending June 2014. Figure is for revenue. And: http://www.gleesonstrategicland.co.uk/ (accessed 13/03/16)

34. Lend Lease and Gleeson Strategic Land are listed as clients of Cratus Communications Limited in 2015, on the Register of Lobbyists: https://registerofconsultantlobbyists.force.com / CLR _ Public _ Profile?id=0012400000CA7mZAAT ; the quote describing Lend Lease is from www.lendlease.com/worldwide/about-us (accessed 13/03/16)

35. In the Register of Interests, as at 02/02/16. He may have mentioned them in speeches in Parliament.

36. http://www.publications.parliament.uk/pa/cm201516/cmhansrd/cm151109/debtext/151109-0001.htm#1511091000622 NB: It is not known how long Gleeson Strategic Land was (or indeed is) a client of Cratus. However, on Cratus's page on the Lobbying Register, Gleeson Strategic Land is named within the period Oct–Dec 2015 i.e. Cratus acted as a consultant lobbyist, as defined by the Act, within this period.

37. http://www.publications.parliament.uk/pa/cm201516/cmhansrd/cm150610/debtext/150610-0002.htm#15061057001602

38. http://www.publications.parliament.uk/pa/cm201516/cmhansrd/cm160105/debtext/160105-0006.htm#16010614000421 NB: As with Gleeson (detailed in the notes above), it is not known how long Land Lease was (or indeed is) a client of Cratus. However, on Cratus's page on the Lobbying Register, Land Lease is named within the period July–Sept 2015 i.e. Cratus acted as a consultant lobbyist, as defined by the Act, within this period.

39. Email to Bob Neill MP (19/01/16)

40. Email to Bob Neill MP (21/01/16)

41. As at 25/01/16

42. Email from Wes Streeting MP (05/11/2015)

43. http://www.theguardian.com/politics/2015/oct/06/michelle-thomson-snp-mp-property-deals-investigated-police

44. Michelle R Thomson: Consulting Ltd, annual return made up to 19/04/15 (latest available at time of writing).

45. Email to Lord Boyce (21/01/16) and Register of Lords Interests (see the page listing amendments).

46. http://www.quest.co.uk/ (accessed 03/02/16). Stevens is non-executive chairman, according to the Register of Interests (as at 03/02 /16). His adviser job for Cameron is also listed on the Register of Interests.

47. Email (19/01/16) sent to generic email address for peers (contacthol-member@parliament.uk) as this was the only address listed on his parliamentary profile. NB: To be clear, the company itself is fully declared, the email was merely requesting a list of clients.

48. He is referring to peers not declaring them, not the companies.

Chapter 11: Lobbying: taking the bait

1. Charlie's name has been changed.
2. http://www.independent.co.uk/news/obituaries/ian-greer-parlia-mentary-lobbyist-whose-successful-business-was-brought-down-by-the-1990s-cash-for-a6741326.html
3. Quoted in: Tamasin Cave & Andy Rowell, *A Quiet Word: Lobbying, crony capitalism and broken politics in Britain* (Vintage, 2015), p.10
4. http://www.telegraph.co.uk/news/obituaries/12001034/Ian-Greer-lobbyist-obituary.html
5. http://www.independent.co.uk/news/world/europe/truth-is-the-first-casualty-in-pr-offensive-1541548.html
6. http://www.theguardian.com/media/2013/dec/09/bell-pottinger-tim-bell-pr-interview
7. Quoted in: Tamasin Cave & Andy Rowell, *A Quiet Word: Lobbying, crony capitalism and broken politics in Britain*, (Vintage, 2015), p.1. NB: This quote is about the lobbying industry in general; not about any of the specific cases or clients I have mentioned.
8. Greg Palast, *The best democracy money can buy: An investigative reporter exposes the truth about globalization, corporate cons, and high finance fraudsters* (Pluto Press, 2002), p.154
9. Lionel Zetter, *Lobbying: The Art of Political Persuasion* (Harriman House Publishing; 3rd revised edition, 2014), Kindle edition.
10. http://www.theguardian.com/politics/2010/feb/08/david-cameron-secret-corporate-lobbying

11. Comparison includes all companies listed on the official Register of Consultant Lobbyists (as at 03/10/15) where the relevant information was available from Companies House (relating to turnover and profit) for accounts ending 2010 and 2014. Where accounts refer to 'fee income' or similar, instead of 'turnover' or 'revenue', this was used instead. I am grateful to the journalist Daniel Kraemer, who worked with me on this analysis, and who is credited in the acknowledgements page.

12. http://www.spinwatch.org/index.php/issues/lobbying/item/5812-uks-lobbying-register-falls-100-000s-short It is also worth noting that, although all these firms are listed on the official Lobbying Register, some of them do more than just lobbying.

13. *Private Eye*, No.1406, 27 Nov–10 Dec 2015, p.38

14. http://blogs.channel4.com/factcheck/whitehalls-revolving-doors-factcheck-qa/13596 NB: Hartnett's appointment was approved both by the Advisory Committee on Business Appointments and by David Cameron and was subject to a number of conditions (these included a ban on advising companies whose cases he was involved with at HMRC). There is absolutely no suggestion that Hartnett has acted against the conditions of his appointment.

15. http://www.dailymail.co.uk/news/article-2331901/Dave-Hartnett-HMRC-chief-gets-job-accountancy-giant-Deloitte.html

16. https://www.gov.uk/government/publications/acoba-recommenda-tion-mark-simmonds-mp-parliamentary-under-secretary-of-state-foreign-and-commonwealth-office/summary-of-business-appoint-ments-applications-mark-simmonds#non-executive-director-african -potash NB: ACOBA noted that Simmonds had met with some (but not all) of the companies while in office but any concerns were dismissed because, it said, he was not involved with any policy decisions relating to any of the companies.

17. Approval generally comes with certain conditions attached, such as advising against lobbying the government for two years after leaving ministerial office.

18. http://www.africanpotash.com/News.aspx?ArticleId=23488430 (accessed 21/01/16)

19. http://www.ihg.co.uk/experience.html (accessed 21/01/16)

20. Speech was first reported in *Private Eye*, No.1406, 27 Nov–10 Dec 2015, p.38. The full speech can be found at: https://www.gov.uk/government/speeches/african-investment-summit. NB: the comment about the African economy offering 'huge potential for British investors' was made in relation to a series of remarks about a range of

different companies including, but not solely, the International Hospitals Group.

21. *Private Eye*, No.1410, 22 Jan–4 Feb 2016, p.37.

22. Quoted in: *Private Eye*, No.1417, 19 April–12 May 2016, p.13.

23. The original quote includes the name of this person, which has been deleted to protect their anonymity.

24. It is not clear from ACOBA's documents whether EDF was a client of MHP at the time Davey had dealings with EDF. There is no suggestion that Davey communicated with MHP while he was a minister.

25. http://www.mhpc.com/blog/former-secretary-of-state-for-energy -and-climate-change-ed-davey-joins-mhp-as-senior-adviser/ NB: There is no suggestion that Davey breached ACOBA's directions in any way, or that he has lobbied for MHP, or that MHP either expected or instructed Davey to lobby or breach ACOBA's ruling. Rather, the point here is that ministers' expertise can be utilised in a perfectly legitimate (if controversial) way, without *having* to break the wishy -washy guidelines set out by ACOBA.

26. There is absolutely no suggestion that he waited for this purpose.

27. http://www.gorkana.com/news/all/people-news/former-health-minister-paul-burstow-joins-mhp-communications-as-senior-adviser/

28. The first two of these are registered as clients on the Statutory Lobbying Register which is updated quarterly: https://registerofconsultantlobby-ists.force.com/CLR_Public_Profile?id=00124000006QOXGAA4. At the time of writing, the first three quarters of 2015 have been published and these companies are named as clients in one or more of these. NB: the names listed are the UK arms of these firms, i.e. Astellas Pharma UK Ltd and Merck Sharp & Dohme Limited (MSD UK). The third client here, AbbVie, is named on MHP's website (as at 22/10/15): http://www.mhpc.com/

29. http://www.mhpc.com/blog/who-won-battle-health-party-confer-ences/

30. http://www.mhpc.com/blog/what-norman-lamb-should-say-to-his-party/

31. Twitter message from Burstow. In full, his final response said: 'I left the department three and a half years ago. My portfolio was not pharma related and I had one unsolicited contact where they were sharing a report produced with the Alzhiemers society. I think the pro bono advice referred to was rhetorical and not actual. I certainly don't recall any advice being rendered. I note in the blog this advice was offered to both the Con and Lab spokespeople too. I didn't work for MHP before

entering parliament or before entering the department and I have no
plans to stand for election again so this is not so much a revolving door.'
He said that he had been made aware of ACOBA's rules regarding
another, separate appointment, and that he sought their approval for
this. There is no suggestion of any wrongdoing on the part of Burstow
or MHP. NB: a comma has been added into the quote used in the main
text, for the sake of clarity.

32. http://www.mirror.co.uk/news/uk-news/david-camerons-gravy-
train-scandal-7153710

33. http://www.telegraph.co.uk/news/investigations/11805083/Former-
ministers-walk-through-revolving-door-into-lobbying.html

34. http://changeopinion.com/jacqui-smith-i-havent-left-politics-ive-left
-parliament-pr-week-interview/ (21/01/16)

35. http://www.parliament.uk/business/committees/committees-a-z/
commons-select/scottish-affairs-committee/news/swift-session/

36. See, for instance, http://time.com/3592098/uber-controversy/ and
http://uk.businessinsider.com/ubers-enemies-have-clifford-chance-
fighting-to-ban-it-here-are-the-5-big-arguments-2015-10

37. Clients listed: https://registerofconsultantlobbyists.force.com/CLR_
Public_Profile?id=00124000005zqpeAAA

38. Turnover, as stated in 'Blue Rubicon (Holdings) Limited', annual
accounts ending Dec 2014. Clients listed at: http://www.bluerubicon.
com/what-we-do/clients/ (as at 23/10/15)

39. http://www.publications.parliament.uk/pa/cm/cmregmem/151026/
haselhurst_alan.htm

40. http://www.bluerubicon.com/what-we-do/projects/improving-
internal-communications-_-william-hill (accessed 21/01/16). My
emphasis.

41. http://www.bluerubicon.com/what-we-do/projects/design-and-roll-
out-of-frist-global-code-of-conduct-_-bae-systems (accessed 21/01/
16). My emphasis.

42. http://www.theguardian.com/uk/2012/dec/25/tory-mp-benefits-
gambling-industry

43. http://www.thetimes.co.uk/tto/news/uk/article4717086.ece

44. The interviewee was asked: 'When an MP gets lobbied . . . what is in
it for them?' In the response, the interviewee talked about various
'outside groups' that lobby MPs, adding that the 'vast majority' of these
are charities.

45. http://www.buzzfeed.com/jimwaterson/jeremy-corbyns-new-poli-
tics-is-bad-news-for-lobbyists#.htkjPEoodq

46. http://www.spinwatch.org/index.php/issues/lobbying/item/5785-corbyn-has-no-mates-in-the-lobbying-business

Chapter 12: Institutional corruption

1. Title of article: http://blogs.spectator.co.uk/2013/08/when-is-corruption-not-corrupt-when-the-establishment-says-it-isnt/

2. http://www.parliament.uk/about/faqs/house-of-lords-faqs/role/

3. Joyce Quin, *The British Constitution: Continuity and Change – an inside view*, (Northern Writers, 2010), p.57

4. http://lordsappointments.independent.gov.uk/media/17348/ucl_report.pdf p.15. NB: the 43% figure for banking, finance and business combines two separate figures given in the report: 'Banking and finance' (20%) and 'Business and commerce' (23%). Percentages include peers who counted these as both primary and secondary professional areas.

5. http://lordsappointments.independent.gov.uk/media/17348/ucl_report.pdf p.19. Again, the figure for banking, finance and business combines two separate figures given in the report: 'Banking and finance' (15%) and 'Business and commerce' (17%). Unlike the total figures for the whole House of Lords, these Conservative Party statistics only refer to 'primary professional area'.

6. http://www.theguardian.com/news/datablog/2014/aug/28/elitism-in-britain-breakdown-by-profession

7. I have cleaned up this quote for the sake of clarity. The complete quote is: 'I remember when we were discussing the – which we managed to stop in both the Lords and Commons – the sort of sell off of the forestry estate.'

8. These two quotes are from an anonymous survey of peers that I conducted in early 2016. The statistical results have not been used in this book since the sample turned out to be very small (about 30–40). This was largely because peers' email addresses were not readily available. Nonetheless, a couple of the anonymous comments have been used.

9. British Airways, accounts ending Dec 2010 (i.e. the year that Soley left this job). The figure represents total revenue and is rounded to the nearest billion.

10. http://www.publications.parliament.uk/pa/ld200607/ldhansrd/text/70614-0001.htm#07061424000063

Chapter 13: Cash for peerages

1. Seth Thévoz did not confirm the identity of the lord, but said he was a Conservative. He said: 'He's still there [in the House of Lords]. The *Observer* did contact him, they know exactly who he is . . . He's been contacted a few times.' NB: The *Observer* has also made reference to Thévoz's job interview without naming the peer.

2. http://www.economics.ox.ac.uk/materials/papers/13888/paper744.pdf

3. Daniel Boffey, *Observer* (22/03/15), pp.8–9, and web version: http://www.theguardian.com/politics/2015/mar/21/revealed-link-life-peerages-party-donations

4. Ibid. NB: This is merely a summary of the *Observer* article and the donation amounts listed here are all taken from that article. I am not endorsing the accuracy of these figures. I am just reporting what the *Observer* printed.

5. http://www.economics.ox.ac.uk/materials/papers/13888/paper744.pdf

6. Let me preemptively answer my critics here. Several politicians I spoke to argued that funding from trade unions was just as big a problem as the donations from individual business tycoons. They told me to write about that instead. So why am I not doing this? Am I just biased? Well maybe. After all, one Tory refused to talk to me because he said I was 'tarred with the lefty brush', having written for the *Guardian* newspaper. But here's my explanation anyway: I am skipping over the issue of trade union funding simply because it's a different subject. It might well be a problem, and someone should definitely write a book about it. But here I want to tell the story of *personal* finances – not *party* funding. I want to know how politicians' own private money affairs impact on British politics. I'm in no way implying that trade union funding should not be scrutinised as well. But it's not the problem I'm investigating in this book. If that troubles you, please feel free to go and write a book about it yourself.

7. Ed Habershon, 'The Honours Salesman Who Went To Jail', *The Sunday Times* (16/04/06, 2nd edition), p.11

8. Cook, Andrew. 'Hawking peerages: Andrew Cook looks at the mysterious career of a man notorious for selling seats in the House of Lords.' *History Today* 56.11 (10/02/16) ; Ben Fenton, 'MI5 still keeps secrets of man jailed for selling peerages', *Daily Telegraph* (25/07/06), p.14

9. http://www.telegraph.co.uk/finance/property/4812864/Inside-story

-Vanity-Fair.html NB: he was never officially seen again. There were, however, unsubstantiated sightings years later.

10. Cook, Andrew. 'Hawking peerages: Andrew Cook looks at the mysterious career of a man notorious for selling seats in the House of Lords', *History Today* 56.11 (10/02/16)

11. Chris Bryant, *Parliament – The Biography: Reform, Volume 2,* (Doubleday, 2014) pp.291–2

12. Andrew Cook, *Cash for honours: the true life of Maundy Gregory*, (History Press, ebook edition, 2008), preface.

13. Matthew d'Ancona, 'Who'll be next in All The Prime Minister's Men?' *Sunday Telegraph* (16/04/06), p.23

14. Quoted in: http://www.theguardian.com/commentisfree/2012/aug/31/honours-system-stroking-bruce-forsyth

15. Matthew d'Ancona, 'Who'll be next in All The Prime Minister's Men?' *Sunday Telegraph* (16/04/06), p.23

16. Robert Peston, *Who Runs Britain?: . . . and who's to blame for the economic mess we're in* (Hodder & Stoughton, 2008)

17. http://www.dailymail.co.uk/news/article-503344/Cash-honours-Labour-deliberately-tried-conceal-secret-loans.html

18. http://news.bbc.co.uk/1/hi/uk_politics/4826680.stm

19. http://news.bbc.co.uk/1/hi/uk_politics/6179911.stm NB: It was an informal interview; Blair was not under caution and he was not accompanied by a lawyer.

20. FOI response (refused) from Metropolitan Police (18/02/16)

21. *Dateline London*, BBC (Aug 2015): https://www.youtube.com/watch?v=pPJ1u9ngVQU

22. FOI response from the Cabinet Office (05/02/16)

23. FOI response from the Attorney General's Office (04/02/16)

24. Attorney General's Office, internal review into the decision to refuse my FOI request (03/02/16)

25. FOI response from Metropolitan Police (18/02/16)

Part Four: Justifying it
Chapter 14: Millionaire mindset

1. Quoted in Introduction.

2. Sir Peter Tapsell, Commons Hansard, 25/02/15: Column 315.

3. http://parliamentarystandards.org.uk/payandpensions/Documents/Ipsa%20final%20report.pdf

4. Owen Jones, *The Establishment: And how they get away with it*, (Penguin, 2014; 2015 edition), pp.47 and 49

5. Feargal McGuinness, 'Social Backgrounds of MPs', House of Commons Library briefing paper SN/SG/1528 (14/12/10)

6. Ibid.

7. http://www.theguardian.com/society/2015/aug/25/public-sector-workers-pay-rise-greg-hands-treasury

8. My emphasis.

9. My emphasis.

10. http://www.telegraph.co.uk/news/newstopics/mps-expenses/5363883/Anthony-Steen-voters-are-just-jealous-of-my-very-very-large-house-MPs-expenses.html

11. http://www.bbc.co.uk/news/uk-england-devon-33112657

12. http://www.telegraph.co.uk/news/politics/8277371/How-politics-got-posh-again.html ; http://i100.independent.co.uk/article/here-are-some-of-britains-poshest-politicians--gkzEsZQDTx ; http://www.theguardian.com/politics/shortcuts/2012/apr/25/posh-politicians-guide-real ; http://www.dailymail.co.uk/debate/article-1350553/Why-todays-politicians-posh-I-dont-just-mean-Tories.html ; http://www.bbc.co.uk/news/uk-politics-35043879

13. http://www.dailymail.co.uk/news/election/article-1280554/The-coalition-millionaires-23-29-member-new-cabinet-worth-1m--Lib-Dems-just-wealthy-Tories.html

14. http://www.dailymail.co.uk/news/election/article-1280554/The-coalition-millionaires-23-29-member-new-cabinet-worth-1m--Lib-Dems-just-wealthy-Tories.html

15. http://www.telegraph.co.uk/news/politics/9290520/Exclusive-Cabinet-is-worth-70million.html

16. http://blogs.spectator.co.uk/2008/07/the-shadow-cabinet-rich-list-part-2/

17. http://www.dailymail.co.uk/news/election/article-1280554/The-coalition-millionaires-23-29-member-new-cabinet-worth-1m--Lib-Dems-just-wealthy-Tories.html

18. http://www.theguardian.com/politics/2009/sep/08/profile-sir-george-young

19. http://www.dailymail.co.uk/news/election/article-1280554/The-coalition-millionaires-23-29-member-new-cabinet-worth-1m--Lib-Dems-just-wealthy-Tories.html

20. http://www.telegraph.co.uk/comment/personal-view/3602801/Letwins-parents-are-the-key-to-his-soul.html

21. http://www.newstatesman.com/uk-politics/2009/10/oxford-univer-sitywealth-school

22. http://www.independent.co.uk/news/people/oliver-letwin-profile-another-blunder-from-the-tory-king-of-clangers-a6793436.html

23. Oliver Letwin, *Privatising the World: A Study of International Privatisation in Theory and Practice*, (Cassell, 1988)

24. http://www.mirror.co.uk/news/uk-news/bedroom-tax-iain-duncan-smith-1794517

25. http://www.dailymail.co.uk/news/election/article-1280554/The-coalition-millionaires-23-29-member-new-cabinet-worth-1m--Lib-Dems-just-wealthy-Tories.html

26. Ion Trewin, 'Alan Clark: The Biography' (2009) ebook version ; http://www.conservativehome.com/profiles/2015/05/profile-amber-rudd-a-true-believer-in-climate-change.html

27. £12,425. https://www.cheltladiescollege.org/key-information/fees/ (accessed 17/02/16)

28. http://www.telegraph.co.uk/education/educationnews/11598097/Half-of-the-new-Cabinet-went-to-Oxbridge.html

29. Quoted in: Martin Williams, 'In it together: Osborne company's £750,000 loss', *Guardian* (23/12/11), p.30

30. Under the firm's previous name, 'Osborne & Little plc'. Annual Return, report between: 03/08/01 to 02/08/02 as obtained from Companies House ('Full list and share particulars of past and present members, since the date of last return'). There is no suggestion that either Osborne & Little, or any of the shareholders avoided tax or did anything improper.

31. http://www.channel4.com/news/george-osborne-family-business-6m-deal-with-offshore-firm NB: There is no suggestion that Osborne & Little – or anyone associated with the company – dodged any taxes. Simply, that it was involved in a sale to a firm based in a tax haven.

32. Jon Ungoed-Thomas & Lois Rogers, 'Osborne family firm pays no corporation tax', *The Sunday Times* (14/02/16) pp.1,2. NB1: There is no suggestion that the company or anyone associated has done anything illegal or avoided tax in any inappropriate way. *The Sunday Times* points out: 'The company has not paid any UK corporation tax since 2008 partly because it has rolled over losses from previous years and has deferred tax payments.' NB2: figure for profits is rounded down to nearest hundred thousand.

33. http://www.telegraph.co.uk/news/2016/04/06/george-osborne-clarifies

-personal-taxinterests-as-panama-papers/ ; The trust was declared on the
Register of Interests up until April 2010. There is no suggestion this was
offshore, or that it was inappropriate in any way.

34. *Private Eye*, No. 1371, 25 Jul– 7 Aug 2014, p9

35. http://www.ft.com/cms/s/0/abb4cb76-3780-11e5-b05b-
b01debd57852.html#axzz40MytI52Y

36. http://www.manchester.ac.uk/discover/news/illustrious-jewish-roots
-of-tory-leader-revealed

37. http://www.dailymail.co.uk/news/article-1191155/Claims-David
-Cameron-30m-fortune-sit-uneasily-taxpayers-So-truth-money.
html

38. http://www.dailymail.co.uk/news/article-1191155/Claims-David-
Cameron-30m-fortune-sit-uneasily-taxpayers-So-truth-money.html

39. Michael Ashcroft and Isabel Oakeshott, *Call Me Dave: The unauthorised
biography of David Cameron*, (Biteback, 2015), chapter 2

40. Michael Ashcroft and Isabel Oakeshott, *Call Me Dave: The unauthorised
biography of David Cameron* (Biteback, 2015)

41. http://www.theguardian.com/politics/2012/apr/20/cameron-family-
tax-havens NB: This was perfectly legal. There is nothing to suggest
that any tax was avoided, or that he or any of the firms involved did
anything illegal or improper.

42. http://www.theguardian.com/politics/2012/apr/20/cameron-family-
tax-havens

43. http://www.channel4.com/news/cameron-david-ian-jersey-tax-
haven-conservatives

44. http://www.telegraph.co.uk/news/politics/9290520/Exclusive-
Cabinet-is-worth-70million.html NB: these figures are estimates
provided by a specialist consultancy, which are cited in the *Telegraph*
article

45. http://www.itv.com/news/2016-04-07/david-cameron-admits-he-
had-a-30-000-stake-in-his-fathers-offshore-trust/

46. http://www.mirror.co.uk/news/uk-news/cameron-millions-family-
fortunes-tories-206432

Chapter 15: Gang mentality

1. http://www.parliament.uk/business/publications/house-of-lords-
publications/records-of-activities-and-membership/register-of-all-
hereditary-peers/

2. See, for example: http://www.parliament.uk/documents/lords-information-office/2015/Hereditary-peers-by-election-result-Montgomery-of-Alamein.pdf

3. http://www.independent.co.uk/news/uk/politics/the-worlds-most-elitist-election-8395981.html

4. http://www.theguardian.com/politics/2015/mar/04/plebgate-pc-80k-damages-libel-action-andrew-mitchell ; http://www.thesun.co.uk/sol/homepage/news/politics/6138960/andrew-mitchell-whistle-blower-sacked-by-met.html

5. http://blogs.telegraph.co.uk/news/brendanoneill2/100182704/andrew-mitchell-is-a-snobbish-twit-but-the-polices-playing-of-the-victim-card-is-nauseating/; http://www.independent.co.uk/news/uk/home-news/plebgate-politician-andrew-mitchell-whose-privileged-upbringing-and-temper-tantrums-were-his-undoing-9888705.html

6. http://www.independent.co.uk/news/uk/home-news/plebgate-politician-andrew-mitchell-whose-privileged-upbringing-and-temper-tantrums-were-his-undoing-9888705.html

7. http://www.dailymail.co.uk/news/article-2295489/Jacob-Rees-Mogg-JANE-FRYER-meets-poshest-man-politics.html

8. Simon Hoggart, *Send Up the Clowns: Parliamentary Sketches 2007–11*, (Guardian Books, 2011), sketch from 22/03/11

9. http://www.parliament.uk/mps-lords-and-offices/offices/lords/freedom-of-information-in-the-house-of-lords/log/house-of-lords-foi-request-log--disclosed-information/lords-menus-and-bar-tariffs-foi-978/ NB: This quote was specifically used about catering in the House of Lords.

10. For the years 2010/11 to 2014/15. http://www.parliament.uk/documents/facilities/Catering-costs-to-HC-2014-15.pdf

11. http://www.dailymail.co.uk/news/article-2626402/MPs-spend-200-000-doing-exclusive-Commons-dining-room-despite-getting-millions-food-drink-subsidies.html

12. http://www.parliament.uk/documents/facilities/Proativepublication-menus/Christmas%202015%20menus/Strangers-Dining-Room.pdf

13. http://www.parliament.uk/documents/facilities/Proativepublication-menus/Christmas%202015%20menus/Terrace-Cafeteria-2015-12-09.pdf

14. Paul Flynn, *How to be an MP*, (Bitebank, 2012), p.107

15. Latest House of Lords menus; FOI response (13/01/16)

16. Paul Flynn, *How to be an MP*, (Bitebank, 2012), p.103

17. Referenced in 'Alcohol Concern's response to the MPs' Pay and Pensions consultation': http://parliamentarystandards.org.uk/transparency/Our%20consultations/Pay%20and%20Pensions/Pay%20and%20Pensions%20Consultation%20July%E2%80%93Oct%202013%20(redacted%20responses)/Organisations/Alcohol%20Concern.pdf

18. Parliament alcohol prices: http://www.parliament.uk/site-information/foi/foi-and-eir/commons-foi-disclosures/catering-services-retail/alcohol-prices-2014/; Average price of pint in London: http://www.theguardian.com/money/2014/sep/04/good-pub-guide-londoners-76p-pint-more-than-herefordshire NB: both sources are from 2014.

19. http://www.sunnation.co.uk/order-order-cost-of-pints-at-parliament-up-just-0-5-while-mp-pay-up-10/

20. http://www.parliament.uk/business/committees/committees-a-z/other-committees/works-of-art/role/ (accessed 10/01/16)

21. Information was previously disclosed under FOI by House of Commons (02/06/15), but unavailable online. Copy of response provided by Commons press office.

22. House of Lords. Response to previous FOI request that was not available online (FOI 1174) provided by Lords press office.

23. Statement from Parliament, not Bercow himself. http://www.parliament.uk/site-information/foi/foi-and-eir/commons-foi-disclosures/other-house-matters/the-cost-of-the-speakers-state-portrait/

24. http://www.edeandravenscroft.com/ceremonial-dress/peers-robes/ (accessed 10/01/16)

25. Response to a previous FOI request to the House of Lords (FOI 1160). Not available online, but details provided by House of Lords on 06/10/15.

26. 'Comments Report: all staff survey 2014', prepared for the House of Lords Administration by BMG Research. (FOI)

27. 'Comments Report: Members Survey 2014', prepared for the House of Lords Administration by BMG Research. (FOI)

28. House of Lords, previous response to FOI (3/13/15) for catering complaints received.

29. NB: Champagne quote is not from Refreshments Committee correspondence but is separate. See: 'Comments Report: Members Survey 2014', prepared for the House of Lords Administration by BMG Research. (FOI)

30. 'Comments Report: Members Survey 2014', prepared for the House of Lords Administration by BMG Research. (FOI)

31. http://www.mirror.co.uk/news/uk-news/house-lords-zero-hour-jobs-6346580?utm_content=bufferf69c6&utm_medium=social&utm_source=twitter.com&utm_campaign=buffer

32. 'Narrative Report: all staff survey 2014', prepared for the House of Lords Administration by BMG Research. (FOI)

33. Ibid.

34. Assorted quotes taken from anonymous comments included in the 'Comments Report: all staff survey 2014', prepared for the House of Lords Administration by BMG Research. Previously released under FOI (8/19/14) but not publicly available; but was subsequently released again in Oct 2015.

35. Ibid.

36. Ibid.

37. Ibid.

Part Five: Expenses forever
Chapter 16: The scandal that never left

1. http://www.bbc.co.uk/news/uk-politics-25492017

2. Ibid.

3. https://twitter.com/denismacshane (accessed 2015)

4. http://www.mirror.co.uk/news/uk-news/george-osborne-denies-flipping-second-399508; http://www.mirror.co.uk/news/uk-news/george-osborne-included-a-horses-paddock-1477294

5. http://www.theguardian.com/politics/2012/dec/07/taxpayers-paid-george-osborne-paddock-mortgage

6. http://www.telegraph.co.uk/news/newstopics/mps-expenses/5364847/MPs-expenses-John-Bercow-claims-maximum-allowance-for-540000-flat.html

7. http://news.bbc.co.uk/1/hi/uk_politics/8051027.stm

8. http://www.telegraph.co.uk/news/politics/4557354/Jacqui-Smith-claimed-allowance-for-living-with-sister.html

9. http://www.telegraph.co.uk/news/politics/labour/11416788/Ed-Balls-among-12-shadow-cabinet-members-who-claimed-expenses-without-receipts.html

10. http://www.telegraph.co.uk/news/newstopics/mps-expenses/shadow-cabinet-expenses/5634046/Eric-Pickles-expenses.html

11. https://www.youtube.com/watch?v=94JgL0jmX0w

12. https://www.youtube.com/watch?v=94JgL0jmX0w

13. https://www.youtube.com/watch?v=b48I7QHqgSg

14. https://www.youtube.com/watch?v=iADOrCEV82Q

15. https://www.youtube.com/watch?v=MT74OG1maj8 My emphasis.

16. There are stories of MPs being pressured to claim expenses (see later in Chapter 16), but it was ultimately a personal decision to fiddle expenses. In criminal law, professional pressure is not a defence against guilt, and nor is it for non-criminal acts like many of the abuses exposed in the expenses scandal.

17. Total gross cost of MPs' Business Costs and Expenses Scheme (including staff expenses). Rounded up to nearest million. Figures verified by IPSA's press office

18. Based on figures in IPSA's annual reports

19. http://www.telegraph.co.uk/news/newstopics/mps-expenses/5298258/Gordon-Brown-Cleaning-cash-for-brother-was-legitimate.html NB: a No. 10 spokesperson said, in 2009: 'There is nothing unusual or wrong about this relationship.'

20. https://twitter.com/IPSA_watch. First quote is from the Twitter profile, the second is from the earliest post available (as at 26/12/15), which was on 19/12/12.

21. The dispute was settled after an independent assessment ruled that Jackson did not owe any money. http://www.bbc.co.uk/news/uk-england-cambridgeshire-26406354

22. IPSA, Annual Report and Accounts, 2014–15. NB: salaries are disclosed within £5,000 brackets, so 'up to' refers to the upper end of this bracket.

23. https://www.youtube.com/watch?v=IrTER7vUfVc (accessed 30/12/15)

24. IPSA, Annual Report and Accounts, 201415

25. http://www.bbc.co.uk/news/uk-wales-21851088

26. http://www.theguardian.com/society/2015/aug/27/thousands-died-after-fit-for-work-assessment-dwp-figures

27. http://www.independent.co.uk/news/uk/politics/dwp-fit-to-work-assessments-cost-more-than-they-save-report-reveals-a6801636.html

28. Ken Olisa (IPSA) letter to John Bercow (Speaker), 13/11/12. Available under FOI: http://parliamentarystandards.org.uk/transparency/FOI/2014-15%20Freedom%20of%20information%20requests%20and%20responses/wF1415-053%20-%20Annex%20A.pdf

29. All 'free text' responses to this survey were released under FOI by IPSA. A report of the key findings of the Annual User Survey 2014, which was published the previous month, is available on IPSA's website.

At the time of writing (26/12/15) this was the most recent available survey of this kind on its website.

30. Grammar has been corrected in the quote for the sake of clarity: 'IPSA' has been put into capitals and a question mark added on the end of the sentence.

31. Quoted in report of an internal survey of peers. See: 'Comments Report: Members Survey 2014', prepared for the House of Lords Administration by BMG Research.

32. Lord (Paul) Bew, 'The Committee on Standards in Public Life: Twenty Years of the Nolan Principles 1995–2015', *The Political Quarterly*, Vol. 86, No.3, July–Sep 2015. My emphasis. NB: it says the scandal is over 'in the sense that it was understood at the time of our enquiry and the *Daily Telegraph* revelations'. It goes on to say that further improvements do need to be made.

Chapter 17: Penny pinchers

1. FOI response from IPSA (2015). NB1: Although the bill was £15.90, Campbell only claimed £15 on expenses, in keeping with the rules at the time. NB2: photocopied or scanned.

2. Anecdotal evidence from numerous interviewees, including former Lib Dem MP Dr Julian Huppert who said that one cafeteria 'put its prices up to £15, no matter what you ate'. There is no suggestion whatsoever that Kennington Tandoori or any other restaurants that are named in this book did this.

3. NB: On the interview recording, a few inaudible words are mumbled between 'a nice three seater' and 'and a double seater'. It is not clear what is being said, but is most likely to be another item of furniture.

4. Actually, Ronnie Campbell's latest tenancy agreement that I could get hold of from IPSA says his rent is more than this. The contract says he pays £1,408.34 per month, for a term of 17 months and 4 days, commencing 3 Dec 2013.

5. NB: This quote about cleaning is from a phone conversation with Ronnie Campbell and was not part of the same interview as the surrounding quotes. He repeated the same remarks in the interview, with very similar wording, but the quotes from the phone conversation were used because they were fuller and more succinct.

6. http://ratings.food.gov.uk/business/411158 NB: the hygiene rating was given in Feb 2016, after both mine and Danczuk's visits to the restaurant.

7. FOI response from IPSA, 27/11/15. According to the FOI, the latest documents they hold say that Danczuk's rent was set to increase to £2,142.40 per month from 20/05/14.

8. FOI response from IPSA, 02/11/15. NB: he only claimed £15 on expenses, in line with the rules. The remaining 40p was not claimed on expenses.

9. http://www.mirror.co.uk/news/uk-news/millionaire-mp-jeremy-hunt-claims-2803300

10. IPSA data. Claim for Rapesco foldback clips (26/06/13)

11. IPSA data. Claim for metal single hole pencil sharpener (30/06/13), claim reference: Payment to Supplier. And: http://news.sky.com/story/1522677/mps-expenses-they-claimed-for-that

12. http://www.dailymail.co.uk/news/article-2545664/30p-doughnut-4p-driving-176-yards-And-Camerons-7p-bulldog-clip-Proof-expenses-loving-MPs-STILL-dont-it.html

13. http://www.southwalesargus.co.uk/news/gwentnews/10657775.display/ (accessed 22/12/15)

14. http://paulflynnmp.typepad.com/my_weblog/2013/08/councillor-ron-jones-1935-2013.html (accessed 22/12/15)

15. IPSA data. (Claim reference number: 304919. Date: 05/09/13)

16. It's worth noting also that, even if this wasn't a mistake, it is still not a breach of the rules.

17. Flynn's full comment in response to this (08/03/16): 'The inclusion of this claim for four miles was a mistake by a member of staff of which I had no knowledge or consent. If you are searching in such detail you may have noticed there are no claims for my Constituency office for council tax, heating, lighting or rent. This is an under claim of about £15,000 every year. As these minute amounts attract excessively bad publicity that's impossible to refute, it's [sic] inclusion would almost certainly create a misleading impression.'

18. All claims mentioned by Morrice: IPSA data, 2013/14. All are travel costs only.

19. FOI response from IPSA (13/11/15)

20. IPSA data and IPSA response to FOI request (13/11/15). John Denham's claim: 06/08/14; claim no. 375730. Margot James's claim: 21/05/14; claim no. 374299

21. IPSA data and IPSA response to FOI request (13/11/15). Claim date: 17/08/14; claim no 389037

22. http://www.independent.co.uk/news/uk/politics/revealed-the-british-mps-who-earned-more-than-7m-outside-of-parliament-in-2014-10066802.html

23. *Sun on Sunday*, 08/02/15, p.8
24. http://metro.co.uk/2015/07/20/mp-claimed-9p-for-traveling-down-the-road-from-his-house-5304492/
25. http://metro.co.uk/2015/07/20/mp-claimed-9p-for-traveling-down-the-road-from-his-house-5304492/
26. http://www.telegraph.co.uk/news/newstopics/mps-expenses/5431700/MPs-expenses-Boris-Johnson-claimed-16.50-for-Remembrance-Sunday-wreath.html and http://www.telegraph.co.uk/news/newstopics/mps-expenses/5380085/MPs-expenses-Ed-Ballss-claim-for-Remembrance-Sunday-wreaths.html
27. http://www.bbc.co.uk/news/uk-england-south-yorkshire-31895703
28. NB: the claim that British Legion officials do not pay for poppy wreaths themselves is one being made by this former MP, not by me. I do not claim to make any suggestions about what its officials do, or do not, pay for out of their own money. However, the quote is included here to highlight the mindset of politicians, by showing the comparisons they seek to make with other institutions (whether or not those comparisons are correct).

Chapter 18: Big spenders

1. IPSA data, 2014/15
2. Rounded up to nearest £1,000. The name of this hotel chain is included in some of the details of MPs' expenses claims, as published in IPSA's database for 2014/15 expenses. However, not all claims contain this information, so the actual amount spent in this hotel will be more than this. NB: I am choosing not to disclose the names of specific hotels if they are *regularly* inhabited by MPs (like this one is) for the sake of security.
3. NB: A 12-month period, not a calendar year.
4. IPSA data, 2013/14. NB1: The 165 nights were not consecutive. NB2: The hotel bill may, in fact, have been more than this with anything extra topped up by Bridgen out of his own money. This amount (£24,750) represents the total amount claimed on expenses, according to IPSA.
5. IPSA data, 2015/16
6. It is not clear which hotel they stayed at. IPSA data simply says: 'RITZ CARLTON The Ritz Carlton Hotels'
7. http://www.theritzlondon.com/en/ (accessed 14/01/16)

8. According to Google Maps.

9. https://www.hotelduvin.com/locations/glasgow/ (accessed 28/12/15)

10. IPSA data, 2014/15 and IPSA response to FOI request (23/09/15). There is no suggestion that Joyce knowingly attempted to breach IPSA rules.

11. IPSA data, 2014/15

12. IPSA data, 2014/15

13. 'Hampton by Hilton', which is part of Hilton Worldwide's portfolio of hotel chains. IPSA data, 2014/15

14. My interview with Andrew Bridgen was on 23/11/15. There is no suggestion that this arrangement has, or has not, continued beyond this date. Indeed, IPSA suggested that they might raise the issue with him at some point in the future, to suggest he makes expenses claims for his staff.

15. Phone call with IPSA source

16. Letter from Simon Danczuk to IPSA, dated 06/05/14, released under FOI (27/11/15)

17. IPSA. NB: There is no suggestion that Paisley necessarily always claims the full amount on expenses.

18. Rounded to nearest £1

19. http://www.theguardian.com/politics/2014/aug/11/tory-foreign-office-minister-quits-intolerable-expenses-rules

20. http://www.channel4.com/news/mps-expenses-46-claim-in-london-despite-owning-a-property

21. http://www.channel4.com/news/mps-expenses-46-claim-in-london-despite-owning-a-property. NB: Chris Bryant did not respond to Channel 4's request for comment at the time of the report.

22. http://www.theguardian.com/politics/2012/oct/19/mps-expenses-row-defend-arrangements

23. I.e. revealed in the media. The details had previously been disclosed in a database on the Speaker's website, but had not been written about more widely.

24. http://content.tfl.gov.uk/tube-dlr-lo-adult-fares.pdf

25. http://www.dailymail.co.uk/news/article-3370292/Lord-Speaker-claimed-230-expenses-chauffeur-driven-car-waiting-outside-opera-FOUR-hours.html and http://www.thesun.co.uk/sol/homepage/news/politics/6819448/Baroness-charges-230-for-chauffeur-driven-car-to-wait-outside-the-opera.html

26. http://www.theguardian.com/politics/2015/dec/22/lord-speakers-expenses-reveal-hundreds-spent-on-chauffeured-cars

27. https://chandlersopticians.co.uk/biogs/stephen.php (accessed 29/12/15)

28. Clearly, therefore, there is no suggestion that these claims were against the rule.

29. Email from Jeremy Hunt (09/03/16). (I had asked him 'whether you consider these expenses claims to be reasonable?')

30. http://www.dailymail.co.uk/news/article-2587010/Spectacular-excess-MPs-charge-taxpayer-hundreds-pounds-designer-glasses.html

Chapter 19: Money for old robe

1. 2014/15 (Parliament data).

2. In 2015.

3. Lords expenses and attendance data for the year 2014/15, as published on Parliament's website.

4. http://www.parliament.uk/documents/lords-information-office/2013/Guide-to-Financial-Support-For-Members-2013.pdf

5. http://www.parliament.uk/biographies/lords/lord-paddick/4288 (as at 29/12/15)

6. http://www.britishairways.com/en-gb/information/travel-classes/business/club-world

7. http://www.britishairways.com/en-gb/information/travel-classes/business/club-world (accessed 29/12/15). NB: details of the Club World service may have changed between Lord Paddick's flight and this date. Therefore, there is no suggestion that he necessarily benefitted from any of these specific items or offers.

8. http://www.publications.parliament.uk/pa/ld201415/ldhansrd/text/140926-0001.htm

9. For instance, Baroness Symons of Vernham Dean had said earlier in the debate that: 'ISIS is neither Islamic nor is it a state. By implication we justify its existence when using its own terminology, and I hope that we will find a different way to refer to this murderous group.'

10. http://www.publications.parliament.uk/pa/ld201415/ldhansrd/text/140926-0002.htm#14092614000148

11. All details of expenses claims from documents disclosed to me by the House of Lords under the FOI (09/11/15). The total amount claimed is also mentioned on the spreadsheet of expenses published on the House of Lords website.

12. Direct Twitter message from Brian Paddick (08/03/16). After this book was first published in May 2016, Paddick finally issued a statement when the *Sunday Times* picked up on the story. He said: 'I sought the advice of the chief whip and the House of Lords authorities before travelling. I was advised what class of travel I was entitled to. I gave up two days of my holiday to speak in an important debate in parliament. The claim simply covered the cost of travel. I did not gain financially myself from the claim.'

13. http://news.bbc.co.uk/1/hi/uk_politics/8060003.stm

14. http://www.publications.parliament.uk/pa/ld200809/ldselect/ldprivi/88/8803.htm

15. In the main chamber. This does not include any interventions he may have made in committees or elsewhere.

16. publicwhip.org.uk

17. http://www.data.parliament.uk/dataset/33

18. http://www.theguardian.com/politics/2011/jul/01/lord-hanningfield-jailed-nine-months

19. http://www.mirror.co.uk/news/uk-news/video-ex-tory-lord-hanningfield-exposed-2934895

20. http://www.theguardian.com/politics/2015/sep/30/lord-hanningfield-alleged-false-expenses-claims-to-be-charged NB: Hanningfield's lawyer is quoted by the *Guardian* saying that Hanningfield 'conducted parliamentary work both prior to, and after, attending the House on the requisite dates in July 2013.' He added: 'Any day where he left the House after a short amount of time was linked to his continuing ill health, which was documented in evidence given to the Scotland Yard inquiry.'

21. http://www.mirror.co.uk/news/uk-news/lord-hanningfield-expenses-scandal-there-2934870

22. http://www.telegraph.co.uk/news/2016/07/18/ex-tory-peer-lord-hanningfield-cleared-over-false-expenses-after/

23. Editorial, *Daily Mirror* (19/07/2016), p.8

24. The Parliamentary year of 2014/15 ran from June 2014 to March 2015 (it was not a full 12 months because of the General Election). See: http://www.parliament.uk/about/faqs/house-of-commons-faqs/business-faq-page/recess-dates/recess/. These dates have been applied to all the data analysis on Silent Lords in this section. NB: The data I have used includes all categories of expenses, including the daily attendance allowance.

25. http://www.publications.parliament.uk/pa/ld/ldstat.htm and Hansard (does not include committees)

26. Rounded to nearest thousand. Actual amount: £43,110

27. Rounded to nearest thousand. Actual amounts: £40,893 and £36,417

28. Rounded to nearest thousand. Actual amount: £33,300

29. Parliament expenses data (2014/15), and Lords Hansard (2014/15). NB: this refers only to speeches in the main chamber that are recorded by Hansard, and does not include any contributions to committees or other parliamentary activities. There is no suggestion that they have 'fiddled' their expenses – merely that they have not participated in Parliament as actively as some might expect.

30. Total expenses: £13,895 (2014/15)

31. Parliament expenses data (2014/15), and voting data from www. publicwhip.org. NB1: this refers only to speeches in the main chamber that are recorded by Hansard, and does not include any contributions to committees or other parliamentary activities. There is no suggestion that they have 'fiddled' their expenses – merely that they have not participated in Parliament as actively as some might expect. NB2: According to his parliamentary biography, Earl Stair was a member of the 'EU Sub Committee F – Home Affairs, Health and Education' during this period.

32. Parliament expenses data (2014/15) and voting data from www. publicwhip.org.

33. http://www.sunnation.co.uk/two-peers-claim-thousands-in-taxpay-ers-cash-despite-never-voting-or-speaking-in-the-house-of-lords/ (Through sheer bad luck, this story was published a week after I'd finished my own data analysis on Silent Lords! It covered a slightly different time period.)

34. As at 30/12/15, according to Hansard and publicwhip.org. This does not include any contributions to committees or other parliamentary activities.

35. Flights checked on 30/12/15 for Glasgow–London return flights for the following week, using http://www.skyscanner.net/, the cheapest 12 options were all £44, and; FOI request to House of Lords for invoice documents and booking information held concerning various (but not all) expenses claims Macfarlane made in 2014 and 2015. All of the fight details listed in this FOI response were over £300 return. The £362 figure is rounded to nearest £1.

Part Six: Damage assessment
Chapter 20: Confirmation

1. Register of Interests, as at 08/02/16.
2. Register of Interests, as at 08/02/16. NB: Some MPs donate earnings from completing surveys to charity. It is not known whether Peter Bone did this, so there is no suggestion that he has personally profited from the surveys. NB2: There is no suggestion that Bone will only do surveys if he is paid, he is used merely as an example of an MP who has declared payment for surveys.
3. Rounded to nearest whole number.
4. They selected this from a multiple choice option.
5. https://yougov.co.uk/news/2013/05/24/mps-due-raise-public-says-no/
6. Numbers have been changed from digits to words for the sake of stylistic continuity.
7. 11.3%
8. For this question, MPs were able to tick as many options as they liked, so the results do not add up to 100%. The most popular answer was: 'A small number of politicians are greedy, which gives everyone a bad name,' which was selected by 63% of respondents.
9. A few of the students wrote more than one word. There were 19 students altogether. All the words have been included.
10. National Opinion Poll survey, 'The Teenagers', for the *Daily Mail* (1967), cited in: Bernard Davies, 'Non-Swinging Youth', *New Society* (1969)

Chapter 21: What's next?

1. http://www.theguardian.com/politics/blog/live/2016/apr/08/cameron-offshore-tax-panama-resign-hypocrisy-labour-accuses-cameron-of-hypocrisy-after-he-admits-profiting-from-offshore-trust-politics-live?page=with:block-57075801e4b08e2711ce65e7#block-57075801e4b08e2711ce65e7
2. http://www.bbc.co.uk/news/uk-politics-31589282
3. http://www.publications.parliament.uk/pa/cm201415/cmhansrd/cm150225/debtext/150225-0002.htm#15022597001011 ; http://www.publications.parliament.uk/pa/cm201415/cmhansrd/cm150225/debtext/150225-0003.htm

4. http://www.publications.parliament.uk/pa/cm201415/cmhansrd/cm150225/debtext/150225-0003.htm

5. http://www.publications.parliament.uk/pa/cm/cmregmem/150223/duncan_alan.htm NB1: The Register only said: 'Rental income from residential property in London.' The phrase 'substantial income' is taken from the then rules for financial interest declaration, which instructs MPs to declare any land or property 'from which a substantial income is derived'. Those rules can be found at: http://www.publications.parliament.uk/pa/cm201012/cmcode/1885/188504.htm#a21 NB2: It is not known how much income Duncan received, or if he was the owner of the property. There is no suggestion that he misled the House or broke any rules by not mentioning this.

6. http://www.bbc.co.uk/news/uk-politics-31624695

7. http://www.islingtongazette.co.uk/news/politics/islington_north_mp_jeremy_corbyn_is_the_country_s_lowest_expenses_claimer_1_748369

8. Paul Flynn, *How to be an MP*, (Bitebank, 2012), p.19

9. Short Money (see: http://blogs.spectator.co.uk/2015/07/nigel-farage-overruled-ukip-nec-short-money/)

10. There is no suggestion of any wrongdoing on the part of UKIP, UKIP Parliamentary Resource Unit Limited, or anyone involved in it. The company secretary, Mark Reckless, told me: 'The purpose of the UKIP Parliamentary Resource Unit Limited of which I'm the operational head is to support the work of the UKIP Parliamentary Party. It's sort of funded through Short money and that's the requirement for use of the money. And the company is a special purpose vehicle to sort of segregate funds and make sure they're all . . . properly used for that purpose and seen to be.' He added: 'When I incorporated the company, on behalf of the two directors, I sought and received permission from the Parliamentary authorities that is the clerk of the House of Commons and his equivalent in the House of Lords to use the word "Parliamentary" in the company description, because "Parliament" is one of the words restricted by Company House, such that you need official permission to use it, which was granted in our case . . . Our office in at the House of Commons, so hence that's why it's registered as our office address on Companies House.'

Afterword

1. http://www.telegraph.co.uk/news/politics/11873040/Sir-Malcolm-Rifkind-and-Jack-Straw-lobbying-inquiry-Whos-who.html
2. http://www.telegraph.co.uk/news/2016/10/20/commons-watchdog-chair-sir-kevin-barron-breached-mps-code-of-con/
3. http://www.parliament.uk/documents/commons-commission/House-of-Commons-PCS-news-release.pdf
4. http://www.parliament.uk/documents/pcfs/not-upheld/gisela-stuart.pdf
5. http://www.publications.parliament.uk/pa/ld201617/ldselect/ldprivi/28/28.pdf

Index

An invitation from the publisher

Join us at www.hodder.co.uk, or follow us
on Twitter @hodderbooks to be a part of
our community of people who love the very
best in books and reading.

Whether you want to discover more about a book
or an author, watch trailers and interviews, have the
chance to win early limited editions, or simply browse
our expert readers' selection of the very best books,
we think you'll find what you're looking for.

And if you don't, that's the place to tell us what's missing.

We love what we do, and we'd love you to be a part of it.

www.hodder.co.uk

@hodderbooks

HodderBooks

HodderBooks